CHEVROLET
SMALL-BLOCK

David Lewis

Motorbooks International
Publishers & Wholesalers
Osceola, Wisconsin 54020, USA

First published in 1989 by Motorbooks International Publishers & Wholesalers Inc, P O Box 2, 729 Prospect Avenue, Osceola, WI 54020 USA

Printed and bound in the United States of America

The information in this book is true and complete to the best of our knowledge. All recommendations are made without any guarantee on the part of the author or publisher, who also disclaim any liability incurred in connection with the use of this data or specific details

We recognize that some words, model names and designations, for example, mentioned herein are the property of the trademark holder. We use them for identification purposes only. This is not an official publication

Library of Congress Cataloging-in-Publication Data
Lewis, David.
    Chevrolet small-block V-8 interchange manual / David Lewis.
      p. cm.
    ISBN 0-87938-357-7
    1. Chevrolet automobile—Parts—Handbooks, manuals, etc.
I. Title.
TL215.C5L48 1989   89-3271
629.28'722—dc20   CIP

On the front cover: The slightly modified small-block V–8 350 ci engine in the Corvette owned by Bobby Walden of Borger, Texas. *Jerry Heasley*
On the back cover: Chevrolet small-block V–8 interchange comparisons.

Motorbooks International books are also available at discounts in bulk quantity for industrial or sales-promotional use. For details write to Special Sales Manager at the Publisher's address

Contents

Acknowledgments

Special thanks to my wife, Ann, for her encouragement and patience during the difficult job of typing my unreadable copy. My father Robert Lewis, who deserves publication more than I. Richard Hennessey of Hennessey's Performance Center, Norwalk, Conn. Bob and Rick of H&L Chevrolet Parts Department, Darien, Conn. Jerry Castro of Storm Crankshaft Service, Mt. Vernon, N.Y. Richard Hipp of the General Motors Training Center, Tarrytown, N.Y. Dave Hederich, manager of Product Publicity at Chevrolet Motor Division, Warren, Mich. T. Willie Hutchens, public relations manager at Erson Cams, Carson City, Nev. Ron Hoyt of Danbury, Conn., and Mannys Auto Parts, Brien Stefanko of Norwalk, Conn., and his friend Jimmy. Erin Welti of Ridgefield, Conn. Rick of In Motion Performance, Danbury, Conn. All the guys at RHS Auto Shop. My sister Diane.

General Motors, Chevrolet Division
Erson Cams
Edelbrock
TRW Automotive Aftermarket Division
Haynes Publications
AC-Delco Division of General Motors
General Motors Publications
Moroso
Total Performance
Alliance Cams

Camonics Cams
Competition Cams
Cam Techniques
Crane Cams
Crower Cams
Engle Cams
Herbert Cams
Isky-mega Cams
Lunati Cams

Preface

Unless you have experienced it there is no way to explain the feeling of accomplishment and pride when a project is completed.

From the earliest stages of selecting the engine you intend to rebuild, until it is installed and running in your project vehicle, you will feel discouraged, frustrated and fatigued. You may even regret ever having started such a demanding task.

My best advice to you is to relax, enjoy yourself and take pride in your work. Do the best job you can and be meticulous with every detail no matter how insignificant.

When the work is completed you will have every reason to be proud of your accomplishment and what you have created, and you'll be proud to show off your work to friends and relatives. But only you—and other true enthusiasts who have successfully completed similar projects—can truly appreciate what you have built and the work involved.

History of the small-block

1

The Chevrolet small-block has been the choice of racing champions for more than thirty years and the reasons are simple. The small-block is just that—small. It measures approximately 25 in. deep by 25 in. wide by 25 in. high, including clearance. (Your personal choices for induction system, exhaust system, water pump and front drive accessories will alter these figures slightly.) The small-block is light, weighing in at about 550 lb., with all cast-iron equipment. The most important characteristic of this engine is the ease of parts interchangeability from both factory and aftermarket sources.

The engineers at Chevrolet designed the most popular V-8 engine of our time back in 1955, when the 265 ci engine was introduced. The engine had a bore of 3.750 in. and a stroke of 3.000 in. This engine was in production only in the 1955 and 1956 model years.

In 1957, the 283 ci engine was released. It was also a 265 but with a new, larger 3.875 in. bore and the same 3.000 in. stroke. In 1962, with the demand for more performance came the 327 ci engine. The 327 had a 4.001 in. bore with a new stroke depth of 3.250 in. In 1967 the 350 and 302 engines arrived. The 350 used the same bore as the 327 (4.001 in.) with a stroke increased to 3.480 in. The 302 also had a 4.001 in. bore but it used the shorter stroke of the old 283 engine (3.000 in.) to make it a race engine for the newly popular Trans-Am race series of five-liter size limit.

These engines all shared small journal diameter measurements. The crankshaft connecting rod journal size was 2.000 in., and the main bearing journal size was 2.300 in. Compression heights varied but the connecting rod lengths were all the same at 5.703 in., and the bore spacing stayed at 4.400 in.

In 1968, Chevrolet engineers made a major design change in the block, crankshaft and connecting rod areas. To help reduce bearing loading, they increased the crankshaft journal diameters to 2.100 in. for the rod and 2.450 in. for the main bearing. From this new large-journal design came the reliability of the Chevrolet small-block of today, as well as a new assortment of bore and stroke combinations to fit vehicle needs through the seventies and eighties. This book deals exclusively with the large-journal small-block from 1968 to 1988—the last twenty years of small-block history and interchangeability.

The 327 ci engine (1962-67) was upgraded in 1968. It now used the new, large-journal, cast-iron or steel crankshaft (depending on performance level), and the large-journal connecting rods fit exclusively into a two-bolt main bearing cap block. With these improvements, the 327 was used in two more production years of service: 1968 and 1969.

Street rodders usually choose the Chevy small-block. The engine here is customized even more than it appears: it is a 378 ci with a combination of a 400 ci block and 350 ci crankshaft, the block bored 0.030 in. I used 487 casting 74 cc 2.02I and 1.60E heads to help the forged, 1970 style pistons yield an approximate 9:1 compression—before boost. The blower is underdriven by about 20 percent.

Get to know these guys, they are your local Chevrolet Parts men. Many parts departments don't care about performance, won't answer questions and lack the kind of enthusiasm that helps you enjoy your hobby. Shop around and find enthusiastic guys like these who will help you with what you need to know and sell you what you need to buy. Your money is well spent at their counter because GM parts are usually of high quality.

The 302 engine of 1967 also received the large-journal modification in 1968. The only crankshaft available was a special heat-treated, forged-steel unit now installed in the new, heavier four-bolt main bearing cap block with thicker main bearing webs. This engine came with many other special

parts and was intended for racing use only. The 302, like the 327, was dropped from production after the 1969 model year.

In 1968, the 350 received the large-journal treatment. The crankshafts offered were either cast iron or forged steel in the heavy block of two-bolt or four-bolt main bearing cap design. This engine is in production today.

In 1968, Chevrolet introduced a new bore-and-stroke combination. This was the first production year of the 307 ci V-8. The 307 was a combination of the 283 and the 327: the bore was 3.875 in. and the stroke was 3.250 in. This much-neglected combination of bore and stroke went out of production after the 1973 model year.

In 1970, Chevrolet created 400 ci from the small-block's original external dimensions by joining the cylinders together. This increased the strength of the relatively thin wall castings, but it also created some special problems. Siamesing the bores allowed the bore spacing of 4.400 in. to remain common with that of other small-blocks. The engineers were able to squeeze out a 4.126 in. bore size, and to stroke the engine to a 3.750 in. depth. This giant small-block was in production until the end of the 1980 model year.

In 1975, Chevrolet released the 262 ci V-8. Its bore of 3.671 in. and stroke of 3.100 in. were too small to power any wheelbase over 110 in. For that reason, Chevrolet dropped the 262 V-8 from production after the 1976 production year.

The replacement for the 262 engine was the 305 ci engine, released in 1976. With a 3.736 in. bore and a 350 engine stroke of 3.480 in., this five-liter small-block was a good idea for providing the horse-

Chevy small-block oil pans awaiting treatment at Moroso Performance Products in Guilford, Connecticut.

Moroso is a rapidly expanding company building custom engine accessories. Moroso divisions include induction engineering, Herb Adams suspension, and competition engineering. Moroso's warehouse is well stocked.

There are many custom kit car manufacturers that encourage the use of the small-block Chevy. One such company not too far from my home is Total Performance. Many Total Performance kits have motor mounting pedestals designed for Chevy engines.

The only true test to rate horsepower is with a dynamometer. The dyno room at Moroso is working a six-cylinder Buick stock car racing engine. Dick Moroso assures me that this room has seen its share of small-blocks.

power, torque and acceptable emission levels required at the time. This engine is still in production.

In 1979, Chevrolet again tried a 4.3 liter V-8. The 267 ci used the 350 stroke of 3.480 in. with the smallest bore of any small-block at 3.500 in. With good emission results but little power, this engine was discontinued at the end of the 1981 production year.

With the information supplied here, the Chevy enthusiast should be able to select or build the small-block engine desired. Small-block Chevrolet parts interchange well, and there are some great combinations and good parts available from the factory, as well as from aftermarket suppliers.

The following chapters discuss at length blocks, heads, crankshafts, rods, pistons, cams, manifolds, water pumps, pulleys, flywheels, motor mounts and bore-and-stroke combinations. They describe where the small-block will fit, and where it won't. They also tell you how to identify parts at a glance and how to save time and money when selecting parts. Step-by-step instructions cover reliable com-

binations of parts and explain which combinations work best. There are discussions of power versus economy and how to get the best of both worlds. Pictures, data tables and advice accompany the text.

Horsepower formula

If you would like to know what kind of horsepower your engine is developing but can't afford dynamometer time, try this peak horsepower formula:

$$\text{Peak hp} = \frac{\text{vehicle weight} \times (\text{mph})^2}{10,000 \times \text{ET}}$$

I wish I could credit the unknown author of this formula, but I have no idea where this came from. One of my students brought it to me and asked if it worked. Having had my big-block Chevelle engine tested on a dyno, and knowing what my vehicle weight and quarter-mile elapsed time were, I decided to try the formula. To my surprise, the answer when using the formula was within 1.39 hp of dyno calculations. It may be a coincidence but I got a laugh out of it. Anyway, it makes you wonder.

Chevrolet small-block engines 1968-88

Year	Engine size (ci)	Bore and stroke (in.)	Compression ratio	Carburetor	Horsepower* @ rpm
1968	302	4.000×3.000	11:1	H4V	290@5800
	307	3.875×3.250	9:1	R2V	200@4600
	327	4.001×3.250	8.75:1	R2V	210@4600
		4.001×3.250	8.75:1	R4V	250@4800
		4.001×3.250	10:1	R4V	275@4800
		4.001×3.250	10:1	R4V	300@5000
		4.001×3.250	11:1	H4V	325@5600
		4.001×3.250	11:1	H4V	350@5800
	350	4.001×3.480	10.25:1	R4V	295@4800
1969	302	4.000×3.000	11:1	H4V	290@5800
	307	3.875×3.250	9:1	R2V	200@4600
	327	4.001×3.250	9:1	R2V	210@4600
		4.001×3.250	9:1	R2V	235@4800
	350	4.001×3.480	9:1	R4V	255@4800
		4.001×3.480	10.25:1	R4V	300@4800
		4.001×3.480	11:1	H4V	350@5600
		4.001×3.480	11:1	H4V	370@5800
1970	307	3.875×3.250	9:1	R2V	200@4600
	350	4.001×3.480	9:1	R2V	250@4800
		4.001×3.480	10.25:1	R4V	300@4800
		4.001×3.480	11:1	H4V	350@5600
		4.001×3.480	11:1	H4V	360@6000
		4.001×3.480	11:1	H4V	370@6000
	400	4.125×3.750	9:1	R2V	265@4400
1971	307	3.875×3.250	8.5:1	R2V	200@4600
	350	4.001×3.480	8.5:1	R2V	245@4800
		4.001×3.480	8.5:1	R4V	270@4800
		4.001×3.480	9:1	H4V	330@5600
	400	4.125×3.750	8.5:1	R2V	255@4400
1972	307	3.875×3.250	8.5:1	R2V	130@4000
	350	4.001×3.480	8.5:1	R2V	165@4000
		4.001×3.480	8.5:1	R4V	175@4000
		4.001×3.480	8.5:1	R4V	200@4400
		4.001×3.480	9:1	H4V	255@5600
	400	4.125×3.750	8.5:1	R2V	170@3800
1973	307	3.875×3.250	8.5:1	R2V	115@4000
	350	4.001×3.480	8.5:1	R2V	145@4000
		4.001×3.480	8.5:1	R4V	175@4000
		4.001×3.480	8.5:1	R4V	190@4400
		4.001×3.480	9:1	H4V	245@5200
		4.001×3.480	9:1	H4V	250@5200
	400	4.125×3.750	8.5:1	R2V	150@3200
1974	350	4.001×3.480	8.5:1	R2V	145@3600
		4.001×3.480	8.5:1	R4V	160@3800
		4.001×3.480	8.5:1	R4V	185@4000
		4.001×3.480	8.5:1	R4V	195@4400
		4.001×3.480	9:1	R4V	245@5200
		4.001×3.750	9:1	R4V	250@5200
	400	4.125×3.750	8.5:1	R2V	150@3200
		4.125×3.750	8.5:1	R4V	180@3800
1975	262	3.671×3.100	8.5:1	R2V	110@3600
	350	4.001×3.480	8.5:1	R2V	145@3800
		4.001×3.480	8.5:1	R4V	155@3800
		4.001×3.480	8.5:1	R4V	165@3800

Year	Engine size (ci)	Bore and stroke (in.)	Compression ratio	Carburetor	Horsepower* @ rpm
		4.001×3.480	9:1	R4V	205@4800
	400	4.125×3.750	8.5:1	R4V	175@3600
1976	305	3.736×3.480	8.5:1	R2V	140@3800
	350	4.001×3.480	8.5:1	R2V	145@3800
		4.001×3.480	8.5:1	R4V	165@3800
		4.001×3.480	8.5:1	R4V	185@4000
		4.001×3.480	8.5:1	R4V	195@4400
		4.001×3.480	9:1	R4V	210@5200
		4.001×3.480	8.5:1	R4V	270@4400
	400	4.125×3.750	8.5:1	R4V	175@3600
1977	305	3.736×3.480	8.5:1	R2V	145@3800
	350	4.001×3.480	8.5:1	R4V	170@3800
		4.001×3.480	8.5:1	R4V	180@4000
		4.001×3.480	9:1	R4V	210@5500
1978	305	3.736×3.480	8.5:1	R2V	135@3800
		3.736×3.480	8.5:1	R2V	145@3800
	350	4.001×3.480	8.2:1	R4V	160@3800
		4.001×3.480	8.2:1	R4V	170@3800
		4.001×3.480	8.2:1	R4V	175@3800
		4.001×3.480	8.2:1	R4V	185@4000
1979	267	3.500×3.480	8.2:1	R2V	125@3800
	305	3.736×3.480	8.4:1	R2V	125@3200
		3.736×3.480	8.4:1	R2V	130@3200
		3.736×3.480	8.4:1	R4V	155@4000
		3.736×3.480	8.4:1	R4V	160@4000
	350	4.001×3.480	8.2:1	R4V	165@3800
		4.001×3.480	8.2:1	R4V	170@4000
		4.001×3.480	8.2:1	R4V	175@4000
		4.001×3.480	8.9:1	R4V	195@4000
		4.001×3.480	8.2:1	R4V	195@4000
		4.001×3.480	8.9:1	R4V	225@5200
1980	267	3.500×3.480	8.3:1	R2V	120@3600
	305	3.736×3.480	8.6:1	R4V	155@4000
		3.736×3.480	8.5:1	R4V	180@4200
	350	4.001×3.480	8.2:1	R4V	190@4200
		4.001×3.480	9:1	R4V	230@5200
1981	267	3.500×3.480	8.3:1	R2V	115@4000
	305	3.736×3.480	8.6:1	R4V	150@3800
		3.736×3.480	8.6:1	R4V	165@4000
	350	4.001×3.480	8.2:1	R4V	175@4000
		4.001×3.480	8.2:1	R4V	190@4000
1982	267	3.500×3.480	8.3:1	R2V	115@4000
	305	3.736×3.480	8.6:1	R4V	145@4000
		3.736×3.480	9.5:1	RFI	165@4200
	350	4.001×3.480	9:1	RFI	200@4200
1983	305	3.736×3.480	8.6:1	R4V	150@3800
		3.736×3.480	9.5:1	RFI	175@4200
	350	4.001×3.480	9:1	RFI	200@4200
1984	305	3.736×3.480	8.6:1	R4V	150@3800
		3.736×3.480	9.5:1	R4V	190@4800
	350	4.001×3.480	9:1	RFI	205@4300
1985	305	3.736×3.480	8.6:1	R4V	150@4000
		3.736×3.480	8.6:1	R4V	165@4200
		3.736×3.480	8.6:1	R4V	165@4400
		3.736×3.480	9.5:1	R4V	180@4800

Year	Engine size (ci)	Bore and stroke (in.)	Compression ratio	Carburetor	Horsepower* @ rpm
		3.736×3.480	9.5:1	R4V	190@4800
		3.736×3.480	9.5:1	RFI	215@4400
	350	4.001×3.480	9.5:1	RFI	230@4000
1986	305	3.736×3.480	9.5:1	R4V	150@4000
		3.736×3.480	9.5:1	R4V	165@4200
		3.736×3.480	9.5:1	R4V	180@4400
		3.736×3.480	9.5:1	R4V	190@4800
		3.736×3.480	9.5:1	RFI	205@4800
	350	4.001×3.480	9.5:1	RFI	230@4000
1987	305	3.736×3.480	8.6:1	R4V	150@4000
		3.736×3.480	9.5:1	R4V	205@4800
	350	4.001×3.480	8.2:1	R4V	205@4800
		4.001×3.480	9:1	RFI	225@4400
		4.001×3.480	9.5:1	RFI	240@4000
1988	305	3.736×3.480	9.3:1	R4V	180@4000
		3.736×3.480	9.3:1	R4V	200@4800
		3.736×3.480	9.3:1	RFI	205@4800
	350	4.001×3.480	9.3:1	RFI	230@4400
		4.001×3.480	9.5:1	RFI	245@4000

*From 1972 to present, horsepower ratings are net as installed in vehicle.

Engine blocks

2

Beginning with the 1968 model year, Chevrolet cylinder blocks have been available in six bore sizes. The bore diameters measure from 3.500 in. to 4.126 in. in diameter with bore spacing remaining constant at 4.400 in. The external dimensions of these blocks are the same; the only differences are the internal bore and stroke combinations.

Identification

For twenty years these blocks have been available in two- or four-bolt main bearing cap designs in a variety of different metal alloy combinations. Determining two- or four-bolt design is just a mat-

ter of counting bolts on the three center main bearing caps. In most cases, two-bolt main blocks are fine to use, especially if they have a high nickel content. The only reason you would choose a four-bolt block would be for resale or because you intend to use your engine for racing. I have never seen a broken main cap, and General Motors has reported that two-bolt blocks will hold up to 500 hp, so a four-bolt block is not required for street use or even for some drag strip use.

Metal alloy identification is usually located on the front face of the block under the timing chain cover. This identification indicates the presences of

A comparison of two 305 ci small-blocks showing off the subtle differences in castings. Here are the rear main crankshaft seal areas of the early model 305 engine, left, *and late-model 305 engine, right. Notice how the block on the right changed. The flat area with four holes is to mount the new-style (1986 and later) rear seal appliance.*

This 1988 GMC block, 838, was parked near the dumpster. It has four-bolt main caps and the new rear seal appliance. Notice the crankshaft casting number labeling this a cast-iron shaft. A forged-steel crank is available for this block.

A two-bolt main bearing cap 327 ci block.

tin and nickel. (Tin helps the cast iron heat and cool more evenly; nickel hardens and polishes the bore surfaces so the ring seal is better and less wear occurs.)

If two numbers, 10 and 20 (one over the other), are located near the camshaft bore, then ten per-

Although they have similar outer dimensions, the 350 ci engine block, left, and the 400 ci engine block, right, have enough subtle internal and external differences to be recognized immediately. Notice the large round freeze plug bosses on the center of each side of the 400 block. Internally, the 400 has wider center caps and larger main bearing saddles.

If you look closely, you can see the four bolt holes where the main caps fit. The caps are off at the machine shop being shortened by a few thousandths of an inch as this block is about to be align-honed.

The cast-iron bow-tie small-block.

This is a bow-tie aluminum block with cast-iron cylinder liners. It is available under part number 366300.

cent tin and twenty percent nickel are present in the block. If only one number is present, 10 or 20, this number represents the percentage of nickel in the casting. Any other numbers under the timing cover are casting identification. The absence of the numbers 10, 20 or both indicates that only trace amounts of other metals are present.

The block you choose will depend on your application and on how many cubic inches you want. The 4.001 in. and 4.126 in. bore blocks are available in two- and four-bolt main design. From these bore sizes, 302 ci, 327 ci, 350 ci, 372 ci, 383 ci and 400 ci are possible, depending on crankshaft selection.

Blocks

Bore diameter (in.)	Engine (ci)	Main bearing cap design	Year
3.500*	267	Two-bolt	1979-81
3.671*	262	Two-bolt	1975
3.736*	305	Two-bolt	1976-88
3.875*	307	Two-bolt	1968-73
4.001	327	Two-bolt	1968-69
	350	Two-bolt	1968-88
4.001 (2.45 in. main saddles)	302	Four-bolt	1968-69
	350	Four-bolt	1968-88
4.126 (2.65 in. main saddles)	400	Four-bolt	1970-72
		Two-bolt	1973-80

Available in two-bolt main bearing cap design only.

Used blocks

Your choices at the local wrecking yard include the 267 ci engine with the smallest bore size of 3.500 in., which was produced from 1979 to 1981. Its external dimensions are identical to those of other small-blocks, and all high-performance parts from larger engines will physically interchange onto the 267 ci engine. However, because of the 267's small bore size, the large valves used in high-

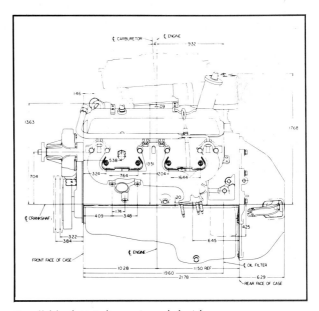

Small-block V-8 dimensions, left side.

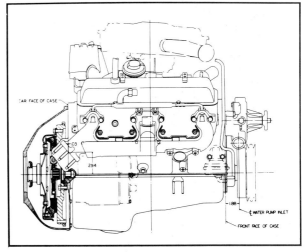

Small-block V-8 dimensions, right side.

The LT1 small-block, still available from Chevrolet.

This 1979-80 400 ci block is difficult to recognize when the engine is fully assembled. There is no third freeze-plug hump. Always look at the harmonic balancer or flywheel—if visible—to check for the unbalanced units that are standard on the 400 engine. This block is labeled 509.

When a block comes out of the hot tank, casting numbers and other identifying marks are more easily visible. It is important that you know what you are buying: bring some scrapers so that you are able to read numbers before leaving the wrecking yard.

performance heads will hit the edge of the 267's bore. In addition, the larger combustion chamber sizes used with larger-cubic-inch engines cause a severe drop in compression when installed on the smaller 267 ci engine. The 267 engine is so small that any high-performance camshaft that will run smoothly in a larger engine would be a radical selection; your money is better spent elsewhere. The 3.500 in. bore is too small, the 3.480 in. stroke is too deep for the bore size and the cylinder temperatures with this combination are too high. Better choices are available that will cost the same amount to build.

The 3951511 casting number identifies this block as a 1970-74 400 ci of either two- or four-bolt main bearing cap design.

Don't forget this number on the extended patch of the block deck surface. It will tell you what year and vehicle the engine came from.

Here is a two-bolt main bearing cap 327 ci block, casting number 3914678. GM never built a four-bolt main 327 ci engine. You can build one by using a 350 four-bolt block with 327 engine internals. The 302 ci, 327 ci and 350 ci blocks all share a 4 in. bore and similar crankshaft main web diameters. Everything will interchange from 1968 to 1985.

A close-up of the casting mark on the 1986 and later 305 ci five-liter G engine. Notice the G style pistons.

This is how the 1986 and later 350 ci 5.7 liter G engines are marked. The new block marks make it easy to identify what motor you have. The 1986 and later engines have the displacement cast on the flywheel housing.

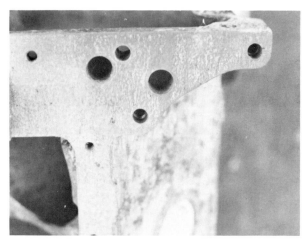

This block has two starter motor bolt patterns—very handy! Be sure that the block you have selected has all the features needed for your accessories.

This is a single-starter-motor bolt pattern. This block will only accept a starter for a 14 in. diameter flywheel.

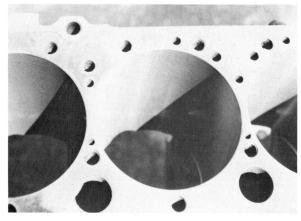

Here are the cylinder deck steam holes on the 400 ci block. The larger hole at the bottom, between the cylinders, measures about 0.250 in. in diameter. The top hole measures about 0.141 in. in diameter. These holes are aligned with similar holes in the head.

This two-freeze-plug 400 ci engine has a raised center hump which is the third freeze plug boss. The block has a casting number of 330817.

This is a three-freeze-plug 400 ci block. Both two-bolt and four-bolt main bearing design blocks had a casting number of 3951511.

When upright on the stand, the 509 casting number 400 ci engine displays the necessary steam holes. Notice that the gasket also has holes. If block, gasket and head can pass steam, the engine should not encounter any sealing problems.

This is a 1980 truck 350 ci block. Just above and to the right of the 207 casting number is a shorty dipstick entry that is on the opposite, or passenger, side of the engine as it is installed in the vehicle.

Here is a close-up view of the shorty dipstick access hole. This hole can be blocked with a steel dowel that comes with the oil pan and has its own access hole for dipstick mounting.

The 262 ci engine has the same set of problems as the 267 ci engine. Although the stroke is not as deep at 3.100 in., and the bore is larger at 3.671 in., it is also not cost-effective to build this engine. Chevrolet engineers may have thought this, too, since the 262 engine was available only for the 1975 production year. The 262 block—although small—ran well with little cylinder bore wear because of the use of nickel in the block.

The 305 ci engine with a 3.736 in. bore is available in several casting alloys. It is also used in many performance applications. This engine has been in production from the 1976 model year, and is easily available at most junkyards. Many 305 ci engines are labeled 305 just above the fuel pump mounting boss.

The 305 ci and 350 ci engines share the same 3.480 in. stroke. This means that the special high-

This engine will have a GMC blower installed, hence note the use of the GM stud kit. Cylinder pressures will be extreme so every precaution is taken to preserve the head gasket seal. These stud kits fit all blocks and are especially recommended for the aluminum bow-tie block.

This truck block was so badly overheated that the deck surface had to be refinished. The cylinders were bored to a 0.030 in. oversize and the main webs were checked. Both of the 991 heads from this engine were cracked. Be sure to examine discarded engine parts thoroughly.

Here is a 1986 305 ci short block assembly with the rear seal appliance removed to expose the round crankshaft flange. Notice how the block is recessed and how narrow the rear main cap is. The number 331 is cast on the sides.

This is the seal appliance that fits the 1986 and later five-liter and 5.7 liter engines.

This is a 1970 350 ci engine. Notice how different the accessory mounting became after the 1969 models were released. When interchanging engines, it is best to keep them as complete as possible.

If you look directly at the freeze plug hole in the center of this picture, you will notice the clutch linkage pivot ball holes to the left and right. Make sure your block has these if you need them.

performance crankshaft of the 350 engine will fit the 305. Be careful when interchanging cylinder heads because the bore size is still small compared with that of a 350. The small-chambered inter-mediate-performance 327 ci or 350 ci heads should clear the sides of the bore. The 305 is a good choice for the mild street-performance engine.

The 307 ci engine, with a bore size of 3.875 in. and the same 3.250 in. stroke as the 327, is a better choice. The only problem with the 307 engine block is the absence of nickel in the casting. The block will show wear after 60,000 miles or so, but a

Front view of a 1968 327 ci engine. The bracket and accessory mounting arrangement shown here was abandoned in 1969, a prime example of why it is important to buy complete engines from the junkyard when selecting an engine to rebuild.

Disassembling a junkyard engine is a dirty job. This $100 special didn't get a chance to mess up the inside of the shop—we tore it down in the driveway.

We found that our 350 ci engine was far dirtier on the outside than the inside. In fact, upon closer examination we discovered that the cam, lifters and timing chain were brand new. If you should ever wish to reuse cam and lifters, be sure to label the lifters so as to keep everything in order. When lifters are reinstalled exactly where they had previously run, no additional break-in wear occurs.

well-prepared 307 ci engine will run circles around an equally well-prepared 305 ci engine. The 307 engine has been ignored because no factory high-performance version was ever built and because it was produced from the 1968 model year to the end of the 1973 model year, when higher-horsepower 327 ci and 350 ci engines were plentiful.

The 307 ci engine was created by stroking the 1957-67 283 ci engine to the 327 ci engine's 3.250 in. and using the old 283 engine's bore of 3.875 in. The 307 also boasted the large-journal crankshaft. So, to undo what Chevrolet engineers did and create a 283 engine from the 307, one must use a large-journal 3.000 in. stroke steel crankshaft from a 302 ci engine for de-stroking—but don't bother doing

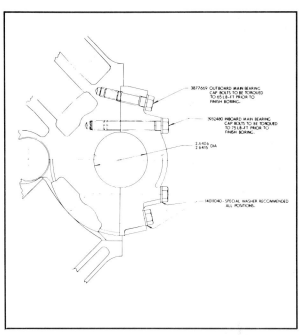

Installation and line boring of splayed-bolt main cap.

Knowing what to look for is a big plus when shopping at the junkyard. I knew there was a good chance that this was a four-bolt main cap block when I picked it out: the block casting number is 3970014.

This Sunnen honer is the best way to get a 45 degree angle crosshatch pattern on your newly bored cylinder walls. Notice how nicely the first cylinder polished up with a 400 grit stone.

this, because a 307 equipped with the best high-performance parts from larger small-blocks is a screamer with reasonable economy.

The 302 ci, 327 ci and 350 ci engines all share the 4.001 in. bore block. Yet you will not find a Chevrolet 302 ci engine at the junkyard, and the large-journal 327 ci engine is almost gone. This leaves the 350 ci engine, which is still manufactured and has been in production for twenty years.

Finding the right block

As stated earlier, the 4.001 in. bore block is available in either two- or four-bolt design. Trucks and vans are a good source for locating used four-bolt main bearing cap blocks. These seasoned blocks are highly prized, so don't look just in a junkyard. Construction companies, General Motors dealerships, marinas or any companies using Chevy trucks that have a small truck fleet and perform their own maintenance may have an old worn-out engine (look near the dumpster at their shops). Such a workhorse with more than 100,000 miles of travel is still worth investigation because it may even have a steel crankshaft in it.

If a two-bolt main cap 350 ci engine is acceptable for your needs, shop around and get your best deal. Sometimes even a neighbor's or friend's old rust bucket will have just what you're looking for clanking away under the hood.

Full-size sedans and station wagons are good places to find 400 ci small-blocks. The 1970-72 engines had four-bolt main caps, and the 1973-80 engines had two-bolt blocks standard. The 400 block can be recognized easily because of the three freeze plugs on each side of the block in early production years and a raised round hump with no plug in later years. Some of the last of these engines produced for truck use have a large 509 cast on the sides of a block that looks like any other smaller engine at first glance.

Finding a usable block at the junkyard is a tough job. If the engine you are looking at is out of the car, the only way to identify it quickly is by the block casting number or engine identification number. The casting number is located on the top

Another view of the 327 ci engine shows the three oil gallery plugs in the front face of the block. Notice that they are new and have been sealed into place with Loctite. The complete block refinishing included the removal of these plugs, front and rear, for cleaning and installation of new cam bearings.

The cylinder walls, now overbored, show a nice cross-hatch pattern. This finish is necessary for proper piston ring seal.

of the flywheel housing just behind the cylinder head of the 1-3-5-7 left side. Engine identification numbers are always located on the small part of the block deck surface that extends beyond where the head mounts on the front of the 2-4-6-8 right side. The two identifying numbers are diagonally across from each other at both ends of the engine. If the numbers are not plainly visible, use a scraper to clean away any rust or grease covering them.

Be careful to examine the sides, back and mounting surfaces of any block outside a vehicle. Junkyards are not known for their careful treatment of parts. Look for dents, cracks or chunks broken away from the outside of the block, because the block may have been dropped to the ground or onto a heap of other engines.

Junkyards are worth a look, but they are usually expensive and sometimes not the best place to get an engine. When I look for an engine, I read the local *Trader, Parts Swapper, Bargain News* and so on. These papers have advertisements for inexpensive cars. (I have purchased cars for as little as $100 that have just the engine and transmission I have been looking for.) This method of selecting a block is the most desirable because the engine is usually running and easy to check out.

Inspection

When you find a "virgin" engine that has 90,000 or more miles on it, you can be sure it was built correctly to begin with. If you're lucky, you may be buying from the original owner who knows the entire vehicle history and has repair records. Make sure the block you are investigating has all the mounting holes and accessories needed for your application.

The pivot ball mounting holes for the clutch linkage are sometimes not located where you need them. Usually the small-block has two pivot ball holes. One is located in front of the oil filter mounting pad, and the other is located above the mounting pad close to the back of the block. Check to see that the block has the mounting hole you need. Many 400 ci engine blocks have bosses for pivot ball mounting, but the holes are not drilled and tapped. You can do the drilling and tapping yourself, but use extreme care.

Be aware of the dipstick location on the side of the block. Late-model small-blocks have dipstick mounting on the opposite side compared with ear-

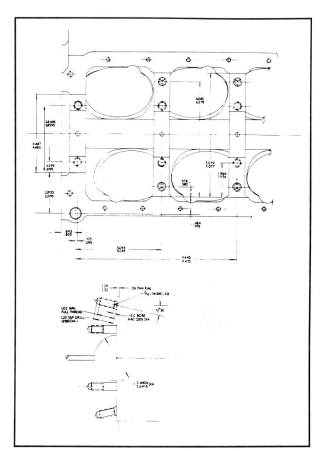

Cylinder block machining for splayed-bolt main cap.

The first main bearing cap is unaltered but the second, third and fourth have been machined flat and had ½ in. steel plates bolted on to strengthen the block. This is probably effective but I have never seen a small-block fail through the main cap.

This is a Target Master engine crate, a brand spanking new engine within. These engines can be acquired for considerably less than list price—especially if you buy more than one at a time. Check with your friends and use the buddy system to lower your cost.

lier blocks. For example, the 1980 and later 350 ci truck blocks numbered 207 on the sides or labeled 5.7LG, and the new 305 ci passenger car blocks labeled 5.0LG, have opposite-side dipstick locations.

Make sure there are no broken-off bolts in any of the engine mount holes on either side of the block, and be sure the transmission flywheel housing bolt holes are undamaged. Also check the con-

dition, location and number of starter motor mounting holes.

When you have a block you think you want to use, take out all removable bolts and knock out the freeze plugs. (Be sure to remove the freeze plugs; don't just knock them in and leave them!) Have the block hot-tanked to remove all the grease and sludge.

Make sure the block is clean, then bolt it into an engine stand and clean out the threaded holes with a bottoming tap. When retapping the thread holes, check for stripped threads or cracks around the holes. Check the main bearing webs and caps, and check the cylinder bores if the engine was not running when you got it.

After inspection, you may want to have the block decked for clean-up or to remove rust pits and other depressions that make the cylinder head mounting surface uneven.

Have the cylinders made round again by having the block bored to a size that removes all cylinder wall taper. New pistons are available in 0.020, 0.030, 0.040 and 0.060 in. oversizes. More than a 0.040 in. overbore is not recommended if you are using a 1980 or later block.

After boring, have the block honed on a machine that will give a nice forty-five-degree-angle crosshatch with a 400 grit stone. While still at the machine shop, have new cam bearings installed.

You should be able to do everything else at home. Start by washing the block again with liquid soap and hot water. Dry the block quickly using a lint-free towel. Oil the block, especially rubbing the oil into the cylinder walls, and cover the block with a plastic bag until you are ready for assembly.

This is how the Target Master 350 looks when the crate is open. These engines are a bargain! They have heavy casted 993 heads and four-bolt main bearing caps.

Here is a close-up of the Target Master casting number. The words, Hecho en Mexico, are printed above the number. These engines are based on pre-1986 part castings and have old-style heavy-duty parts.

I have never found it necessary to grind away sharp edges or "improve" the inside of the block in any way. Deburring your block is unnecessary and can contaminate your engine with metal filings and other grit that can seriously damage an engine. Better leave well enough alone.

New blocks

Buying a new block is an alternative to block hunting at wrecking yards, and many new blocks are available from Chevrolet. The new four-bolt, 350 ci block from the Chevrolet high-performance division is part number 366246. This block features thicker cylinder walls, a thicker deck surface and an iron alloy with a greater percentage of nickel and tin.

An unfinished four-bolt block with siamesed cylinders is available as part number 366287. This block may be bored to 4.125 in., as were earlier 400 ci engines, or it can be finished as a standard 350 ci unit. The advantage of siamesed cylinders is the strength gained by cylinder bores that are connected.

An aluminum 350 ci four-bolt block with center main caps that have splayed outer bolts is available under part number 366300. The cost of this unit is around $4,000. All high-performance and regular production parts will interchange between the cast-iron and aluminum blocks. The aluminum block has cast-iron cylinder liners that will accept up to a 0.030 in. overbore. Use of the aluminum block, aluminum heads (part number 14101127, for example), aluminum intake manifold and thin steel-tube headers will reduce the weight of the small-block considerably.

The new blocks mentioned here will accept only the 2.450 in. diameter main journal crankshafts. Chevrolet no longer offers a replacement bare block that will accept the 2.650 in. diameter main journal 400 ci crankshaft.

Run-in

Remember that new blocks are unused and are subject to some dimensional changes during first running. They also take considerably longer than used blocks to break in because they have not yet heated and cooled enough to stabilize. Allow for as many as 3,000 extra break-in miles for a new block.

When all is considered, used blocks offer many advantages. They have been run-in or seasoned, and are available at a fraction of the cost of a new block.

Partial list of engines available from Chevrolet				
Engine (ci)	Year	Short-block part number	Cylinder head part number	Application
305	1976-79	474169	14034807	General
	1976-80	10054575	Included (Target Master long-block)	
	1980-85	14019868	14034807	General
		10054560	Included (Target Master long-block)	
	1985	14091328	14034807	High output
	1986	14101315	14034807	High output
	1987	14049047	10065207	General
	1988	10104488	10065207	General
307	1968-73	3970651	6272069	General
350	1969-70	3966921	3987376	High performance
	1973-85	10067353	Included (Target Master long-block)	
	1976-79	14034904	14034808	General
	1980-81	14019871	14034808	General
	1982-85	10077067	14034808	General
	1984-85	14083505	464045	Corvette
	1986 First design	10046307	464045	Corvette
		14101310	14101127	Corvette
	1986 Second design	10077064	464045	Corvette
		10077063	14101127	Corvette
	1986	10048971	Included (Target Master long-block)	
	1987	10049050	14101127	Corvette
	1988	10104464	14101127	Corvette

Block-crankshaft-cylinder head casting identification

Casting number	Years used	Engine size	Casting number	Years used	Engine size
330545	71-74	350	3941174	68-73	307, 327
330817	74-76	400	3941182	68-85	350
333882	71-76	350, 400	3946812	69	350
340292	73-77	350	3946813	69-70	350
354431	75-76	262	3947041	69-70	350
354434	75-79	262, 305	3951509	74-80	400
355909	76-79	305	3951511	70-74	400
358741	76-79	305	3951529	70-80	400
361979	75-77	305	3951598	70-71	400
367450	75-77	262, 305	3956618	68-76	350
460776	76-79	305	3958618	68-76	350
468642	76-80	350, 400	3964286	68-76	350
517513	79-80	267	3970010	68-76	350
3770126	68-70	327, 350	3970014	68-72	302, 350
3782461	68	327, 350	3970020	68-73	307
3795896	68-72	307, 327	3970024	68-71	307
3855961	68-76	327, 350	3970126	68-70	327, 350
3891492	68-73	327, 350	3973487	68-71	350
3911001	68-73	307	3973493	71-73	400
3911032	68-69	307, 327	3981462	68	327
3914636	68-73	307	3986388	68-76	307, 350
3914660	68-69	327	3986339	68-76	307, 350
3914678	68-69	327	3991492	69-70	350
3917290	68-69	307, 327	3998916	72	400
3917291	68-70	302, 327, 350	3998991	71-80	307, 350
3917292	68-69	327	3998993	71-76	350
3917293	68-69	307	3998993	85-88	350 Target Master: Hecho en Mexico
3927185	68-75	307, 327, 350			
3927186	68-72	302, 327, 350			
3827187	69-70	302, 350	3998997	72-74	350, 400
3927188	69-70	307, 327, 350	6259425	68-76	350
3928454	68	307	6260856	68-76	350
3928455	68	302, 327	10051101	86 and later	350
3928494	68	327	10066033	80-85	350 Target Master
3928495	68	327			
3931633	68-73	307			
3931635	68-76	350	14010201	85-86	305
3931637	68-69	327	14010207	80-85	350
3931638	68	327	14010509	79-80 and later	400
3931639	68	302	14011049	80 and later	350
3932373	68-73	307	14014415	80-82	267
3932386	68-70	327, 350	14014416	80-84	305
3932388	69-73	350	14022801	80-86	276-305
3932441	68-72	350	14088526	86-88	350
3932442	68-85	305, 350	14088552	86-88	350
3932454	68-69	307	14101128	86 and later	350
3932882	75-76	350, 400	14102191	87-88 and later	350

Crankshafts

3

By 1968, small-block Chevrolet crankshafts all measured 2.100 in. in diameter at the rod bearing journal and 2.450 in. in diameter at the main bearing journal. The only exception was the 400 ci engine (released in 1970), which had a larger main bearing journal diameter of 2.650 in. The large-journal measurements are standard today.

Small-block stroke lengths measure 3.000 in. for the 302 ci engine; 3.100 in. for the 262 ci engine; 3.250 in. for the 307 and 327 ci engines; 3.480 in. for the 267, 305 and 350 ci engines; and 3.750 in. for the 400 ci engine.

Chevrolet crankshafts are available in two material styles: cast nodular iron or forged steel.

The cast-nodular-iron crankshafts are the most common because they are standard in all the base and intermediate-performance engines. Special high-performance and heavy-duty truck engines have the forged-steel crankshafts installed because more severe loading usually occurs in these applications.

Identification

Cast-nodular-iron crankshafts are easily recognized by a thin casting seam extending down the length of the shaft. This is most easily visible on the first crankshaft rod bearing journal and is a result of the two halves of the mold coming together. These

This is only one corner of the crankshaft storage room at Storm Crankshaft in Mt. Vernon, New York. I believe that *this company has at least two of every crankshaft ever made somewhere on the property.*

Ray at Storm Crankshaft prepares to radius oil holes on this 442 cast-iron 350 ci crankshaft. Always have an experienced crank grinder inspect your crankshaft and at the least, have him or her polish the journals and radius the oil holes.

crankshafts are strong and will give good service with proper oiling.

The iron material of the cast-iron crankshaft has the ability to flex under load, and its granular structure dampens torsional vibration when run at high rpm. This feature helps eliminate frequency response problems that occur when an engine is operated under full load and high rpm for a long period of time—for example, in a Grand National stock car engine on a superspeedway. Cast-iron crankshafts will work well in any high-performance street engine, but if you are going to build a race engine for a short-track, drag strip or any serious application, forged-steel crankshafts are more desirable.

Forged-steel crankshafts are easy to recognize owing to their smooth appearance as compared with cast units, and they have a large ribbed parting line instead of the narrow seam of a casting. They are available with a special heat-treating and

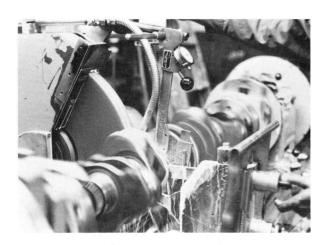

This is not a Chevy crankshaft but it shows the grinding operation at Storm. Crank clearances are critical so consider that a few dollars spent here may save a lot of money later.

The polishing operation eliminates high spots or running lines on journal surfaces. Polishing may remove a little metal but Delco-Moraine (GM) bearings are available in 0.001 in. and 0.002 in. undersizes to compensate for creating larger clearances.

surface-hardening process called Tufftriding. Tufftriding decreases friction, making the treated forged-steel unit the preferred crankshaft in racing.

Forged-steel crankshafts interchange between all blocks except the 400 ci unit. The 400 engine block has larger main bearing saddles, making it necessary to use bearing spacers or thicker-shelled bearings (this is explained further in the piston chapter). Forged crankshafts from Chevrolet are available only in the 3.000 in., 3.250 in. and 3.480 in. strokes. This means that the 302 ci engine uses a steel crankshaft with the 3.000 in. stroke. The 307 ci and 327 ci engines can use a steel crankshaft with the 3.250 in. stroke. The 267 ci, 305 ci and 350 ci engines can use a steel crankshaft with the 3.480 in. stroke.

The only strokes not available in steel from Chevrolet are the 3.100 in. stroke of the 262 ci engine and the 3.750 in. stroke of the 400 ci engine.

Casting numbers are visible on both forged-steel and nodular-iron crankshafts. These are not part numbers but identification numbers assigned to forgings or castings at the manufacturing plant. All large-journal crankshafts are redesigned units as of the 1968 production year. Any casting numbers mentioned were in production between 1968 and 1988.

Crankshafts

Year	Stroke depth (in.)	Construction and materials	Casting or forging number
1968-69	3.000	Forged steel	1178 or 3279
	3.250	Forged steel	1130 or 4672
1968-73	3.250	Cast nodular iron	3911001 or 3941174
1968-75	3.480	Forged steel	2690
1968-85	3.480	Cast nodular iron	3932442
		Forged steel	3941182 or 1182
1970-80	3.750	Cast nodular iron	3951529*
1975-76	3.100	Cast nodular iron	354431
1986-88	3.480	Cast nodular iron	14088526†
		Forged steel	14088552†

*Needs main bearing journal modification before interchange is possible.
†Works only in a 1986 or later block.

On the left is a 3911001 cast 307 crankshaft; on the right is a 3941174 cast 327 crankshaft. These crankshafts with different casting numbers and different-shaped flywheel flanges share a 3.250 in. stroke and are completely interchangeable.

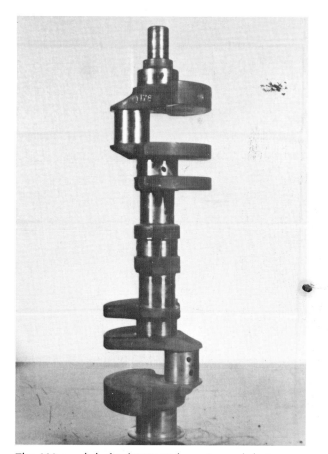

The 302 crankshaft of 1968-69 large-journal design was only available in forged steel. Notice this crank has 1178 on the first counterweight. Chevrolet also produced another large-journal 3.000 in. stroke unit numbered 3279.

On the center of this cast-iron 400 crankshaft is the number 3951529. Notice how large the main bearing journal diameters are.

Bearings

The bearings should be selected on the basis of how you intend to use your engine. Whether a cast-iron or steel crankshaft is used, high-performance engines driven on the street need top-quality bearings such as Clevite 77, Federal Mogul AP, Michigan 77 or original equipment GM 400 bearings. These high-performance bearings will give good service provided they are given frequent oil changes and great care is taken to ensure proper clearances when they are installed.

A good method of selecting bearings is to let the person who resurfaces your crankshaft supply you with the bearings he or she feels are best for your application. According to one of the best crank grinders in the business, the brand of the bearing is unimportant. Most important are the materials used in manufacturing, because these classify the bearings into types for different applications.

If you have questions about how much clearance you should build into your engine, consult the

When installing a 400 crankshaft into a 350 ci block, it is necessary to grind the main journal diameters from 2.650 in. to 2.450 in. This converted 400 crankshaft has been marked by Performance Automotive Wholesalers and is ready to become part of a 383 ci assembly.

This cast-iron crankshaft, marked 354431 on the second counterweight, belongs to the 1975 262 ci V-8. It has large-journal diameters and a 3.100 in. stroke that will interchange if custom rod lengths or custom pistons are used.

GM service manual for your engine. A time-tested method for checking clearances is to use Plastigage. Plastigage is a thin plastic wire that is crushed between the bearing and the crankshaft journal surface: it measures the distance between the two where oil passes. Plastigage kits come with simple instructions and easy-to-use comparison charts.

Flanges

Whether cast iron or steel, all crankshafts before 1968 had round flywheel flanges. The only late-model large-journal crankshaft to retain that design was the 1968-69 steel 3.000 in. stroke 302 ci unit. All the other stroke depths—3.250, 3.480, 3.750 and 3.100 in.—were redesigned with a counterweight on the flange. This redesign created irregular shapes between the different stroke depths, which help identify crankshafts while they are still installed in the engine. The recognizable, irregularly shaped counterweights on crankshaft flywheel flanges were in production for eighteen model years.

According to Chevrolet engineers, the biggest warranty problem on the small-block was crank-

The 1182 forged-steel and the 2690 forged-steel 350 crankshafts differ in weight slightly but both share a 3.480 in. stroke. Sometimes these units are customized for circle track racing so it is important to identify them by number—if someone hasn't ground that off too.

Here are two 327 forged-steel crankshafts. It is unusual to find both 4672, left, and 1130, right, castings in one place. These large-journal (1968-69 only) units are hard to track down.

The numbers on the steel 350 crank, left, and the steel 327 crank, right, are plainly visible. When the numbers can't be seen, another way to distinguish these crankshafts is by the front throw of each shaft: notice the dip in the 327 unit as compared to the built-up top of the 350 shaft.

The 1986 and later 305 five-liter and 350 5.7 liter engines use these round, thick-flanged crankshafts for the re-designed rear-seal blocks. Most engines come with the cast-iron 14088526 unit on the left. Some engines with four-bolt main cap blocks have the forged-steel 14088532 crank on the right.

Two 350 crankshafts: the cast-iron unit on the left has a round protruding knob and a thin cast-parting line; the forged-steel unit on the right has no knob, has a wide seam and is built out on the front journal. The cast crank is numbered 3932442 on the second counterweight and the forged crank is numbered 3941182 or 1182 on the first throw. Both of these crankshafts interchange and fit into the 267 ci, 305 ci and 350 ci engines from 1968-85.

This close-up view of 3.250 in. stroke crankshaft flanges shows a difference that could help identify a junkyard engine more easily. As stated earlier, these are com-pletely interchangeable. The 307 is at left, the 327 at right.

These crankshaft flanges belong to a steel 350 crank, left, and steel 302 crank, right. Notice that the 302 crank flange is round with one notch cut out, as early pre–1968 cranks are. Also notice the round, bronze pilot bushing installed in the 302 shaft. Pilot bushings support manual transmission input shafts. The 302 engine from the factory never came with an automatic transmission.

This close-up view of the 1986 and later 3.480 in. stroke 305 ci and 350 ci crank shows that this small round flange will only accept a flywheel designed specifically for it. The late-model cranks also use dowel pins and have a flywheel with balancing weights attached.

shaft rear main seal leakage. To solve the problem, the rear crankshaft flange was redesigned for the 1986 production year to accommodate a new larger one-piece oil seal. The flange was made smaller and perfectly round.

The new seal was designed to be a bolt-on appliance at the back of the redesigned block. Therefore, 1985 and earlier crankshafts will not fit the new block unless the special adapter kit (part number 10051118) is installed. The adapter allows the installation of the old two-piece oil seal and an earlier crankshaft in the stroke of your choice.

Harmonic balancers

Harmonic balancers, or vibration dampers, are available in at least six different styles. Any balancer

that came with your engine and is not damaged can be reinstalled. The stock harmonic balancer is more than likely adequate for any high-performance street application.

All crankshaft snouts measure 1¼ in. in diameter. In addition, all small-block balancers fit all large-journal crankshafts.

Harmonic balancers come from Chevrolet in two basic hub diameters: 4⅜ in. and 6¼ in. The hub is the support for the outside iron ring that

This is the flange of a 400 cast-iron crankshaft. It is easily recognized by the dowel pin, top center of picture.

Here are the harmonic balancers that come stock on the small-block. From left to right: the 400; 350, 327 and 302 SP HP; 350 HP; 350, 327 and some 305s; 307 and 262; 305 and 267 balancers.

This special high-performance timing cover and balancer is for a 1970 370 hp 350 ci. Notice the older-style timing cover with welded pointer. This set will interchange onto all but the externally balanced 400 small-block.

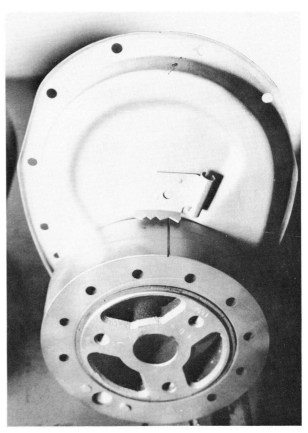

In the late seventies, wide, hollow balancers began showing up on the 305. This timing pointer was in a different location and had a diagnostic machine pickup holder. This must stay together as a set. I would not recommend this balancer for interchange: the outer ring walks back and around the center hub.

The balancer and cover from a late-model truck. This slightly narrower 8 in. balancer is not the largest but it will dampen vibrations at high rpm well. It will interchange onto all but the 400 ci engines.

From left, the 400 balancer, the 262 through 350 balancers, and the 305 balancer. The 400 balancer must stay with the 400 crank. The 262 through 350 balancers are all interchangeable when using the appropriate bolt-on timing mark. Notice the dissimilar timing mark location on the 305 balancer; I don't recommend using this unit.

absorbs vibration from the crankshaft. The ring is fastened to the hub by means of a rubber inlay pressed between the two parts. Crankshaft vibration travels through the balancer hub and diffuses out through the rubber into the outside ring. The hub size is directly related to the length of the rubber inlay and the size of the diffusing ring.

Balancer dimensions vary according to engine size. For the 262 ci and 307 ci engines, a 4⅜ in. hub supports a balancer measuring 6⅛ in. in diameter by ¾ in. in width. The base and intermediate 327 ci and base-only 350 ci engines use the same 4⅜ in. hub but the outer ring is larger and wider—6¾ in. in diameter and 1 3/16 in. in width. The 267 ci and 305 ci engines also have the small 4⅜ in. hub and the 6¾ in. ring diameter, but the ring width is increased to 1 11/16 in.

The remaining balancers all use the large 6¼ in. hub. The intermediate-performance 350 ci balancer measures 8 in. in diameter with a width of 1½ in. The 400 ci small-block has an 8 in. diameter, 1½ in. wide balancer that has been unbalanced by removing weight from one side. This 400 engine balancer should be used only with the 400 crankshaft.

The special high-performance 302 ci, 327 ci and 350 ci engines have the largest balancer because these engines are intended for high-rpm use. High-performance engines come with forged-steel crankshafts that have a denser structure. This heavy-duty structure makes these engines more resistant to component failure during repeated wide-open-throttle acceleration. However, the same feature that makes the engine so tough also makes it more susceptible to frequency vibrations, which could cause other failures, so more vibration damping is necessary. The high-performance balancer is heavy. It measures 8 in. in diameter by 1¾ in. in width.

All but one of the small-block balancers are interchangeable. The exception is the 400 ci unit, which should be used only on a 400 crankshaft.

This harmonic balancer repair kit saves new seals and prevents oil leaks. Notice the crankshaft sleeve on the hub of the balancer. The deep groove is from the oil seal wearing away at the cast iron. When the sleeve seal-saver is installed, the surface is flat again and the chromed surface doesn't wear. I would use this kit on a new balancer to prevent wear and the possibility of developing a leak later.

Do not interchange balancers without checking the timing tag location on the timing cover in relation to the mark on the balancer. During the assembly of your engine, make sure the number 1 piston comes to the top of the cylinder when the timing marks read zero. If an adjustment has to be made to the timing tag alignment, do it before installing the cylinder heads while the pistons are still visible in the bore.

As stated earlier, any high-performance street engine will work well with a stock-size harmonic balancer. If you plan to run your engine for extended periods at high rpm, or if you are going to

Harmonic balancers

Balancer dimensions (in.)	Engine size (ci)	Part number	Use description	Hub size
6⅛×¾	262, 307	6272223	Base performance	4⅜
6¾×1 3/16	305, 327, 350	6272221	Base performance	4⅜
6¾×1 11/16	267, 305	458653	Base performance	4⅜
8×1½	350	6272222	Intermediate performance	6¼
	400 only	6272225	Unbalanced intermediate performance	6¼
8×1¾	302, 327, 350	3947708	Special high performance	6½
		364709	Nodular iron ring, off-road racing	6¼

A 400 harmonic balancer and flywheel for the automatic transmission.

use a steel crankshaft, use the large high-performance balancer (part number 3947708).

When interchanging balancers, take comfort in the knowledge that the triangular three-bolt pattern on the front of any small-block balancer will fit any of the crankshaft pulleys available to drive accessories. In addition, all water pumps for use on the small-block were designed to clear the largest harmonic balancer dimensions. Thus, you can use any size balancer you want, as you won't have any clearance problems.

Flywheels and starters

The basic function of the flywheel is to smooth out the motion of the crankshaft while each cylin-

der turns through the four stroke cycles. Flywheels are interchangeable from the 1968 to 1985 production years. In 1986, a design change created a flywheel bolt pattern of different dimensions compared with that on previous small-blocks.

Chevrolet flywheels are available in two basic sizes: a 12¾ in. diameter, 153 tooth unit, and a 14 in. diameter, 168 tooth unit. These two basic sizes are available as flex plates that attach to torque converters for use with an automatic transmission and as flywheels that attach to pressure plates to squeeze clutch discs for manual transmissions.

Flex plates all weigh about the same, but manual transmission flywheels are available in many different weights. When a heavy flywheel is used, the vehicle pulls away from a stopped position with less rpm loss. If a light flywheel is used, the engine will lose rpm quickly on the start but will gain rpm quickly while accelerating.

The flywheel, when in motion, is where inertia is stored. The use of one with less weight means less stored energy; the use of one with more weight means more stored energy. For drag racing applications, a heavy flywheel will launch the car with more force because the engine is run at high rpm at the starting line when the clutch is released. When the heavy flywheel is turning at high rpm, the great reciprocating mass holds tremendous power. When this power is expended in an instant, the drag car jumps off the starting line.

The reverse applies to a circle track car. A light flywheel will help the car accelerate out of a turn because the light reciprocating mass puts a small load on the engine and allows the engine to gain rpm. Energy is expended instantly because there is

A 400 balancer and flywheel for a manual transmission. The manual and automatic equipment have the same external weights. These pieces must only be used with 400 engine crankshafts.

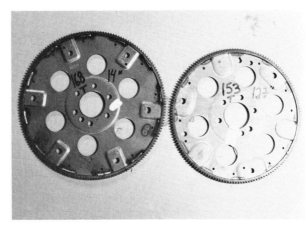

These different-sized flywheels will interchange onto all but 400 engines. The 168 tooth 14 in. flywheel on the left is designed to fit all small-block crankshaft hubs from 1968 to 1985. The 12¾ in. 153 tooth flywheel on the right will fit the same engines but each flywheel requires a different starter nose. Both flywheels are for use with automatic transmissions.

Here are flywheels intended for manual transmissions on all but the 400. Several different weights are available in each size but they measure similarly. The 12¾ in. 153 tooth is at left and the 14 in. 168 tooth is at right. Note that sometimes these are called the 10½ in. and 11 in. fly-wheels: the reason is that these flywheels fit a 10½ in. clutch disc and an 11 in. clutch disc, respectively.

Although these starters are rated at different torque levels and have different-sized armatures, the nose sections interchange from one to the other. As labeled in the photo, the starter on the left is for 12¾ in. flywheels only (notice the straight-across bolt pattern) and the two starters on the right are for 14 in. flywheels only (notice the diagonal bolt pattern). The starter with the cast-iron nose on the extreme right is for 1968-70 special high-performance engines with manual transmissions and heavy-duty 11 in. clutch.

little weight to store the inertia created by the motion of the turning crankshaft.

The use of a manual or automatic transmission does not determine your flywheel diameter choice. Both 12¾ in. and 14 in. diameter setups will work with either transmission. The choice of what fly-wheel to use will depend on how fast you want your starter motor to turn your engine when starting.

If you have a low-compression, 307 ci or smaller engine, the 12¾ in., 153 tooth high-starter-ratio combination will work. More than likely, however, your engine came equipped with the low starter ratio that uses a 14 in. diameter, 168 tooth flywheel.

Most late-model vehicles with air conditioning use the low-ratio starter-flywheel combination. The engines in these vehicles usually have to power an air-conditioning compressor, large alternator and other power accessories, and they get hot in the process. Hot engines and hot starter motors don't turn easily. If a low, or "easy-to-push," ratio is used, the starter works more easily and, as a result,

less wear occurs on the starting components. If you have a large-displacement, high-compression performance engine, the large flywheel and high-torque starter are mandatory.

Mounting

Not every starter fits every flywheel. By 1968, most starters were block-mounted. To use different ratios required mounting the starter motor 0.625 in. toward or away from the crankshaft because of the differences in flywheel diameters. The different mountings were accomplished by the use of two different shaped starter motor nosepieces. Both nosepieces used two of the three mounting holes on the bottom of the block.

Always check the number, location and condition of the starter motor mounting holes on the block you have selected before deciding which flywheel to use.

Pistons and connecting rods **4**

When rebuilding the small-block Chevy engine, so many different pistons are available that it is difficult to make a choice that best suits your needs.

These 305 pistons have been cleaned, glass-bead blasted and, with new rings installed, are about to be placed into the cylinder bores. The pistons are being re-used as they show little sign of wear.

Here are the two basic styles of the 305 piston: the one on the left is from a 1979 H motor; the four-notch piston on the right is from a 1987 G motor.

Carefully evaluate your needs before rushing into your local speed shop.

For everyday transportation, with an occasional Saturday night thrashing, the factory cast-aluminum pistons are completely adequate. These are available from a variety of reputable after-market manufacturers at a reasonable cost, and using them can help keep the cost of a rebuild down.

Cast pistons

Cast pistons come manufactured with steel wrist pin and skirt supports molded into the aluminum on each side. The steel inserts help support the wrist pin bosses and keep the piston skirts equally separated during low- and high-temperature operation. Less thermal expansion allows a tighter piston fit in the cylinder bore. A tighter fit reduces the amount of noise or piston slap the engine has following a cold start. Less piston-to-cylinder-wall clearance also prevents the rings from twisting in the ring grooves, so minimal ring wear occurs. Reduced ring wear increases engine life because cylinder compression pressures remain higher, longer. When rings do their job effectively, the cylinders create less blow-by gases, thereby lowering emission levels.

These features make the cast-aluminum pistons desirable for the street engine. What is not desirable is the pistons' relative weakness when compared with forged-aluminum pistons. Cast pistons are more porous than forged pistons and tend to hold carbon deposits that will change compression figures. They will not resist burning away or pitting under severe cylinder temperatures or detonation pressures, and they may crack or burn through when used under severe conditions.

Forged pistons

All factory high-performance small-block Chevrolet engines come with forged pistons. If you are serious about performance and you intend to build a special engine for use with a turbocharger, blower or nitrous oxide injection system, then forget cast-aluminum pistons and use forged pistons.

Forged high-performance aluminum pistons may distort under extreme detonation or lean con-

The underside of two 350 pistons shows some of the differences in construction between the cast piston on the left and the forged piston on the right. Notice the three reinforcement ribs on each side of the skirt of the forged unit.

Here are some 1970 style forged 400 pistons installed in a 1980 van block using a 1972 crankshaft with one of the two 1976 cylinder heads already installed. We later installed a 1969 intake manifold and carburetor. The interchange possibilities of the small-block are endless.

ditions at high rpm, but for repeated severe use they are the toughest pistons available.

The forged piston can handle severe conditions because of the special construction techniques used in their manufacture. Forged pistons are made by crushing aluminum pellets into piston molds under extreme pressure. This process makes a piston of high density that is able to work with

little distortion when used under extreme conditions.

TRW Corporation has developed forged performance pistons that can be fitted to cylinder walls almost as tightly as can cast pistons. The aluminum alloy used, VMS-75, has the same tough, dense construction as that used for previous pistons, but has less thermal expansion and dissipates heat more effectively. Traditionally, forged pistons had to be fitted with more clearance than cast pistons, and this caused oil control problems. Today's TRW forged pistons have construction features that

This 1976 400 piston creates an 8:1 compression ratio with 76 cc heads. The factory 400 pistons have two other styles that create 8.5:1 and 8.9:1 compression. These L2410 forged pistons are the ones to use if the engine is always run under load.

This 327 piston is rated at 10:1 compression. When used with later-model larger combustion chamber cylinder heads, the resulting lower compression ratio is desirable considering today's fuels.

Pistons

Engine (ci)	Cast-aluminum piston no.	Forged-aluminum piston no.	Dome or relief size	Combustion Chamber Sizes			Rings
				64 cc	68 cc	76 cc	
262	L3075F			8.5:1*			
267	L3031F			8.3:1*			
302		L2210AF	0.450 dome	12.5:1	11.7:1	10.4:1	T9034MM T8325M
305	L3028F	L2432F	Flat	8.5:1*			T8307M
		L2468F	0.250 dome	12:1	11.3:1	10.1	
307	L3023F	L2314F	Flat	10.5:1	10.1:1	9:1	T7556M
		L2272F	0.450 dome	12.5:1	11.7:1	10.4:1	
327	L3020F	L2165F	Flat	10:1	9.5:1	8.75:1	T9013MM T8325M
		L2166NF	0.125 dome	10.7:1	10.25:1	9:1	
		L2211AF	0.380 dome	12.15:1	11.5:1	10.4:1	
		L2326F	Flat with 2 valve relief	9.87:1	9.4:1	8.65:1	T9139MM
350	L3022F	L2256F	Flat with 4 valve relief	10.25:1	9.4:1	8.9:1	T9013MM T8325M
		L2417F	Flat with slot	10.25:1	9.78:1	9:1	
	L3026F	L2403F	Flat with dish	10.1:1	9.5:1	8.5:1	
	L3028F	L2432F	Flat with dish	10.1:1	9.5:1	8.5:1	
	L3084F	L2382F	Flat with dish	9.5:1	8.9:1	8:1	
		L2454F	Flat with slot	10.25:1	9.78:1	9:1	
		L2441F	Flat with large dish	8.95:1	8.65:1	8.2:1	
		L2304F	0.100 dome	11:1	10.4:1	9.75:1	
		L2252AF	0.125 dome	12.5:1	11.75:1	10.6:1	
		L2327F	Flat with 2 valve relief	10.5:1	9.55:1	8.75:1	T9139MM
400	L3024F	L2352F	Flat with dish	9.95:1	9.58:1	8.9:1	T9018MM
	L3024F	L2376F	Flat with dish	9.87:1	9.15:1	8.5:1	T7678M
	L3024F	L2410F	Flat with dish	9.7:1	9:1	8.2:1	
		L2311F	0.500 dome	12.5:1	12:1	11:1	
		L2467F	Flat with 2 valve relief	10.3:1	9.85:1	9:1	

*Actual combustion chamber size as small as 60.5 cc.
This table of TRW pistons shows approximate compression ratios with the average chamber sizes available. Your actual compression ratio will vary because of manufacturing differences between cylinder heads, gasket thickness, block deck height and cam timing. These ratios are approximate using standard bore sizes.

allow a tighter fit and the best ring control of any previously discussed pistons. They create the most efficient sealing of the cylinder, locking in combustion pressures and preventing oil from entering the combustion chamber.

Compression ratio

When making your piston selection, use pistons and cylinder heads that work together to create a maximum compression ratio of 9.5:1, unless you intend to use special fuel on a regular basis. (A 9.5:1 ratio, or lower, is the only way to go for a street-driven engine.) If you have to overbore your engine, remember that the larger bore size created by the overbore will effect the compression ratio.

When calculating the compression ratio of your engine, figure in the amount of overbore (0.020, 0.030, 0.040, 0.060 in.) your block requires for cleanup.

Compression height and connecting rod length

Interchanging pistons from one engine size to another is easy between the 302 ci, 327 ci and 350 ci engines because the bore sizes of these engines are the same at 4.001 in. The connecting rods of the aforementioned engines are also the same length: 5.703 in. The problems begin when you try to interchange crankshafts between pistons without comparing the compression heights of the different engines.

Compression height is the distance from the wrist pin to the deck of the piston. The compression

On the right is a 1969 327 piston; on the left is a 1973 350 piston. With dissimilar compression heights, no interchange of crankshafts is possible. If a 350 crankshaft was used with 327 pistons, the deeper-stroke crankshaft would push the pistons out of the bore by as much as a quarter of an inch.

height of each piston is determined by the stroke of the crankshaft. Therefore, you cannot use a 327 ci piston with a 350 ci (3.480 in. stroke) crankshaft because the piston will protrude from the block by almost 0.125 in. When the piston deck is higher

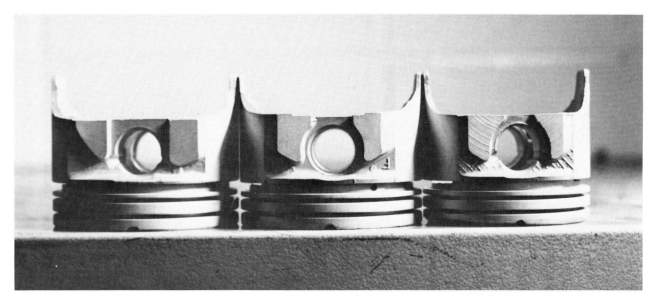

From left, the 350, 400 and 305 pistons, which all share the same compression height (the distance from wrist pin to piston top deck). The 305 and 350 engines share the same 3.480 in. stroke depth and 5.703 in. length rod. The 400 engine has a 3.750 in. stroke depth so it must use a shorter *5.560 in. rod to compensate. This photo illustrates that crankshaft interchange is possible between these engines—provided main bearing journal diameters are taken into consideration.*

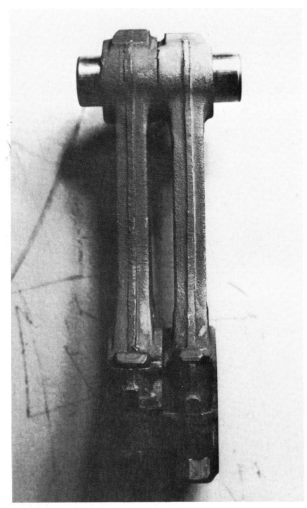

The two connecting rods on the same pin are examples of the 5.560 in. long 400 rod on the left and the 5.703 in. long 350 rod on the right. The difference in length is hard to see but is visible at the journal end parting-line where the two rods are touching. Notice the wide flattened rod bolt on the short rod at left, designed for block clearance.

The L2256 pistons in this block are of light construction. Although forged pistons, they are not intended for racing and have no skirt reinforcements.

than the block deck by 0.125 in., the cylinder heads will contact the pistons and will not allow the engine to turn through one crankshaft rotation. In another example, if you tried to use a 302 ci (3.000 in. stroke) with 350 ci pistons, the piston deck would not reach the top of the cylinder bore and the pistons would fall short by almost 0.250 in.

Compression height is directly related to crankshaft stroke. The only way to interchange pistons on crankshafts is to alter the connecting rod length, as Chevrolet engineers did in the 400 ci engine.

Compression height and connecting rod length

Engine (ci)	Bore (in.)	Stroke (in.)	Rod length (in.)	Compression height (in.)
262	3.671	3.100	5.703	1.750
267	3.500	3.484	5.703	1.560
302	4.001	3.000	5.703	1.800
305	3.736	3.484	5.703	1.560
307	3.875	3.250	3.703	1.675
327	4.001	3.250	5.703	1.675
350	4.001	3.484	5.703	1.560
372 (custom)	4.126	3.484	5.703	1.560
383	4.001	3.750	5.565	1.560
	4.001	3.750	5.703	1.425 (approx.)
400	4.126	3.750	5.565	1.560

Notice the compression height of the 3.484 in. stroked 350 ci engine: 1.560 in. This is possible because the 5.565 in. rod length of the 400 ci engine was substituted for the 5.703 in. rod length common to all other factory small-blocks. This also means that the 400 ci engine will accept the 350 ci stroke size of 3.484 in. in place of the 3.750 in. standard stroke (note the main bearing journal diameter differences) using 400 ci pistons with the 5.703 connecting rods to create a 372 ci engine. The reverse is also possible and is becoming quite common. By using a 400 ci crankshaft stroked to 3.750 in., with the 5.565 in. connecting rods, 383 ci is created from a 350 ci engine. (Note the main bearing journal diameter differences.)

Interchanges

Here are the steps you follow to accomplish the interchange. With a common piston compression height of 1.560 in. between the 350 ci and 400 ci engines, interchange of crankshaft and connecting rod sets is possible. To use a 350 ci crankshaft with a stroke of 3.484 in. in the 400 ci block, TRW bearing kit M53564P must be used. The 400 ci crankshaft with a stroke of 3.750 in. has a main bearing journal diameter of 2.650 in. The 350 ci engine with the 3.484 in. stroke has a main bearing journal diameter of 2.450 in. The 0.200 in. difference requires the use of the TRW thick-shell bearing, or the kit that is a 350 ci main bearing set in the size of your choice (0.010, 0.020 or 0.030 in. undersize), with spacers that lie in the block and main caps underneath. These kits can be expensive, but they provide the best way to de-stroke your 400 ci engine to 372 ci. When a 3.484 stroke is used, the common compression height requires the 5.703 connecting rod length to bring the piston to the top of the bore. The flywheel and harmonic balancer from the internally balanced 350 ci engine must also be used.

The 372 ci engine (4.126 in. bore and 3.480 in. stroke) will gain rpm faster and will be able to produce higher rpm. This is because of the less severe crankshaft and connecting rod geometry that results when a shorter stroke depth is used with a longer connecting rod.

To add cubic inches to the 350 ci engine, substitute the 3.750 in. stroked 400 small-block crankshaft in place of the stock 3.484 in. unit. To accomplish this, some modification is required. The 400 ci crankshaft that measures 2.650 in. in diameter at the main journals must be cut down to the 2.450 in. diameter so that it will fit into the 350 ci block's

These L2441 pistons are intended for racing. Although they are dished to lower compression, the use of bow-tie heads of 64 cc increases the compression ratio only enough to run efficiently on today's fuels. These pistons are intended for use with a turbocharger—or a GMC blower, as is the case here.

A small-block being built up for use with a GMC blower: the demands on the pistons are extreme.

main bearing saddles. Any professional crankshaft grinding company can do this for you.

After the crankshaft is altered to fit the block, shorter 5.565 in. connecting rods must be used in place of the 5.703 in. rods so that the pistons won't extend out of the bore at top dead center (TDC, the highest point the piston will travel up the cylinder wall relative to the crankshaft stroke).

The 400 ci engine is externally balanced. The deep stroke of the crankshaft will not allow enough counterweight to fit inside the limited dimensions of the crankcase, so weight is added or subtracted outside the engine to achieve a balance. The 400 ci flywheel has a weight welded to it that unbalances it, and it should not be used with any other crankshaft. The harmonic balancer, or vibration damper, is a large 8 in. diameter unit with weight removed from one side. The 400 ci balancer should also be used only on the 400 ci crankshaft. The 400 ci crankshaft is now being used in a 350 ci block, so all 400 engine hardware must be used. The crankshaft, connecting rods, flywheel and balancer from the 400 engine are now installed in the 350 engine, creating 383 ci.

The 383 ci engine (4.001 in. bore and 3.750 in. stroke) will create lots of low- and mid-rpm-range torque and horsepower. High-rpm use will be limited by the longer stroke and more severe turning angle of the short connecting rod, but from idle to 5500 rpm, this engine is a real stump puller when properly equipped.

To increase the high-rpm reliability of the 383 ci engine, the longer 5.703 in. connecting rods can be used instead of the 5.565 in. rods. This combination of long stroke (3.750 in.) and long rod (5.703 in.) requires the use of custom pistons with a shorter deck height of 1.425 in. (Remember, the deck height is the distance between the wrist pin and the flat top portion of the piston.) These custom pistons are available in the compression ratio of your choice from many piston manufacturers. Some grinding at the bottom of the block may be necessary to clear the 5.703 in. connecting rod, because the longer rods do not have countersunk bolt heads for clearance, as the short 5.565 in. rods do.

Connecting rods

Recall that Chevrolet small-blocks all have 5.703 in. connecting rods except for the 400 engine, which has the 0.138 in. shorter 5.565 in. rods. All Chevrolet small-block connecting rods from 1968 to the present are of the large-journal size (they fit the 2.100 in. crank journal). The only real difference is in factory preparation, which is described using the terms free-floated, stress-relieved, magnafluxed and shot-peened.

Free-floated means that the wrist pin end of the connecting rod has been machined larger to slide over the wrist pin easily. This additional ease of motion between the connecting rod and the piston is desirable for the high-rpm racing engine. However, special retainers (C-clips or Spirolox) must be used in the piston sides to keep the pin

These components are for a 383 ci engine. The 400 crankshaft has had the main bearing journals turned down from 2.650 to 2.450 in. so that it will fit into a 350 block. The flywheel and harmonic balancer from the 400 engine must be used with this crankshaft. In the foreground are the pistons and the 5.703 in. long 350 connecting rods instead of the 5.560 in. rods of the 400 engine. The longer rod requires custom pistons.

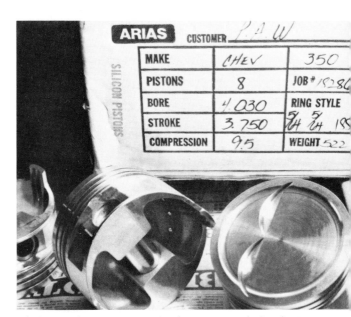

These are the custom pistons that were made for the 383 engine using 5.703 in. rods. They are forged and were made specifically for a custom engine. Standard 350 pistons can be used with a 400 crankshaft when 5.560 in. long rods are used to make the 383 ci combination.

This is a 1970 LT1 type piston, rated at 11:1 compression using 64 cc chambers. It will yield considerably less compression when later-model larger-chambered heads are used. TRW makes a counterpart to this GM part number 3989048 piston.

from sliding out of the rod-and-piston assembly and seriously damaging the cylinder wall. Street engines do not need to be free-floated; leave them press-fitted.

Stress-relieved means that the connecting rods have been heated in a furnace to about 500 degrees Fahrenheit for ten hours or so to relax any torsional twisting that may have occurred during the manufacturing process or when the rod was previously used.

Magnafluxed means that the rod was magnetized by attaching an electromagnet to it while sprinkling metallic dust over it. Any crack in the magnetized rod will attract more metallic dust because a stronger magnetic field is created when magnetism bridges a crack. This process has been used for years and is a good method for locating cracks or other defects.

Shot-peened means the surface of the rod has been blasted with cast-iron shot. This is said to

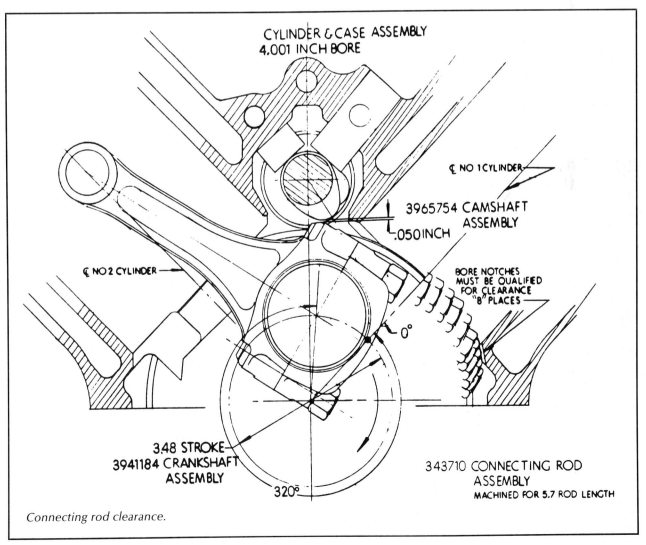

Connecting rod clearance.

This is one of my favorite street/strip performance pistons. It is the 1971-80 L82 forged, flat-top piston with one long valve clearance slot. The GM part number is 474190 but the TRW L 2417F is practically identical.

This TRW L 2327F is a great choice as a circle track piston (when there is a flat-top rule). Its seal does not last too long in a street engine because $\frac{1}{16}$ in. compression ring and a $\frac{3}{16}$ in. oil ring are used. Street and many performance engines should use $\frac{5}{64}$ in. top and second groove rings with a $\frac{1}{4}$ in. oil ring.

increase the surface hardness of the rod and make the rod more resistant to cracking.

Whatever connecting rods came with your engine should be fine to reuse as long as there were no spun bearings in the engine. If the crankshaft bearing end of the rod is damaged because of bearing failure, it can be repaired. However, I have never repaired a small-block Chevy rod because every machine shop I have ever visited has a bucket of good used ones under a workbench. Selecting replacement rods is easy because all stock large-journal small-block rods are made of forged steel and can be interchanged.

Be aware that the 1968 and 1969 stock 302 ci connecting rods were sized at the wrist pin hole at the factory to be free-floating rods. Your local machine shop should be able to enlarge the wrist pin hole and install a bronze or brass bushing so the rod will slide over the pin easily. Dissimilar metals are used to prevent galling if there is a lack of lubrication at any time during engine operation. Factory free-floated rods have bearing material in

the pin hole. They are available under part number 3946841.

Heavy-duty pressed-pin connecting rods are available under part number 14095071. Standard-duty connecting rods, part number 1431310, are also available at a reasonable price.

Super-heavy-duty factory racing rods, part number 14011090, are available at your local Chevrolet parts counter, but the price may be more than your budget can stand. Super-heavy-duty rods have $\frac{7}{16}$ in. diameter rod bolts and require some block modification when used. They are made from a special alloy steel (4340) and are also available in an unfinished version with an elongated pin boss so that the engine builder can alter rod length when the pin hole is drilled.

Whatever type you decide to run, whether new, remanufactured or boiled and reused, small-block rods that are checked for size and defects before being reinstalled almost never fail. Follow a few basic rules—never mix rod caps, number both halves upon disassembly and keep everything spotlessly clean during assembly—and you shouldn't have any problems.

Cylinder heads

5

When choosing cylinder heads for your small-block, keep in mind how you want your engine to perform. From 1968 to the present, Chevrolet has offered four basic combustion chamber sizes to meet various performance needs. These size groups are approximate within 2 cc of volume, larger or smaller, because of differences in manufacturing techniques.

Identification

For the high-performance 302 ci, 327 ci and 350 ci engines with 11:1 compression, 64 cc large-valve heads were standard. Late-model 262 ci, 267 ci and 305 ci engines had slightly smaller combustion chambers, as small as 60.5 cc.

On the intermediate-performance 327 ci and 350 ci engines, with 10:1 or slightly higher 10.25:1 compression, 68 cc heads were standard.

The early 307 ci, 350 ci and 400 ci engines and the late 327 ci engine shared the 74 cc chambered heads. The 74 cc chambers were an early attempt to lower compression for emission control purposes.

After 1971, emission standards forced further reductions in compression ratios, and the 76 cc chambered heads replaced many earlier castings

The 290 chamber shows that this head with 1.71I and 1.50E valves has a large combustion area. These heads are from a 1968 250 hp 327 ci. The larger chamber—about 74 cc—is an attempt to lower emissions by lowering compression.

with smaller combustion areas. The late-model 76 cc heads came as standard equipment on the 307 ci, 350 ci, 400 ci and some 305 ci engines.

Combustion chamber and valve sizes can vary greatly from head to head, even when the same

The 462 casting combustion chamber. These heads came on intermediate and high-performance 327 ci engines. Some of these heads have chambers as small as 60.5 cc and they can have 2.02I and 1.60E, or 1.94I and 1.50E valves as this casting had. These are from a 1968 300 hp 327 ci.

The 291 casting was used on the same engines as were the almost identical 462 heads. In addition to 327 ci applications, these 1.94I 1.50E heads came standard on the 1968 295 hp 350 ci.

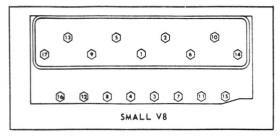

CYLINDER HEAD TORQUE SEQUENCE

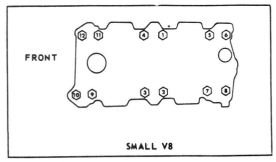

INTAKE MANIFOLD TORQUE SEQUENCE

RECOMMENDED CLEARANCES

Piston to Bore: (Chevrolet Forged Pistons)	.005-.0055" measured at centerline of wrist pin hole, perpendicular to pin. Finish bores with #500 grit stones or equivalent (smooth).
Piston Ring:	Minimum end clearance top — .022, second-.016, Oil - .016.
Wrist Pin:	.0004-.0008" in piston, (.0005-.0007" in rod for floating pin. 0-.005" end play preferred).
Rod Bearing:	.002-.0025" Side clearance, .010-.020.
Main Bearing:	.002-.003", minimum preferred, .005-.007" end play.
Piston to Top of Block: (Deck Height)	.015-.020" average below deck. No part of piston except dome to be higher than deck of block. Deck height specified is for a .018" steel head gasket. If a thicker head gasket is used, piston to cylinder head clearance of .035 should be considered minimum.
Valve Lash:	As shown in text for each camshaft.
Valve to Piston Clearance:	.020" exhaust and intake at 0 valve lash. *Note:* These are to be considered absolute minimum clearances for an engine to run below the valve train limiting speed of 8000 RPM. If you intend to run up to valve train limiting speed, more clearance should be allowed. It is common practice to allow .100" intake exhaust valve clearance for engines used in drag racing.

RECOMMENDED BOLT TORQUE AND LUBRICANT SPECIFICATIONS FOR CAST IRON SMALL BLOCK V-8 ENGINES

	Torque	Lubricant
Main Bearing	Inner 70 ft-lb	Molykote
	Outer 65	Molykote
Con. Rod Bolt 3/8"	45-50 ft-lb (.006" stretch preferred)	Oil
Con. Rod Bolt 7/16"	60-65 ft-lb	Oil
Cylinder Head Bolt	65 ft-lb	Sealant
Rocker Arm Stud (Late HP Head)	50	Sealant
Camshaft Sprocket	20	Oil
Intake Manifold	30	Oil
Flywheel	60	Oil
Spark Plugs (Conventional Gasket	25	Dry
Spark Plugs (Tapered Seat)	15	Dry
Exhaust Manifold	25	Antisieze
Oil Pan Bolt	165 in-lb	Oil
Front Cover Bolt	75 in-lb	Oil
Rocker Cover	25 in-lb	Oil

RECOMMENDED BOLT TORQUE AND LUBRICANT FOR ALUMINUM SMALL BLOCK V-8 ENGINES

	Torque	Lubricant
Main Bearing ...Studs	70 ft-lb	Oil
Bolts (Inner)	70 ft-lb	Molykote
(NF Thd.) (Outer)	70	Molykote
Con. Rod Bolt 7/16" Part 340285	67-73 ft-lb (.009" stretch preferred)	Oil
Cylinder Head Bolt with Hardened Washer ....Long	65	Sealant
Short	60	Sealant
Head Studs - 7/16 NF Thread (Preferred) ......Long	65	Oil
Short	60	Oil
Rocker Arm Stud	50	Oil
Camshaft Sprocket	20	Oil
Intake Manifold	25	Antisieze
Flywheel	60	Oil
Bell Housing	25	Antisieze
Spark Plugs	25	Antisieze
Exhaust Manifold	20	Antisieze
Oil Pan Bolt	165 in-lb	Antisieze
Front Cover Bolt	75 in-lb	Antisieze
Rocker Cover	25 in-lb	Antisieze

A cylinder head stud kit is available from Chevrolet under P/N 14014408. Use with hardened washers #14011040 and nuts 3942410.

Cylinder head bolt torque sequence. Intake manifold bolt torque sequence.

Most 1968 cylinder heads have no threaded end holes for mounting accessory brackets. The single hump mark represents standard-duty small-valve 290 castings with 1.71I and 1.50E valves.

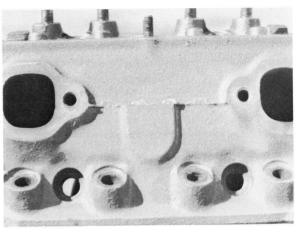

This casting boss, blank in 1968, was drilled and tapped in 1969 and later castings so that temperature sensors could be installed. Notice that this early head also has flat spark plug seats.

casting numbers are present. Chevrolet offers several combinations of intake and exhaust valve sizes. Intake valves range from 1.710 in. to 1.940 in. to the largest at 2.020 in. in diameter. Exhaust valves come in two sizes: 1.500 in. and 1.600 in. in diameter. Any combinations of these valves can come in almost any combustion chamber size.

When replacing one or both heads on your engine, match the casting numbers and valve sizes exactly and the production dates as closely as you can. The closer the production dates are between heads, the more likely the features of the heads will be the same. For example, in the 1971 production year, Chevrolet small-block heads began using 14 mm, 5/8 in. reach tapered-seat spark plugs. Earlier heads used the larger, 14 mm, 3/8 in. reach spark plug, with a washer gasket. Thus you could invest in two cylinder heads of casting number 3991492 and find that one had gasketed-seat plugs and the other had tapered-seat plugs. This would be possible with equal valve and combustion chamber sizes if one head had a production date of E 16 70, and the other A 15 71; this clearly marks them as being one production year apart, 1970 and 1971. The one-year difference would make it necessary to have two different sizes of spark plugs in one engine.

Small valves are standard equipment in most cases and come as regular production items on the

The double hump mark represents either the 462 or 291 intermediate 1.94I and 1.50E valve heads or the high-performance 2.02I and 1.60E valve heads. The two humps were recognized as fuelie heads years ago because they were similar to heads used on engines equipped with Rochester fuel injection.

This 186 casting came on the 1968-69 302 ci, 327 ci and 350 ci high-performance engines with 2.02I and 1.60E valves. Some smaller 1.94I and 1.50E valve versions exist that were used for intermediate horsepower applications. The chamber size is about 64 cc.

Heads casting identification

The casting identification chart represents most of the cylinder heads used from 1968 to 1988. This chart can be helpful at the junkyard when you don't have time to, or the owner won't allow you to, remove every valve cover in the place trying to find heads you want.

The shapes pictured in the casting identification chart can help identify cylinder heads when valve covers are still installed and casting numbers are not visible. These marks or shapes are located at either the front or rear of each head as installed on the engine.

Casting marks usually match the numbers represented in the chart, but you may find some variation or some pre-1968 heads not listed. If you find what you're looking for, remove the valve cover to expose the rocker arm top surface of the head. The date the heads were manufactured is readily visible on all cast-iron parts.

Intake manifolds, exhaust manifolds, blocks and cylinder heads are dated. Look for a letter of the alphabet first: the letters A through L represent the months of production, January through December. The next one or two numbers represent the day of the month the heads were cast. The last number is the year of production. For example, E 29 0 means May 29, 1980 or 1970 (depending on which year the factory was casting that particular number), and D 9 4 means April 9, 1984 or 1974.

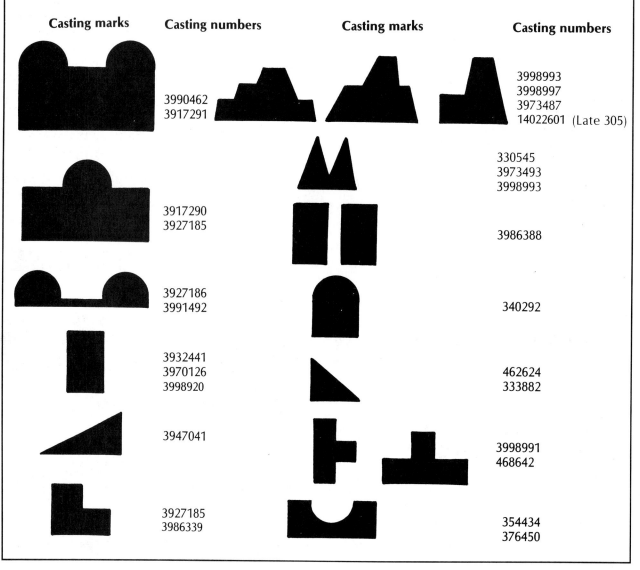

Casting marks	Casting numbers	Casting marks	Casting numbers
	3990462 3917291		3998993 3998997 3973487 14022601 (Late 305)
	3917290 3927185		330545 3973493 3998993
	3927186 3991492		3986388
	3932441 3970126 3998920		340292
	3947041		462624 333882
	3927185 3986339		3998991 468642
			354434 376450

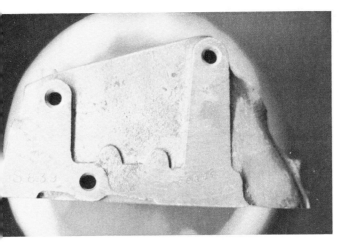

The 1969 and later castings had accessory mounting holes. This end shot shows the holes and the casting identification mark of a fuelie head. This 186 head has been reworked by Crane Cams.

This 492 chamber can have either 1.941 and 1.50E, or 2.021 and 1.60E valves. Here is a large-valve Z28 head that is still available under part number 3987376.

262 ci, 267 ci, 305 ci and 307 ci engines and base production 327 ci, 350 ci and 400 ci engines. These valves measure 1.710 in. intake and 1.500 in. exhaust. They will increase low-rpm performance because they increase the velocity of the mixture flowing in and out of the cylinders.

Any size engine equipped with small valves will run well in the low- and mid-rpm ranges. If economy and crisp, low-rpm throttle response are what you want from your small-block, small-valve heads are what you need. High-rpm operation will be limited, but these heads come in a variety of combustion chamber sizes and will fit all engines past and present.

Intermediate-performance engines, such as the 327 ci, 350 ci and 400 ci units, use larger-valve cylinder heads. A larger intake valve of 1.940 in. and the 1.500 in. exhaust create more horsepower and rpm potential on the small-block. These are available in small and large combustion chamber sizes.

High-performance engines such as the 302 ci, the special high-performance 327 ci and the 350 ci use the 2.020 in. intake valve and the 1.600 in. exhaust valve. These engines used the small combustion chamber sizes in the 1968, 1969 and 1970 (350 ci only) production years. These innovative heads were regular production options for street use.

The Chevrolet replacement parts division developed some special cylinder heads in the early seventies. Many unique features were available on these off-road heads that were not regular production items.

One feature of the new replacement heads was that the spark plug was relocated higher in the

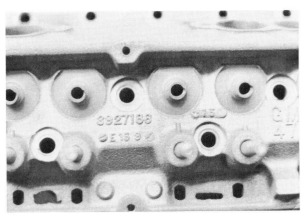

This high-performance 186 head did not have screw-in studs or guide plates. Notice where pins were added to prevent the pressed-in rocker studs from pulling out. I wouldn't recommend stud pins. Instead, have screw-in studs installed.

The top view of the 492 casting shows the production date of May 23, 1973. Note also the machined-down tapped holes for screw-in and guide plates.

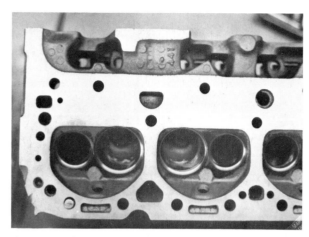

The 441 cylinder heads of 1969 have a combustion chamber like the 1968 290 casting. At about 74 cc in size, 441 has larger 1.94I and 1.50E valves when installed on the 350 engine. This particular head is from a 1969 255 hp 350 ci. All 400 cylinder heads have steam holes, not shown here. If you don't mind using large $\frac{13}{16}$ in. socket flat-seat spark plugs, the 441 makes for a great street performance head.

This is the 041 casting from a 1970 300 hp 350 ci. It has a combustion chamber shaped like the 462, 291 and 186 castings. Many machine shops have fitted larger than the 1.94I and 1.50E valves that came stock in these 1969-70 only heads. The 041 heads are my favorite intermediate heads. They work beautifully on 307 ci, 327 ci, 350 ci and, when drilled for steam holes, 400 ci engines. They have a combustion chamber that measures approximately 68 cc and they use the larger $\frac{13}{16}$ in. spark plugs.

This 441 has just been finished and is ready for assembly. The heavier casting is desirable.

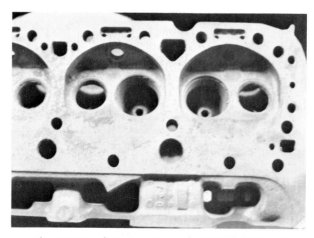

Another 1.94I and 1.50E casting is the 126. The 126 castings were used on 1969-70 engines. With a spark plug hole modification, they also appeared on 1971 engines.

chamber and set on an angle toward the more turbulent exhaust valve area. This helped create better flame travel around a high-compression piston dome. With more compression and better flame travel in the chamber, better valve control became necessary. The standard 1.280 in. diameter valve spring pocket was enlarged to a 1.440 in. diameter. With a larger valve spring, an engine equipped with these heads could gain more rpm and some ten to twelve additional horsepower. Early angle-plug heads also had screw-in studs to mount rocker arms and guide plates for pushrod support.

By 1973, Chevrolet created a head with no heat riser passage and with larger intake and exhaust ports. This head was based on a new casting (casting number 340292) and was called the turbo head. Many professional racers feel this was the best head ever produced by Chevrolet.

In 1980, the turbo head was replaced with the bow-tie head. This head featured the same design lacking a heat riser yet with a thicker deck surface and an exhaust port with a flattened floor instead of the conventional oval shape. The bow-tie, casting number 14011034, also comes in a factory aluminum version, casting number 14011049. These heads have only 64 cc chambers. To use them, dish-top-style pistons must be installed. You can do yourself a favor if you keep the compression ratio low enough so that the engine will run without detonating on the fuel available from a gas station pump.

Cylinder heads have an effect on exhaust emissions. Therefore, as emission controls and standards have changed, so have the designs of the heads.

When compression ratios were changed to 9:1 or lower in the 1971 model year, many good designs

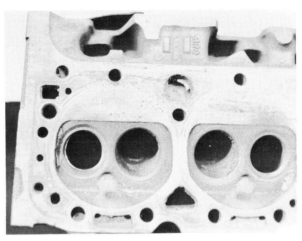

This head is designed for high torque at low speeds. It is the 388 casting of the late sixties and early seventies 350 ci engine intended for truck use. The 1.71I and 1.50E valves are mounted in what appear to be 74 cc chambers.

were available with the large 76 cc emission chambers. These heads, available with 5/8 in. tapered-seat plugs and the large valve sizes, were regular production heads, so they should be plentiful at your local junkyard. The most popular casting numbers are 3973487, 3973493, 3998993 and 3998997. Heads with these casting numbers came as standard equipment on intermediate-performance 350 ci and 400 ci engines. They are great street-performance heads.

The 3998993 and 3998997 castings were available until the end of the 1974 production year. When you find a set of these heads, check between the chambers on the head deck surface for steam holes. Heads that were previously used on a 400 ci

A small-valve head with 1.71I and 1.50E is the 185 casting. The 185 is almost exclusively for the 1968-72 307 ci engine. I would not attempt to use this head for anything other than an economy or low-speed torque application.

The front view of the 388 casting shows an odd hole arrangement; this hole pattern is also shared by the 642 casting. These extra holes must be for mounting special truck accessory brackets.

Another intermediate and high-performance 350 ci and 400 ci head of 1971-73 was the 330545 casting. This top view shows the casting number, screw-in studs and guide plates. These heads had chambers measuring 74 cc with shapes and valve sizes like the 487, 493, 993 and 997 heads.

Here is the 642 casting, similar to the 388 casting but available only with small ⅝ in. tapered-seat spark plugs. This particular head was used on a 1976 400 ci engine (notice the steam holes between chambers). The 642 is a heavy casting that was used on the 400 in cars and trucks until 1980. A light, cast head with similar valve sizes and combustion chambers is the 991.

An intermediate and high-performance head of 1971-72 was the 487. Either 1.94I and 1.50E, or 2.02I and 1.60E, as in this head, were available. This head has just been assembled and is ready for installation on a 1971 L82 350 ci.

An intermediate 1.94I and 1.50E valve head that had 993 and 997 on it: the 3998993 casting. I believe this to be the best small-spark-plug, 74 cc, medium-performance head. It has few failures due to its heavy casting.

engine can be installed on a 350 ci or smaller engine if a composition head gasket is used to seal the steam holes. The steam holes are necessary, however, if you intend to put the heads back on a 400 ci engine.

If your heads don't have steam holes, and you intend to use them on a 400 ci engine, use a 400 head gasket as a template and drill the six holes you need. These holes must be drilled: without steam holes, the 400 small-block will heat unevenly because of trapped steam. Head cracking, cylinder damage and, most certainly, blown head gaskets will result when there are no holes to allow the steam to escape between the bores.

In 1975, small-block heads were redesigned to be lighter. One characteristic of this redesign was to allow more exhaust flow through the heat riser passage. When the heads were redesigned, the

A replacement high-performance head available from 1973-80 was the angle plug, non heat-riser, 340292 casting. This view shows large spring pockets, absent heat-riser passage, production date, and the mounting pads for studs and guide plates.

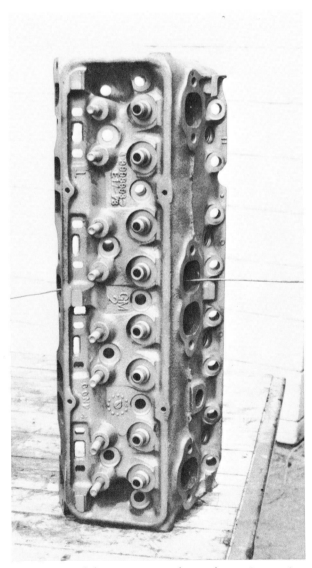

A top view of the 993 casting shows the entire casting number, production date and smaller tapered-seat spark plug holes. Another feature of the heavy casting is the temperature sensor boss (threaded holes) and single heat-riser passage (see welding rod).

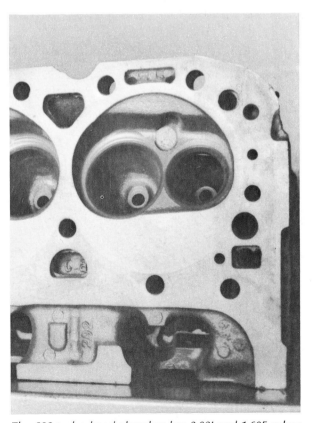

The 292 turbo head chamber has 2.02I and 1.60E valves and measures 64 cc. It is a heavy, performance casting with angled spark plug entry.

In 1975, a lighter cast head was released sporting 1.94I and 1.50E valves; the casting number was 333882. The 882 heads were installed on the 350 ci and 400 ci engines (400 heads had steam holes). The 882 castings had a double heat-riser passage (see welding rods) and were prone to cracking because they ran so hot. If you have these on your engine, get rid of them.

A chamber view of the 882 heads shows the 74 cc to 76 cc chamber size. If you want to replace these heads with others that have similar features, the numbers that interchange are the 487, 493, 993, 997 and 330545 from the 1971–74 model years.

uppermost cooling passage under the rocker arm studs was eliminated. The former cooling passage became part of the intake passage before the mixture reached the valve.

The new 1975 and later regular production heads have an irregularly shaped intake port that doesn't permit the mixture to flow smoothly at high rpm. They also run hotter than other heads. The additional cylinder head heat keeps combustion temperatures higher, thereby reducing exhaust emission levels. Furthermore, late-model carburetor adjustments are leaner, which creates more heat. The exhaust flows less freely because of the catalytic converter in the exhaust system, and this causes even more heat. As a result, with cooling passages eliminated and high engine temperatures, cylinder head cracking is a real problem. Better heads are available for the high-performance engine from earlier small-blocks than these 1975 and newer street-issue heads.

Another light-casted cylinder head released in the late seventies is the 462624 casting. These 624 heads are even lighter than the 882 units. I do not recommend these for any high-performance application where the engine may get exceptionally hot; these heads will crack all around the exhaust seats when exposed to extreme temperature.

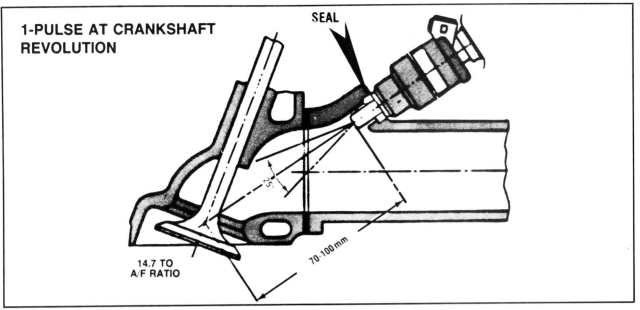

Typical small-block fuel injector installation.

Common heads

Year	Casting number	Valve sizes Intake	Exhaust	Performance	Engine (ci)
1962-68	3990462	1.94, 2.02	1.50, 1.60	Intermediate, high	327
1967-68	3917290	1.71	1.50	Base	327
	3917291	1.94	1.50	Intermediate	327, 350
1968-72	3927186	2.02	1.60	High	302, 327, 350
1968-73*	3991492	1.94, 2.02	1.50, 1.60	Intermediate, high	327, 350
1968-76	3927185	1.71	1.50	Base	307, 327, 350
	3986388	1.71	1.50	Base	307, 350
	3998991	1.71	1.50	Base	307, 350
	3986339	1.71	1.50	Base	307, 350
1969-70	3947041	1.94	1.50	Intermediate	350
	3970126	1.71	1.50	Base	350
1969-72	3932441	1.94	1.50	Intermediate	327, 350
1971-73	3973487	1.94, 2.02	1.50, 1.60	Intermediate, high	350, 400
	3998997	1.94	1.50	Intermediate	350, 400
	3973493	1.94	1.50	Intermediate	400
1971-present†	3998993	1.94	1.50	Intermediate	350, 400
1972-75	330545	1.94	1.50	Intermediate	350
	3998920	1.94	1.50	Intermediate	350
1973-80	340292	2.02	1.60	High	350
1975-77	333882	1.94	1.50	Intermediate	350, 400
1975-80	354434	1.71	1.50	Base	262, 267, 305
1976-present	468642	1.71	1.50	Base	350, 400
1977-79	367450	1.71	1.50	Base	350
1980-86	14022801	1.71	1.50	Base	305
1977-present‡	462624	1.94, 2.02	1.50, 1.60	Intermediate, high	350
1980-present§	14011034	2.02	1.60	High	350
1982–86	14022601	1.71	1.50	Base	305

*Available as service part number 3987376, straight plug, 68 cc, 2.02 intake, 1.60 exhaust.
†Cast in Mexico today for use on the Target Master replacement engine.
‡Available as service part number 464045, straight plug, 76 cc, 2.02 intake, 1.60 exhaust.
§Available as service part number 14011058, angle plug, 64 cc, 2.02 intake, 1.60 exhaust.

To identify these light-casting, or smog, heads quickly, put your finger into the intake port and reach toward the nearest rocker stud from inside the port. If you feel a small pocket and the bottom of the rocker stud, you have found a light-casting head.

Another way to identify these heads is to look into the two center exhaust ports. If both ports have small passages leading to the center of the intake manifold, you have found the double-ported heat riser passage of the late-model smog head.

The most common smog heads have the casting number 333882 on the 350 ci and 400 ci engines,

and casting number 462624 on the 350 ci engine only.

The 262 ci, 267 ci and 305 ci engines came equipped with either casting number 354434 or 367450. These cylinder heads also had cracking problems. Even more serious, however, were the excessive valve guide wear and valve seat distortions that plagued the 1976 and 1977 305 ci engines. If you have to use these heads, have them thoroughly checked. Fortunately, other small-chambered heads will fit the 305. Be careful to check the clearance of the intake valve to the cylinder bore when installing earlier large-valve heads; some cylinder bore notching may be necessary to clear a high valve lift.

Head reconditioning

It is quite probable that the cylinder heads you intend to reuse on your 1975 or later engine are cracked. The procedure for reconditioning heads is simple and should start with cleaning and crack inspection.

A top view of the 624 casting shows screw-in studs and guide plates. A production date of April 3, 1980, is also visible. These 624 heads came with both 1.94I and 1.50E intermediate valves (without screw-in studs and guide plates), or 2.02I and 1.60E high-performance valves, as shown. Extreme heat will ruin these heads. This means no turbo, no nitrous oxide, no blower or lean condition that may super-heat cylinders. The high-performance 624 heads are the cast-iron Corvette issue heads from the late seventies and early eighties (current part number 464045).

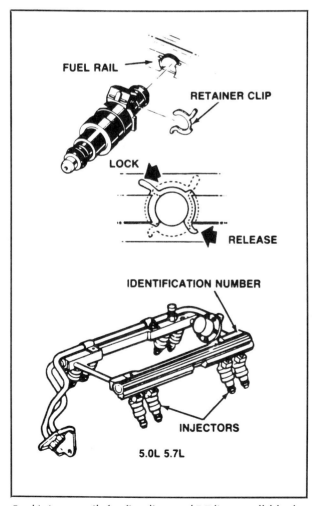

Fuel injector rails for five-liter and 5.7 liter small-blocks.

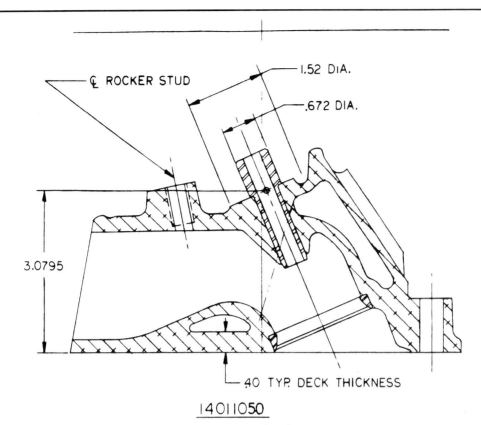

CL ROCKER STUD

1.52 DIA.

.672 DIA.

3.0795

.40 TYP. DECK THICKNESS

14011050

Inlet port dimensions, small-block aluminum cylinder head.

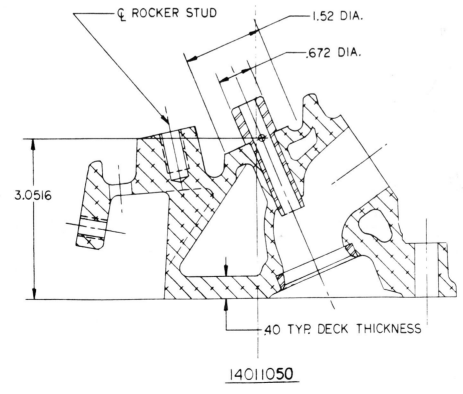

CL ROCKER STUD

1.52 DIA.

.672 DIA.

3.0516

.40 TYP. DECK THICKNESS

14011050

Exhaust port dimensions, small-block aluminum cylinder head.

The cylinder head to use for any extreme condition is this racing bow-tie head. Casting number 14011034 has angle spark plugs, 63 cc chambers, thicker head deck surface, no heat-riser passage and a heavy casting with enlarged cooling passages that make the bow-tie the perfect choice. I wish Chevrolet would make one of these with 74 cc chambers. The factory engineers discourage street use of this head by keeping combustion chambers small and fuel requirements high because of the compression created—even while using flat-top pistons.

A top view of Corvette 624, left, and bow-tie, right, shows the standard diameter valve spring and pocket, left, and large diameter spring and pocket, right. Both heads accept screw-in studs and guide plates (already installed, left).

After the heads are disassembled, they should receive the hot-tank treatment. A hot tank will loosen and soften the baked-on grease and carbon that cannot be removed in a cold parts washer. (Note: Never put assembled heads into the hot tank because the caustic solution will seize the parts together permanently.)

After removing the heads from the tank, jet-spray them with water. Dry them quickly and thoroughly or they will rust.

When dry, the heads are ready to be glass-bead blasted or sandblasted. Glass-beading the heads will help locate any cracks: the blasting process brings back the light, clean cast-iron color of the head and makes cracks appear as dark lines. If addi-

The 624 head, foreground, and bow-tie head, in the background, couldn't be more dissimilar. The 74 cc 624 head is much lighter than the 63 cc bow-tie.

The exhaust face of these heads shows the extra exhaust manifold mounting hole on the 624 head, top. The bow-tie head without the extra hole is on the bottom. Be sure when you order parts that all the features you need are present.

tional crack checking is desired, have the heads magnafluxed.

Cracks usually occur on the exhaust seat in the combustion chamber of the head. It is not uncommon for 400 ci heads to crack between steam holes on the deck surface. Some high-performance heads crack between the intake and exhaust seats because metal is thin there, and the engine was probably run too lean and the head got too hot. If either or both of the heads are cracked, look for others. Heads from 400 ci engines usually have more cracks than do other heads because these engines run hotter as a result of the siamesed cylinders and longer stroke.

Target Master cylinder heads based on the 993 casting do not carry the traditional marks to identify them.

This is a head removed from a 1988 Target Master 350 engine. I was pleasantly surprised to see that these heavy-duty replacement engines come with heavy casted 993 heads. Made in Mexico.

New 993 Target Master heads have the third hole necessary to fit all exhaust manifolds.

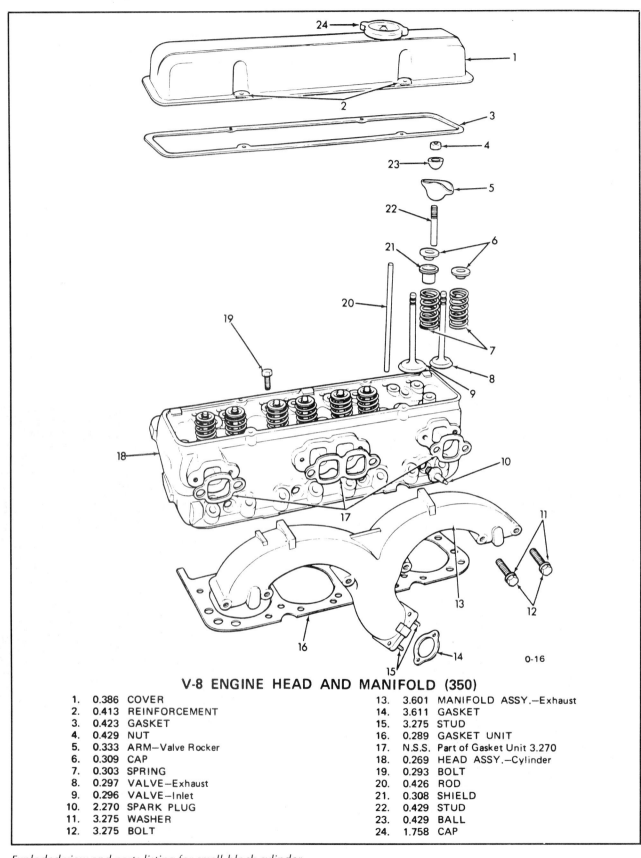

V-8 ENGINE HEAD AND MANIFOLD (350)

1.	0.386	COVER	13.	3.601	MANIFOLD ASSY.—Exhaust
2.	0.413	REINFORCEMENT	14.	3.611	GASKET
3.	0.423	GASKET	15.	3.275	STUD
4.	0.429	NUT	16.	0.289	GASKET UNIT
5.	0.333	ARM—Valve Rocker	17.	N.S.S.	Part of Gasket Unit 3.270
6.	0.309	CAP	18.	0.269	HEAD ASSY.—Cylinder
7.	0.303	SPRING	19.	0.293	BOLT
8.	0.297	VALVE—Exhaust	20.	0.426	ROD
9.	0.296	VALVE—Inlet	21.	0.308	SHIELD
10.	2.270	SPARK PLUG	22.	0.429	STUD
11.	3.275	WASHER	23.	0.429	BALL
12.	3.275	BOLT	24.	1.758	CAP

0-16

Exploded view and parts listing for small-block cylinder head and manifold.

Valve guides and angles

When you find heads that you can use, the next step is to determine how worn the valves and valve guides are. To check valve guide clearances, the valves must be perfectly clean.

Valves can be hot-tanked and glass-beaded, but be sure to use masking tape to cover the stems. Never glass-bead blast the chrome plating on the valve stems. Glass-beading will destroy the smooth, hard-chrome finish, and a rough valve stem will cause friction, ruining the valve guide.

When too much clearance causes the valve to wobble in the guide, the guide can be reamed out to a larger uniform size. Once all the guides are enlarged, bronze inserts can be installed to bring them back to standard size. If the valves are worn out, new valves with oversized stems can be installed and the bronze inserts won't be needed.

Another method is to knurl the guide and custom-fit each valve. This is the least desirable method, as the knurling cuts the support of the guide in half. Although they are expensive, I prefer the new valves and the bronze inserts.

Much has been written about valve angles and seat angles. For the street engine, a forty-five-degree angle, 0.060 in. wide face on the intake valve and a forty-five-degree angle, 0.090 in. wide face on the exhaust valve are all you need.

If you want to do a nice job cleaning up the valve pocket, use a seventy-degree refacing stone in the pocket, a forty-five-degree stone for the seats and a fifteen-degree stone to smooth away any rough lip around the seat. Do not grind away lots of metal—just touch up what the factory did when the heads were manufactured. Try to keep the valves raised on the seats. A raised valve will permit the mixture to flow faster and more efficiently.

The equipment for reconditioning heads is expensive, and not everyone should attempt to use it. The only reason it is mentioned here is to spare you a machine-shop lecture about three angles,

The combustion chambers of the Target Master 993 heads are identical to the original 1971-74 units.

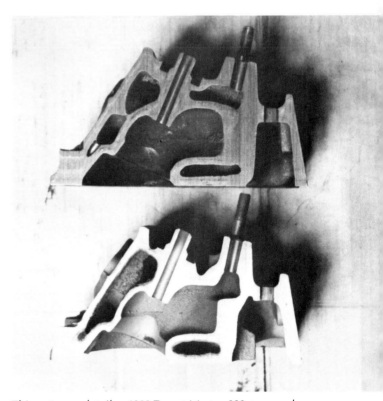

This cutaway details a 1988 Target Master 993, top, and a 1980 passenger car 624, bottom. The cutaway is to illustrate light casting on the 624 versus heavy casting on the 993. The heavy casting has an additional cooling passage under the rocker studs. The light casting is not only thinner, with less cooling, but it also has an irregular-shaped intake port that costs horsepower.

The newest 1988 cast-iron regular production 350 cylinder head. The combustion chambers are further squared and the exhaust seats are special to resist cracking.

special porting and whatever else you don't need for everyday driving.

If you are serious about building a race engine, chances are you already know what special work is needed to get the job done. If you don't, and you need race-prepared cylinder heads, ask around. Get references from any head service you are considering, and check the references out to make sure those people are happy with the work performed for them.

Another option that can save you all this work is to go to the Chevy parts department and buy new heads—that way the work has already been done for you.

The top valve cover lip is raised and the valve covers bolt to the center on the new 1988 350 head.

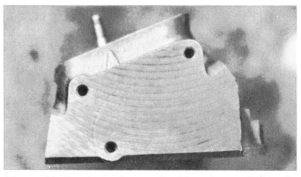

The end holes are in the standard location and a regular production casting mark is present on the new 1988 350 head.

Unfortunately the iron casting on the new 1988 350 iron head is still light. Maybe with improved exhaust seats less cracking will occur.

This casting mark is present on most 305 ci 354434 and 376450 cylinder heads. These heads had many valve guide problems in the late seventies so inspect them carefully before spending any time on them.

Casting identification is a little different on 305 heads. The numbers are there but in a different location and have a production date that is harder to read. Does that say May 2, 1977, or does that big eight to the right of the year make it May 27, 1978? You decide—I don't like 305 heads.

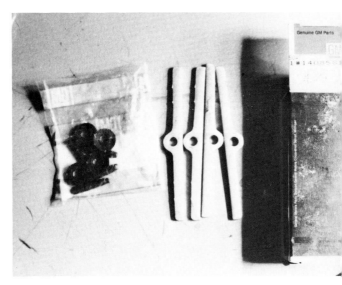

If your pre-1987 valve covers are leaking, try this stud nut reinforcement kit, part number 14085816.

Replacement studs and nuts to hold down valve covers are available. These are a great alternative to fumbling around with bolts.

Here is the typical 305 combustion chamber. Some 305s have combustion areas as small as 60.5 cc.

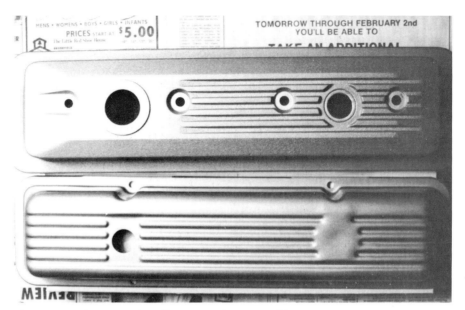

The upper valve cover fits all newer-style 1987 and later center bolt heads. The lower cover will fit 1986 and earlier outer lip bolt heads.

The production Corvette aluminum head, based on the bow-tie casting. The current part number is 14011127.

The 3974290 rocker fits all small-blocks and will work equally well with either pressed-in or screw-in studs.

A 1987-88 and later head, albeit with a production date of September 10, 1986, on the casting. This head will accept center screw valve covers. The casting number is 14102191.

Camshafts

6

Of all the interchangeable parts discussed in this manual, the camshaft has the greatest effect on engine performance. Its function of opening and closing valves controls cylinder pressure and, therefore, horsepower.

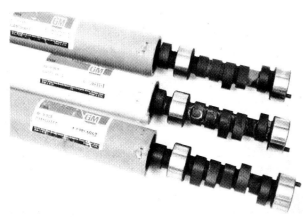

From top to bottom, Chevrolet camshafts LT1-3972178, L79-3863151 and L82-3896962. These camshafts are interchangeable between all small-blocks.

The Sealed Power replacement cam and lifter kit about to be installed is a reproduction of GM cam number 14060651. The lifters are reproductions of the old-style GM hydraulic cam number 5232670, which is no longer produced. Use only GM timing gears or true roller sprockets.

Camshafts are not described in fractions, as some cam manufacturers insist on doing for advertising purposes. They are measured in terms of valve lift in inches and valve duration in degrees. Valve lift is the distance off the seat that the valve is opened. Valve duration is the time during crankshaft rotation that the valve is open. The highest-lift cam for regular production engines from Chevrolet was the Corvette high-performance hydraulic cam (part number 3896962) at 0.450 in. intake lift and 0.460 in. exhaust lift.

Cam selection

Many mistakes are made by enthusiastic camshaft purchasers. Don't buy a camshaft because of an advertisement or because it works well for the local street drag race king. And don't try to fit the largest possible cam into your engine. If your goal is a loping idle to impress your friends, you will be sacrificing most of your low-rpm performance and all of the driving comfort your vehicle may have had.

The term that is most important with regard to camshaft selection is overlap, the time in degrees during crankshaft rotation when both valves are open at the same time. Overlap is what causes the loping idle. What happens inside the engine to cause the rough, loping idle is simple. When both valves are open for a long degree time in relation to crankshaft speed, idle vacuum and exhaust pressure in the cylinders pulse some exhaust back into the intake manifold. When raw fuel and partially burned gases mix in the intake manifold, weird rich-lean intake charges are created. This condition causes the cylinders to run at different power levels and produce the uneven, rough, or loping, idle.

When selecting a camshaft, try to complement your application. Read the description in the cam catalog. Compare the stock lift and duration figures for your engine with what you're looking at. If you don't vary too much from the stock figures, you should not have a problem.

In cam specs, the lift and duration figures are accompanied by some technical information for the experienced buyer. The other figures are the opening and closing points (in crankshaft degrees) of both valves, maybe an overlap figure, and an effective duration figure usually measured at 0.050

in. valve lift. This barrage of information can be confusing. If you are having a problem figuring out what it all means, call the technical assistance number in the cam catalog. Give the technical adviser a description of your car, and tell him or her what you want your engine to do for you. There is no charge for this service, and a tremendous amount of information is available for the asking. Working closely with the manufacturer can help ensure the best possible performance from your engine, because the manufacturer can direct you toward the camshaft you need.

Many factors affect camshaft selection: engine size, induction system, type of transmission, rear-end gear ratio and weight of the vehicle. All these must be considered before an intelligent selection can be made.

For example, if your vehicle is heavy, use a cam for a heavy recreational vehicle or one for a towing application. These cams are designed for lower-rpm power; they have less overlap and more lift than some stock Chevrolet camshafts. Using a smaller cam or being conservative in your selection won't hurt a street machine's performance and may help fuel economy and emission levels considerably.

Vehicles equipped with automatic transmissions are sensitive to overlap and require special consideration for you to select a cam that will develop the proper low- and mid-rpm-range torque. Camshafts with high lift and short duration are a good choice. Cams designed for this application may sacrifice some potential high-rpm power, but this is the price that must be paid for the best all-around performance.

Vehicles equipped with manual transmissions are less sensitive to overlap and therefore can be equipped with camshafts that have a broader power curve. Without having to idle as low as 600 rpm, a cam installed in a manual transmission vehicle can afford to have longer duration. Longer duration will increase the overlap figure, but because the valve is open longer, more mid-range and upper-rpm power is possible.

Basic rules

Remember these basic rules: High lift and short duration will create low-rpm torque; high lift and long duration will create high-rpm horsepower. The key to knowing approximately what a cam will do in your engine is directly related to the duration figure and the overlap figure. Advertised duration is not as important as effective duration at 0.050 in. lift.

The overlap figure is most important. This can be calculated (if it is not given) by adding the intake open figure to the exhaust close figure. Any number more than sixty will cause the engine to have an irregular idle.

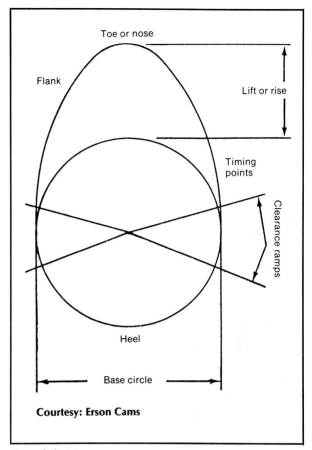

Courtesy: Erson Cams

Cam definitions.

Finding the right power band, or the rpm range where your engine will do most of its running, is important. Many camshaft selection charts have operating ranges for each profile listed; if you know how fast your engine will be running, you can better select the right cam design.

Chevrolet makes four different flat lifters and two different roller lifters for the small-block. From the left is the 5232720 hydraulic, 5231585 edge-orifice mechanical, 5232695 piddle-valve mechanical and 366253 mushroom mechanical.

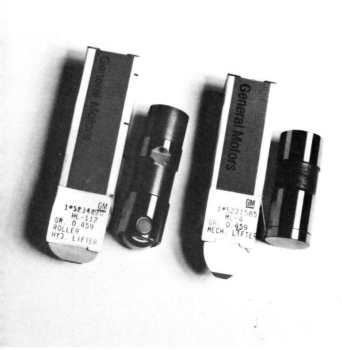

A comparison between a GM hydraulic roller lifter, left, and a flat lifter, right.

Factory and aftermarket camshafts

Today there are four types of camshafts. There are cams designed to run with flat mechanical or solid lifters, flat hydraulic lifters, roller mechanical lifters and roller hydraulic lifters.

Solid cams and lifters

Years ago, the most common cam and lifter type used for high-performance applications by both Chevrolet and the aftermarket manufacturers was the flat mechanical. This cam and lifter type performed well then and, if installed today, will again. The advantages of a mechanical cam and lifter are more rapid rpm gain and the ability to change engine running characteristics easily by altering valve lash. Some possible disadvantages of the mechanical cam and lifter setup are increased maintenance and noise of operation.

Hydraulic cams and lifters

Hydraulic camshafts are practically the same as mechanical camshafts. The major difference is that they use hydraulic lifters which contain adjusting devices to maintain zero valve stem clearance at the rocker arm. Because of the zero lash adjustment, hydraulic camshafts make no noise. Many enthusiasts will use hydraulic camshafts because of their silent operation and because they don't want to be bothered with the added maintenance of adjusting clearances. Even with these advantages, hydraulic cams and lifters have some limitations.

Hydraulic lifters are adjusted to zero clearance and are then additionally loaded to depress the internal lifter plunger. This method of adjustment ensures absolute silence during operation.

Because of this adjustment, hydraulic lifters tend to pump up if the engine is operated above 5000 rpm. At this high rpm, valve float occurs because the lifter attempts to adjust out clearance caused by components not intended for high-rpm use. If this condition occurs, the valves will be held off the seats and power loss will result until the lifter-plunger returns to the adjusted height. Valve float can be corrected by adjusting the hydraulic lifters to a just-off lash setting. This zero-clearance-only adjustment will not load down the plunger, thus eliminating the possibility of pumping up.

A disadvantage of hydraulic high-performance cams is their loping idle and low vacuum at idle as compared with an equivalent mechanical cam. Street machines with large hydraulic cams and automatic transmissions may even encounter power brake loss in traffic resulting from low vacuum to the booster. This low-vacuum condition can be avoided by using a shorter-duration (less-overlap) hydraulic cam or a mechanical cam and lifter setup (maybe even a higher-stall torque converter).

Roller cams and lifters

For the ultimate performance, roller mechanical cams are available. Chevrolet does not offer these cams as production items. However, in the 1987 production year, some small-blocks in Corvettes and in full-size or heavy vehicles came equipped with roller hydraulic camshaft and lifter assemblies.

Roller cams and lifters have been available for more than sixty years. They are the most desirable valve control system for any racing application, and will work equally well on the street. A roller lifter has less friction than does a flat lifter because of the wheel mounted on its bottom. With little or no friction, rpm gain is much faster, high-rpm operation is more easily accomplished and less oiling is required.

From a design standpoint, the roller lifter camshaft is the most efficient camshaft. Valve lifts and valve opening rates that are impossible with a flat lifter design are easily possible with a roller system. Because of these characteristics and minimum friction, higher valve spring pressures can be used. Higher valve spring pressures can provide extended high-rpm operation, often in excess of 8000 rpm.

The primary disadvantage of the roller cam and lifter setup is the cost. Roller cams are usually made of steel instead of cast iron, and the roller lifters are expensive to manufacture (GM part number 5234890 roller lifters cost more than $15 each). The complete roller kit can be as much as five times the cost of a flat mechanical lifter with comparable valve motion.

Components

Aftermarket camshaft manufacturers offer flat mechanical, flat hydraulic, roller mechanical and roller hydraulic kits. These kits usually include the cam, lifters, valve springs, retainers and keepers.

Cam manufacturers like to sell these complete packages because doing so ensures the compatibility of the parts and makes a successful installation more likely. Many camshaft manufacturers will sell a cam only, or a cam and lifters only, but they

---

Racing cam installation

The following is an explanation of racing cam installation as given by Erson Cams.

The installation of a racing cam is not extremely difficult and may be undertaken by anyone with a reasonable understanding of auto mechanics, a representative selection of tools, a manual covering disassembly and assembly of the engine in question, and sufficient patience to follow instructions.

The first factor to consider is the condition of the engine. Since the installation of a racing cam may increase horsepower by as much as twenty percent and allow up to 2000 more rpm before valve float, it stands to reason that the engine must be in first-class condition before making any modifications that will increase stress on the engine components.

Inspection

Once the old camshaft is out of the engine, it is an ideal time to inspect the various components of the valvetrain. Check the timing sprockets and chain for wear or damage. If the engine has accumulated fairly high mileage, it would be good insurance to replace the chain and sprockets at this time with a heavy-duty setup to ensure proper valve timing and long chain life.

Give the bearing journals on the camshaft you remove a thorough visual inspection. The condition of the journals is indicative of the condition of the bearing inserts in the block which are almost impossible to check with the engine assembled.

Check the distributor drive gear on the old camshaft and the gear on the distributor. If they show any sign of wear, it is wise to replace the gear on the distributor before installing the new cam; running against a worn gear will destroy the camshaft gear.

Also, check the condition of the valves and valve guides. The racing cam will have more lift, higher spring pressure and an increased rate of lift compared to the stock cam just removed. The valves and guides must be in perfect shape before installing a hot cam.

We cannot overstress the importance of using the complete component part kit recommended for the installation. Using parts that are not designed for the installation will greatly increase the chances of damaging the cam and engine. Component parts supplied by the cam manufacturer are mechanically and metallurgically compatible with each other and will mate in, and guarantee, long and troublefree service.

The information and suggestions here are generalized due to the great variety of engines currently produced and are not intended to cover all aspects of camshaft installation. It is absolutely necessary to have a detailed manual covering the operations to be performed. Care must be exercised when installing a new cam and valvetrain components, or severe damage to the cam and the engine may result.

Installation

Assuming all the components mentioned earlier have been checked and found satisfactory or replaced with new parts, we can proceed with the actual camshaft installation.

First, install the camshaft sprocket on the cam, including any thrust plate if used on the engine, and check the thrust plate for proper end clearance. Although the sprocket will have to be removed after the camshaft has been installed to facilitate fitting the chain, it is necessary to have the sprocket on the camshaft when checking the cam in the engine. The sprocket also serves as a convenient handle during installation. Coat the lobes and distributor drive gear with special break-in compound supplied with the cam and coat the bearing journals with motor oil.

Install the camshaft in the engine, taking care not to damage the soft surface of the cam bearings in the block. When the camshaft is fully installed, check to be sure the thrust surface of the sprocket touches the block.

Rotate the cam several turns by hand. It should turn easily and no binding should be felt when rotating. Next, coat the cam face of each lifter with break-in compound and insert them into their bores. Apply pressure against the cam sprocket to be sure that the thrust faces are in contact and rotate the cam again. There should be no hard spots or interference to rotation. If interference can be felt at this time, check for contact between the sides of cam lobes and the lifters. The cam drive sprocket may now be removed to facilitate installing the timing chain.

These are late-model valve springs, the valve spring on the left for exhaust only. This picture compares the spring height difference and the balance achieved once the rotator cap, left, and standard cap, right, are installed. The right side assembly can be used on the exhaust side if rotator caps are not desired.

will not guarantee their parts unless the entire kit is used.

Most of these kits come with aluminum retainers and keepers. When I buy cam kits, I call the technical adviser and ask to substitute steel parts if they are available. It is usually possible to do this without voiding the warranty. I do not use aluminum retainers or keepers in any engine I build because I have found aluminum shavings in competi-

From left: valve springs one and three are part number 6263796; springs two and four are another standard diameter spring numbered 3911068; the fifth spring is the larger diameter 330585 spring to fit the bow-tie heads. A steel Erson retainer is installed to 330585 instead of the GM-suggested aluminum piece.

tors' engines when these parts were used, even when no bearing failure had occurred.

Super-duty pushrods are available from the manufacturers of the cam kits. If you plan to increase the valve spring pressure drastically, then use pushrods offered by the kit manufacturers to avoid problems. If your demands are not too far from high-performance Chevrolet equipment, the stock pushrods or heavy-duty pushrods, part number 3796243, should be adequate.

Valve springs

Chevrolet offers many good valve springs. Before you select springs, however, you must know the cruising rpm at which your engine will be running. This will help you decide whether or not you need to use rotator caps on the exhaust springs. Some street-performance engines that will have considerable slow-speed running, or idle, time will benefit from rotator caps with part number 14042575.

Rotator caps must be used with the exhaust valve spring (part number 6263796). The rotators move the exhaust valve slowly around the seat. This movement helps reduce the possibility of burning a valve. If you plan on running at high rpm, or under reduced load, the standard valve cap (part number 14003974) and valve spring (part number 3911068) will work on all valves, and not just the intake valves. In either case, all the aforementioned springs and caps, the stock oil shield (part number 10007818), the valve keepers (part number 3947770) and the rocker arms (part number 3974290) will interchange onto all regular production Chevrolet heads.

Chevrolet has some high-performance valve springs (part number 3927142) that work well with mechanical cam part number 3972178 or cam 3927140. Rpm potential with use of these mechanical camshafts and valve springs can be as high as 7500 rpm without valve float. Valve springs to fit the larger valve spring pockets of the bow-tie heads are available under part number 330585. These springs have a spring-retainer made from an aluminum alloy (part number 330586), but I'm sure you can locate aftermarket steel retainers in their place.

Lifters

Chevrolet offers four different lifters for the flat cams. The hydraulic lifter is available under part number 5232720. Some of these lifters have a black anodized plunger cap, and all have a hardened cam lobe contact area. The mechanical lifters offered are the high-oil-volume piddle valve lifter (part number 5232695) and the oil-restrictive edge orifice type (part number 5231585).

The piddle valve lifters are to be used with the stock ball-and-socket pivot rocker arms. The edge orifice lifters should be used only with roller rockers that have needle bearing pivots that need less oiling. Do not use edge orifice lifters with stock pivot rockers because these lifters flow about twenty percent less oil through the pushrods to lubricate the rocker arms. The same is true of the mushroom lifter (part number 366253) with a 0.960 in. diameter lobe contact area. (A word of caution: The mushroom lifters cannot be installed into the block from the top because the lobe contact area is larger than the lifter bore.)

All flat mechanical and hydraulic Chevrolet cams and lifters interchange. For that reason, pre-1968 camshafts appear on the Chevrolet reference chart. Other cams that may be used in the Chevrolet small-blocks are listed in the aftermarket cams chart.

Cam profiles

Chevrolet and aftermarket camshaft manufacturers offer different lift and duration profiles for different valves, so that on the same camshaft, the intake valve may have one profile while the exhaust valve has slightly more lift and a few degrees more duration. These dual-pattern cams are usually the result of performance tests, but are sometimes simply designs that cam manufacturers think might sell to the public.

Intake and exhaust valve sizes and port flow characteristics also vary. Historically, Chevrolet has used dual-pattern camshaft designs for the small-block. (The only exception is the high-performance 327 camshaft [part number 3863151], which has a single pattern.) With the dual-pattern cam, opposite pressures feed and clear the cylinders. Vacuum pressure moves the fuel mixture past a large open intake valve while combustion and compression pressures move exhaust past the smaller valve. Different size valves and different shape and length ports make a dual-pattern camshaft able to match the flow of these different pressures to create the desired performance.

Valve timing and lobe spacing are extremely complicated. To begin with, the camshaft is driven by the crankshaft at a 1:2 ratio. There are thirty-six teeth on the camshaft gear and eighteen teeth on the crankshaft gear. The two gears are connected by the timing chain, and the marks on the gears must be aligned before the chain is installed. Special bushings and keys are available to alter cam timing, but installing the cam in the straight-up position almost always works the best.

Remember, one camshaft revolution and two crankshaft revolutions make one complete engine cycle. During this cycle, the crankshaft completes 720 degrees of rotation. To start the cycle, the intake valve begins opening before the piston reaches top dead center. This ensures a full-open position when the piston begins the downward intake stroke. The intake open motion occurs at about thirty degrees before top dead center on a mild street grind. If you want the engine to run in a higher rpm range, the intake open figure should be increased to as much as forty-four degrees before top dead center, as in the Chevrolet first-design racing cam (part number 3927140). If the opposite effect, or low-rpm power, is desired, the intake valve could open as late as twenty degrees before top dead center. (The same principle applies to the intake valve closing point. The sooner the intake valve closes in relation to bottom dead center, the higher low-rpm compression pressures will be. Therefore, more low-rpm horsepower will be available because the piston is able to begin compression immediately upon reaching the bottom of the stroke.)

When the piston changes direction in the cylinder from an upward to a downward motion (or vice versa), the crankshaft, although turning, leaves the piston almost motionless. During this degree-rotation time, camshaft movement continues. The continuing valve action makes further cylinder induction possible. Selecting a long or short duration will depend on what rpm range you want your power developed in.

When the fuel mixture is compressed and the charge is ignited, both valves are in the closed position. Almost all of the explosive power is then transmitted to the piston within the first half of the downward power stroke. Before the piston reaches the bottom of the stroke (bottom dead center), the exhaust valve usually begins to open so that the expanding gases can help expel exhaust from the cylinder. This helps reduce the work the piston must do to clear the cylinder. By the time the piston has reached the bottom, the exhaust valve is well open and most of the expanding exhaust is out of the cylinder.

When the exhaust stroke is near completion and before the piston reaches the top of the cylinder, the intake valve begins to open again. When the piston reaches top dead center, the intake valve is well open and the exhaust valve is almost closed. The time when both valves are open simultaneously (the overlap) helps create additional low pressure before the piston begins its downward intake stroke at high rpm. As the piston's downward speed increases, vacuum pressure inducts a new fuel charge, and the four cycles are again underway.

Lobe spacing

When a lobe-spacing figure is given, the manufacturer is referring to the distance in degrees between the intake and exhaust lobe centerlines for one cylinder. The small-block will have lobe center spacing that ranges from 106 degrees to 114 degrees.

Altering the distance between lobes has a drastic effect on engine performance. Camshafts designed with closer lobe centers have more overlap at the beginning of the intake stroke.

Timing tags

The following is an explanation of the timing tag as given by Erson Cams.

All racing cams from reputable manufacturers include a timing tag with figures relating to the camshaft. These figures are necessary to the engine builder if he or she wishes to get the most from the engine. I have found that many people do not understand the timing tag and are therefore unable to use the information available to full advantage.

The following explanation of the timing tag is intended to bring you a clearer understanding of the information contained thereon.

All Erson racing cams are supplied with a four-page timing folder. Page one of the folder gives the following information: recommended valve clearance; gross lift at the valve; and a timing diagram which represents one complete cycle, two complete revolutions (720 degrees), of the crankshaft.

The timing diagram graphically illustrates the relationship between the valve opening and closing points, and the piston travel, measured in degrees of crankshaft rotation. The valve opening and closing points are always given in relation to top dead center of the piston or bottom dead center (BDC). Intake valves open before TDC and close after BDC; the exhaust valves open before BDC and close after TDC. The heavy black line on the outside of the timing diagram indicates the open period of the intake valve, and the double black line on the inside indicates the open period of the exhaust valve.

To determine the intake duration from the sample timing tag, use the following procedure. Start at the upper left-hand corner of the diagram, marked intake open. Note that the figure 30 means that the intake valve opens 30 degrees before TDC. Now simply follow the black line in a clockwise direction past TDC and BDC to the point in the lower left-hand corner of the diagram, marked intake closes. Note that the figure 70 means that the intake valve closed 70 degrees past BDC. Now by adding the total distance traveled in degrees, we can tell what the total duration of the intake opening is as follows: 30 degrees + 180 degrees + 70 degrees = 280 degrees duration. (The number of degrees between TDC and BDC is always 180 degrees)

To determine the exhaust duration, you simply follow the same procedure beginning in the lower right-hand corner, marked exhaust opens. If you add these figures (70 degrees + 180 degrees + 30 degrees) you will find the exhaust duration to be 280 degrees. How about overlap? Add the intake opening before TDC (30 degrees) to the exhaust closing after TDC (30 degrees) and you have the overlap, 60 degrees.

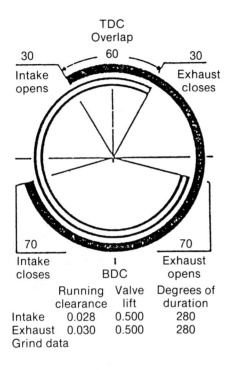

Grind data	Running clearance	Valve lift	Degrees of duration
Intake	0.028	0.500	280
Exhaust	0.030	0.500	280

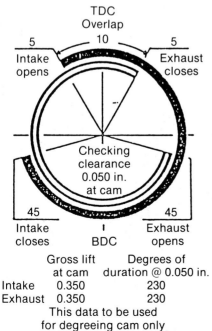

	Gross lift at cam	Degrees of duration @ 0.050 in.
Intake	0.350	230
Exhaust	0.350	230

This data to be used for degreeing cam only

Therefore, cams with this tighter spacing traditionally exhibit profiles with less lift and duration. The exhaust lobe is retarded and the intake lobe is advanced, which causes the exhaust to open and close later and the intake to open and close earlier. The higher cylinder pressures at lower rpm guarantee low- and mid-range horsepower.

The opposite effect occurs when lobe centers are wide apart. The lobes are then tipped farther apart, which decreases overlap and allows for larger profiles to be used without adverse effects on mid-range performance.

The full potential of lobe center changes can be demonstrated by someone who is willing to grind the same profile on several camshafts with different lobe spacing.

If you have questions relating to any aspect of cam selection, call the cam manufacturer's technical adviser.

Timing chain and gears

Stock Chevrolet timing chain and gear sets are available in three different styles: aluminum and plastic cam gear with production chain; hardened-iron cam gear with production-link-type chain; and steel double-row roller cam sprocket with #35 type chain.

The aluminum and plastic gear is the most common production piece. This set has a quiet operation and should withstand 100,000 miles of normal driving. The plastic gear teeth dampen vibrations transmitted from the crankshaft to the camshaft, and for this reason some racers prefer these sets. Using this type of low-performance cam gear requires periodic inspection to make sure the plastic gear teeth have not started to chip or break off the aluminum hub.

If you wish to run at high rpm or you initially install heavy-duty parts, choose one of the other Chevrolet timing chains. I use the hardened-iron cam gear (part number 340235) with the production-type link chain (part number 346261) and the steel crankshaft gear (part number 464617). If the steel crankshaft gear is unavailable, the iron gear (part number 3896959) is all right to substitute. The

GM parts 340235 upper gear, 346261 timing chain and 3896959 lower gear installed. Notice the darker shade around the gear teeth on the cam gear. These pieces are flame hardened and are resistant to wear.

only reservations I have are that the iron is more brittle and is subject to cracking if used in extreme performance situations. The hardened-iron production-style chain parts are usually found in high-performance car applications.

Heavy-duty trucks usually come with the double-row roller camshaft sprocket (part number 3735412) with the double-row chain (part number 3735411) and the steel double-row roller crankshaft sprocket (part number 3735413). These #35 roller link chain sets will interchange to any other small-block, but when they run, they are noisy.

Valve lash adjustment

Recall that mechanical lifter camshafts need clearances set between the valve stem and the rocker arm, and that altering the valve lash will change engine running characteristics. If the clearance is increased between the valve stem and the rocker arm, the valve will open later and close earlier. This action shortens the duration of the valve opening, and as a result, cylinder pressures are altered. This alteration will increase low- and mid-range power.

If the clearance is decreased, duration will increase because the valve will now open sooner and close later. This adjustment will increase upper-rpm power slightly at the expense of some low- and mid-range power.

Valve clearances usually range from 0.010 to 0.032 in. If the cam manufacturer recommends a clearance of 0.018 intake and 0.022 exhaust and you wish to increase your upper-rpm performance, you can adjust down in increments of 0.002 in. to 0.016 intake and 0.020 exhaust. If the engine responds in a way you consider favorable, further adjustment to as much as 0.010 in. less clearance is possible.

From a design standpoint, clearance reduction won't hurt the valvetrain, but you will have to judge how much low-end power you can afford to sacrifice. Don't get carried away; leave enough clearance between the rocker arm and the valve stem so

This bow-tie GM chain is overrated. The lower sprocket is steel but the upper sprocket shows no signs of being hardened. In any case, the weak part in this assembly is the double-row #35 link chain. Like so many replacement parts of this non-roller type, this chain stretches excessively within the first few thousand miles.

The best timing chain assembly uses a true roller design. Cloyes and others make these sets. They are worth the extra money because they do not stretch more than a degree or two after as many as 40,000 miles.

that the valves are not held off the seats. If your cam clearances are as little as 0.012 intake and 0.014 exhaust, be conservative when reducing clearances. Use your head and act cautiously.

If you wish to increase clearance, therefore creating more low-rpm power, a setting of 0.022 can be increased to as much as 0.028 in. When increasing clearances, be aware that you are also increasing the shock of the pieces working together. If you find that the engine runs better with more clearance, it may be possible to advance the cam a few degrees to achieve the same result. This condition of improved performance with looser clearances usually indicates the selection of a camshaft that is too large.

Remember, you can go as much as 0.010 in. tighter in clearance, but no more than 0.006 in. looser. Tighter clearances will quiet valve noise and smooth out valvetrain operation. Looser clearances will increase valve noise and increase valve stem wear slightly because of the additional shock the components get with more lash. Don't increase clearance that is already at 0.032 in. lash.

Make all valve adjustment when the engine is hot.

Rocker arm geometry

Small-block Chevrolet rocker arms (part number 3974290) are of the ball and socket type. A 1.5:1 ratio is built into the rocker, and the rocker's stud mount is self-compensating for changes in valve lift. The stock rockers and mounting studs will accommodate up to a 0.500 in. lift without interference. If you plan to use more lift, it will be necessary to use aftermarket long-slot rocker arms.

Many high-lift cams require greater spring pressures than Chevrolet offers. These pressures cause tremendous loading on the rocker stud, and may cause the stud to pull out of its pressed-in position. The solution is to install screw-in studs (part number 3973416). To do this, the old studs must be pulled, the stud mounts machined down and the holes tapped to screw in the new parts. Most machine shops are equipped to perform this operation for you.

Installing the screw-in studs usually costs around $75. At the same time, pushrod guide plates (part number 3973418) can be installed. Guide plates from Chevrolet require that you use hardened pushrods. Flexible hard-plastic guide plates are available from aftermarket suppliers. They eliminate the need for hardened pushrods.

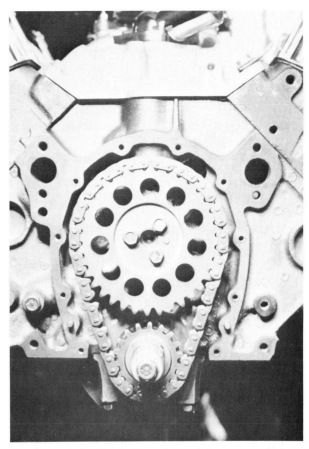

The least desirable timing chain and gear assembly is shown here. I don't know what company manufactures these pieces but many of these multi-holed wonders are made from baked powdered metal and usually don't provide proper cam timing for very long at all.

Conclusion

When all the parts that you have selected are installed, run your engine. If you have to disassemble the engine again, keep the lifters in order. Each lifter must be reinstalled on the cam lobe where it ran before. If the lifters are mismatched, excessive wear or failure of the cam may occur.

Never install used lifters on a new camshaft for the same reason. Lobe failure may occur because the break-in pattern on the lifter does not match the cam lobe. If a hydraulic lifter has failed internally and must be replaced, it is all right to put a new lifter on an old cam if the lobe is good. However, it is best to replace the cam and lifters at the same time.

Chevrolet cams

Camshaft part number and lifter type	Cam lobe and lash adjustment (in.)	Opening point (degrees)	Closing point (degrees)	Duration figure (degrees)	Duration at 0.050 in. lift	Gross lift (in.)	Application
14060653 Hydraulic	Intake 0 lash	29 BTDC	71 ABDC	290	176	0.357	Stock 305 cam, high-torque & fuel economy
	Exhaust 0 lash	78 BBDC	47 ATDC	305	194	0.390	
14060655 Hydraulic	Intake 0 lash	23 BTDC	91 ABDC	294	201	0.403	High-output 305 cam, good torque & power
	Exhaust 0 lash	72 BBDC	42 ATDC	294	206	0.414	
14060651 Hydraulic	Intake 0 lash	26 BTDC	90 ABDC	296	195	0.390	Used in 307-400, good street cam, old 929
	Exhaust 0 lash	84 BBDC	46 ATDC	310	202	0.410	
3863151 Hydraulic	Intake 0 lash	40 BTDC	100 ABDC	320	221	0.447	Used in high-performance 327, good torque & power
	Exhaust 0 lash	92 BBDC	48 ATDC	320	221	0.447	
3896962 Hydraulic	Intake 0 lash	40 BTDC	100 ABDC	320	224	0.450	Used in high-performance 350 Z28 & L82, good power
	Exhaust 0 lash	90 BBDC	50 ATDC	320	224	0.460	
3736097 Mechanical	Intake 0.012 lash	35 BTDC	72 ABDC	287	222	0.381	Used in early Corvette, good small-cube cam
	Exhaust 0.018 lash	75 BBDC	28 ATDC	283	221	0.380	
3972178 Mechanical	Intake 0.024 lash	36 BTDC	91 ABDC	307	229	0.452	Used in LT1 350, good high-rpm street cam
	Exhaust 0.030 lash	97 BBDC	42 ATDC	319	237	0.455	
3927140 Mechanical	Intake 0.024 lash	44 BTDC	92 ABDC	316	243	0.481	Short-track racing cam, not for street use
	Exhaust 0.026 lash	92 BBDC	51 ATDC	323	254	0.486	
3965754 Mechanical	Intake 0.024 lash	47 BTDC	97 ABDC	324	249	0.503	Road race cam, not for street use
	Exhaust 0.026 lash	93 BBDC	51 ATDC	324	258	0.508	
3662293 Mushroom mechanical	Intake 0.025 lash	50 BTDC	95 ABDC	325	354	0.560	Long-track racing cam, not for street use
	Exhaust 0.025 lash	88 BBDC	67 ATDC	335	262	0.575	
14093643 Roller hydraulic	Intake 0 lash						1987 Stock roller hydraulic
	Exhaust 0 lash						
10066049 Roller hydraulic	Intake 0 lash						1988 Stock roller hydraulic
	Exhaust 0 lash						

Caution: General Motors cams should be evaluated by the duration at the 0.050 in. figure. GM calculates valve motion differently than the aftermarket manufacturers do; therefore, overlap calculations are exaggerated.

Aftermarket cams

Alliance Cams

Application	Valve overlap	Intake lobe C/L	Duration As advert. in./ex.	At 0.050 in. lift in./ex.	Gross valve lift in./ex.	Valve lash in./ex.	Part number
Chevrolet 1955-87							
265, 283, 302, 305, 307, 327, 350, 400 ci V-8; 1.5:1 rocker arm ratio							
Fuel efficiency	31	107	250/260	184/194	0.368/0.398	0.000	611488
Fuel efficiency	34	108	256/262	194/203	0.390/0.410	0.000	611495
High torque	41	107	260/270	194/204	0.398/0.420	0.000	611497
High torque	45	108.5	266	203	0.412	0.000	611500
High torque	51	107	270/280	204/214	0.420/0.433	0.000	611502
Street performance	60	105	280	214	0.443	0.000	611501
Street performance	61	107	280/290	214/224	0.443/0.465	0.000	611503
Street performance	64	105	284	218	0.457	0.000	611504
Street performance	55	112	284	230	0.453	0.000	611505
Street performance	78	110	306	222	0.447	0.000	611510
Street performance	60	114	292/288	224	0.450/0.460	0.000	611512

Camonics cams

Application	Duration (degrees)	Valve lift (in.)	Part number	Type
265, 283, 305, 207, 350, 400; 1.5:1 rocker arm ratio				
Super gas saver	254	0.405	HE-2754-C	Hydraulic
Super gas saver	258	0.415	HE-2758-C	Hydraulic
Super gas saver	260	0.420	HE-2860-C	Hydraulic
Stock replacement	242-254	0.390-0.410	HE-100-C	Hydraulic
Street performance	270	0.450	CH-3070-C	Hydraulic
Street performance	277	0.450	CH-3077-C	Hydraulic
Street performance	268	0.460	CH-3078-C	Hydraulic
Street performance	282	0.465	CH-3171-C	Hydraulic
Street and strip	272	0.470	CH-3172-C	Hydraulic
Street and strip	274	0.475	CH-3174-C	Hydraulic
Street and strip	282	0.450	CH-3082-C	Hydraulic
Street and strip	284	0.485	CH-3284-C	Hydraulic
Street and strip	294	0.485	CH-3290-C	Hydraulic
Street	250	0.445	CM-2950-C	Solid
Street performance	260	0.450	CM-3160-C	Solid
Street and strip	266	0.485	CM-3162-C	Solid
Street and strip	264	0.472	CH-3164-C	Solid
Street and strip	278	0.485	CM-3178-C	Solid
Street and strip	280	0.485	CM-3180-C	Solid
Street and strip	296	0.530	CM-3496-C	Solid
Street and strip	290	0.508	CM-3490-C	Solid

continued

Camonics cams

Application	Duration (degrees)	Valve lift (in.)	Part number	Type
265, 283, 305, 207, 350, 400; 1.5:1 rocker arm ratio				
Street and strip	296	0.530	CM-3496-C	Solid
Street and strip	300	0.530	CM-3500-C	Solid
Street	300	0.485	CR-3200-C	Roller
Street and strip	286	0.520	CR-3486-C	Roller
Street and strip	298	0.520	CR-3498-C	Roller

Cam Techniques
MPG—RV cams
Computer designed hydraulic lifter cams

Grind number	Valve lift in./ex.	Advertised duration in./ex.	Duration at 0.050 in. in./ex.	Application
MPG	0.383/0.405	252/262	192/202	Gas mileage
RV-1	0.408/0.408	262/262	202/202	High torque
RV-2	0.426/0.426	284/284	212/212	Mid-torque, highway

Performer cams

Grind number (cam lift)	Valve lift in./ex.	Advertised duration in./ex.	Duration at 0.050 in. in./ex.	Lobe separation	Valve lash in./ex.
Chevrolet V-8 283-400 cubic inch					
		Hydraulic			
PH-298	0.447/0.447	296/296	222/222	114	0.000/0.000
PH-320	0.480/0.480	298/298	230/230	108	0.000/0.000
		Flat tappet			
PS-334	0.501/0.501	296/296	246/246	108	0.028/0.030

Hi-Tech Performer cams
Computer designed hydraulic lifter cams, specially designed to provide the perfect combination for fuel efficiency and performance.

Grind number	Valve lift in./ex.	Advertised duration in./ex.	Duration at 0.050 in. in./ex.	Lobe separation
Chevrolet V-8 283, 400 ci				
HTP-1	0.420/0.442	270/280	204/214	112
HTP-2	0.442/0.465	280/290	214/224	112

Super Tech
Specially designed cams for Super Gas, Super Pro and Super Power

Grind number (cam lift)	Valve lift in./ex.	Advertised duration in./ex.	Duration at 0.050 in. in./ex.	Lobe separation	Valve lash in./ex.
Chevrolet V-8 283-400 ci					
		Flat tappet			
F-382/386-8	0.573/0.579	304/308	268/272	108	0.022/0.024
F-394/400-8	0.591/0.600	312/316	276/280	108	0.024/0.026
		Roller tappet			
R-435-8	0.652/0.652	314/314	274/274	108	0.024/0.026
R-420-8	0.630/0.630	318/318	280/280	108	0.024/0.026

continued

Oval track/Road racing cams

These are computer designed cams especially for use in oval track and road racing. This is a list of the most popular cams we offer for each of the popular engines.

Grind number (cam lift)	Valve lift in./ex.	Advertised duration in./ex.	Duration at 0.050 in. in./ex.	Lobe separation	Valve lash in./ex.
Chevrolet V-8 283, 400 ci					
		Hydraulic			
H-320-6	0.480/0.480	298/298	230/230	106	0.000/0.000
H-324-6	0.486/0.486	302/302	236/236	106	0.000/0.000
F-336/350-6	0.504/0.525	295/300	254/262	106	0.024/0.026
F-361/370-8	0.542/0.555	298/303	261/266	108	0.022/0.024
		Mushroom tappet			
FM-393/406-6	0.590/0.612	280/288	252/260	106	0.024/0.026
GN-6	0.618/0.618	308/314	276/282	106	0.022/0.024
		Roller tappet			
R-372-2-6	0.558/0.558	284/296	250/260	106	0.022/0.024
R-422/404-6	0.633/0.606	297/308	262/268	106	0.022/0.024
R-426/400-6	0.639/0.600	303/314	268/274	106	0.024/0.026

COMPETITION CAMS

Camshaft Part Number	Camshaft Grind Number	Application	Type Idle	Max. RPM	Duration In Degrees In.	Duration In Degrees Ex.	Duration @ .050 In.	Duration @ .050 Ex.	Lift In.	Lift Ex.
High Energy Cams										
Chevrolet 1957 to present										
V-8 S/B 262-400; Rocker Ratio: 1.52 Magnum										
12-300-4	CS-240H-8	Strong torque, excellent mileage for 262-305 c.i.	Smooth	4,500	240	248	192	196	.400	.400
12-205-2	CS-252H-10	Strong torque, excellent mileage for 327-400 c.i.	Smooth	5,300	252	252	206	206	.431	.431
12-206-2	CS-260H-10	Power for vans, pickups & towing, 350 cu. in.	God	5,700	260	260	212	212	.446	.446
12-210-2	CS-268H-10	High perf. cam, mild street & towing applications.	Noticeable	6,000	268	268	218	218	.460	.460
Magnum Cams										
Chevrolet 1957 to present										
V-8 S/B 262-400										
12-210-2	CS-268H-10	High performance, mild street machines.	Noticeable	6,000	268	268	218	218	.460	.460
12-212-2	CS-280H-10	Street machine, works with headers.	Choppy	6,500	280	280	230	230	.486	.486
12-213-3	CS-292H-10	Street/strip special, needs converter.	Rough	7,000	292	292	244	244	.507	.507
12-214-4	CS-305H-10	Pro street/bracket racing only.	Racy	7,500	305	305	253	253	.532	.532
Rocker Ratio: 1.52 Magnum										
12-222-4	CS-270S-10	Excellent torque, high performance street.	Noticeable	6,500	270	270	224	224	.474	.474
12-223-4	CS-282S-10	Good all around power, street ideal.	Choppy	7,000	282	282	236	236	.501	.501
12-224-4	CS-294S-10	Maximum street performance.	Rough	7,200	294	294	248	248	.532	.532
12-225-4	CS-306S-10	Good power for street & strip.	Racy	7,500	306	306	260	260	.562	.562
Rocker Ratio: 1.5 Hi-Tech										
12-700-8	CS-268AR-10	Excellent throttle response, the most versatile	Noticeable	6,000	268	268	224	224	.525	.525
12-702-8	CS-280AR-10	Street/strip performance, broad applications.	Choppy	7,000	280	280	236	236	.550	.550
12-705-8	CS-300AR-10	Excellent choice for maximum street effort.	Racy	7,500	300	300	255	255	.575	.575
Chevrolet, 1957 to present										
V-8 S/B 262-400										
12-210-2	CS-268H-10	Mild street, towing, high performance.	Noticeable	6,000	268	268	218	218	.484	.484
12-212-2	CS-280H-10	Street machine, works with headers.	Choppy	6,500	280	280	230	230	.512	.512
12-213-3	CS-292H-10	Street/strip special, needs converter.	Rough	7,000	292	292	244	244	.534	.534
12-214-4	CS-305H-10	Pro street/bracket racing only.	Racy	7,500	305	305	253	253	.560	.560
Rocker Ratio: 1.8 Magnum										
12-222-4	CS-270S-10	High performance street, excellent torque.	Noticeable	6,500	270	270	224	224	499	499

continued

COMPETITION CAMS

Camshaft Part Number	Camshaft Grind Number	Application	Type Idle	Max. RPM	Duration In Degrees In.	Duration In Degrees Ex.	Duration @ .050 In.	Duration @ .050 Ex.	Lift In.	Lift Ex.
Rocker Ratio: 1.52 Magnum										
12-223-4	CS-282S-10	Ideal for street, all around power.	Choppy	7,000	282	282	236	236	.528	.528
12-224-4	CS-294S-10	For maximum performance.	Rouh	7,200	294	294	248	248	.560	.560
12-225-4	CS-306S-10	Good power to street & strip.	Racy	7,500	306	306	260	260	.592	.592
Rocker Ratio: 1.8 Hi-Tech										
12-700-8	CS-268AR-10	Good vacuum & excellent throttle response.	Noticeable	6,000	268	268	224	224	.560	.560
12-702-8	CS-280AR-10	Broad range of applications, street/strip.	Choppy	7,000	280	280	236	236	.586	.586
12-705-8	CS-300AR-10	Excellent choice for maximum street effort.	Racy	7,500	300	300	255	255	.613	.613

CRANE CAMS

57-85 Chevrolet V-8
262-267-283-302-305-307-327-350-400 cu. in.

Application	Basic RPM Range*	Cam Pt. No.	Series and Grind No.	Deg. Dur. @ .050 Cam Lift Int.	Exh.	Deg. Adv. Dur. Int.	Exh.	Deg. Lobe Center Line	Run'g. Clearance -HOT- Int.	Exh.	Gross Valve Lift Int.	Exh.
Hydraulic—Smooth idle, daily usage, fuel economy, 1600-2200 cruise RPM.	1000 -3500	113971	EconoPower HMV-248-2-NC	912	204	248	260	112	.000	.000	.400	.427
Hydraulic—Replacement for factory 300 H.P. 327 cu. in. camshaft.	1000 -3200	968711	BluePrinted 3896929	195	202			112	.000	.000	.390	.410
Hydraulic—Smooth idle, daily usage, off road, light towing, economy, also mild turbocharged, 2200-2700 cruise RPM.	1500 -4000	113901	EconoPower HMV-260-2-NC	204	216	260	272	112	.000	.000	.427	.454
Hydraulic—Good idle, daily usage and off road, highway towing, performance and fuel efficiency, 2600-3200 cruise RPM.	2000 -4500	113941	EconoPower HMV-272-2-NC	216	228	272	284	112	.000	.000	.454	.480
Hydraulic—Replacement for factory 350 H.P. 327 cu. in. camshaft.	2200 -5200	967601	BluePrinted	222	222			114	.000	.000	.447	.447
Hydraulic—Good idle, daily performance usage, mild bracket racing, 3200-3800 cruise RPM.	2200 -5700	113801	EconoPower HMV-278-2-NC	222	234	278	290	114	.000	.000	.467	.494
Hydraulic—Fair idle, moderate performance usage, good mid-range H.P., bracket racing.	2200 -5500	114201	Hi Intensity	224	224	280	280	114	.000	.000	.460	.460
Hydraulic—Rough idle, moderate performance usage, good mid-range H.P., limited oval track, bracket racing.	2800 -6000	110551	H-228/320-6	228	228	284	284	106	.000	.000	.480	.480
Hydraulic—Rough idle, moderate performance usage, good mid-range H.P., incrased compression ratio advised.	3000 -6200	113821	Hi Intensity HIT-284-2-NC	228	236	284	292	114	.000	.000	.490	.510
Hydraulic—Rough idle, performance usage, good mid-range H.P., increased compression ratio required.	3000 -6500	114561	Commander CCH-304-2-NC	234	244	304	314	112	.000	.000	.488	.508
Hydraulic—Rough idle, performance usage, good mid & upper R.P.M. H.P., limited oval track, bracket racing, increased compression ratio required.	3200 -6400	110651	H-238/3347-6	238	238	294	294	106	.000	.000	.502	.502
Hydraulic—Rough idle, performance usage, good mid & upper R.P.M. H.P., increased compression ratio required.	3200 -6700	114051	Hi Intensity HIT-296-2-NC	240	248	296	304	114	.000	.000	.520	.540
Hydraulic—Rough idle, performance usage, good upper R.P.M. H.P., increased compression ratio required.	3500 -7000	114571	Commander CCH-314-2-NC	224	254	314	324	114	.000	.000	.508	.532
Hydraulic—Moderate competition only, good upper R.P.M. H.P., high compression ratio required.	4000 -7200	114581	Commander CCH-324-NC	254	254	324	324	108	.000	.000	.532	.532

continued

Application	Basic RPM Range*	Cam Pt. No.	Series and Grind No.	Deg. Dur. @ .050 Cam Lift Int.	Exh.	Deg. Adv. Dur. Int.	Exh.	Deg. Lobe Center Line	Run'g Clearance -HOT- Int.	Exh.	Gross Valve Lift Int.	Exh.
Mechanical—Fair idle, moderate performance usage, good mid-range H.P., bracket racing.	3000 -6500	113841	Hi Intensity FHI-284-2-NC	238	248	284	294	114	.010	.012	.500	.520
Mechanical—Rough idle, moderate performance usage, good mid-range H.P., incr. comp. ratio advised, limited oval track, bracket racing.	3200 -6800	110921	F-244/3454-2S-6	244	252	280	288	106	.026	.026	.518	.536
Mechanical—Rough idle, moderate performance usage, good mid-range H.P., increased compression ratio advised.	3400 -6800	114681	Commander CC-280A-NC	244	252	280	288	112	.026	.026	.518	.536
Mechanical—Rough idle, moderate performance usage, good mid-range H.P., increased compression ratio advised.	3800 -7200	113861	Hi Intensity FHI-294-2-NC	248	258	294	304	114	.010	.012	.520	.540
Mechanical—Rough idle, perfor. usage good mid-range H.P., incr. compr. ratio req., short oval track, brck. racing w/ auto. trans.	4000 -7000	110981	F-252/3574-2S-6	252	260	288	296	106	.026	.026	.536	.554
Mechanical—Rough idle, performance usage, good mid-range H.P., increased compression ratio required.	4000 -7500	114691	Commander CC-290A-NC	252	260	290	298	112	.026	.026	.536	.554
Mechanical—Replacement for factory 290 H.P. 302 cu. in. Z-28 camshaft.	4000 -6800	967251	BluePrinted 3849346	255	255			114	.030	.030	.485	.485
Mechanical—Replacement for factory off road special camshaft.	4200	968821	BluePrinted	257	269			112	.022	.024	.493	.512
Mechanical—Rough idle, perfor. usage good mid & upp. R.P.M. H.P., incr. comp. ratio req., oval track, brack. racing w/auto trans.	4500 -7500	111431	F-260/3694-2S-6	260	268	296	304	106	.026	.026	.554	.572
Mechanical—Rough idle, performance usage, good upper R.P.M. H.P., increased compression ratio required.	4500 -8000	114701	Commander CC-300A-NC	264	272	300	308	112	.026	.026	.563	.581
Roller—Good idle, daily performance usage, mild bracket racing.	2400 -5800	118041a	Hi-Roller R-224/3335-12	224	224	286	286	112	.022	.022	.500	.500
Roller—Fair idle, moderate performance usage, good mid-range H.P. bracket racing.	3000 -6500	118021a	Hi-Roller R-234/3335-2-12	234	244	296	306	112	.022	.022	.500	.500
Roller—Rough idle, moderate perfor. usage, good mid-range torq. & H.P., incr. compress. ratio advised, ltd. oval track, bracket racing.	3600 -7000	118131b	Track-Roller TR-242/3867-2S-6	242	250	282	290	106	.022	.022	.580	.600
Roller—Rough idle, perfor. usage, good mid-range H.P. incr. compr. ratio req., short oval track, brac. racing w/auto trans.	4000 -7400	118171b	Track-Roller TR-250/400-2-6	250	260	290	300	106	022	022	600	625
Roller—Rough idle, perfor. usage, good mid & upper R.P.M. torque & H.P., incr. comp. ratio req., late model sportsman & all-pro unlimited carb., bracket racing w/auto trans.	4000 -7800	118251b	Track-Roller TR-256/4167-2-6	256	266	296	306	106	022	022	625	625
Roller—Rough idle, perfor. usage, good mid & upper R.P.M. torque & H.P., incr. comp. ratio req., NASCAR late model sportsman small carb., bracket racing w/auto trans.	4000 -7800	118161b	Track-Roller TR-260/4167-2-4	260	270	300	310	104	022	022	625	625
Roller—Rough idle, perfor. usage, good mid & upper R.P.M. torque & H.P., incr. comp. ratio req., ov. trk., brc. racing w/ auto trans.	4200 -8000	118151b	Track-Roller TR-260/4167-2-6	260	270	300	310	106	022	022	625	625
Roller—Rough idle, perfor. usage, good mid-range torque & H.P., incr. comp. ratio req., oval track, bracket racing w/auto trans.	4000 -7800	119301b	Inverted-Roller IR-260/4168-2S-6	260	268	296	304	106	.010	014	625	625

continued

Application	Basic RPM Range*	Cam Pt. No.	Series and Grind No.	SPECIFICATIONS									
				Deg. Dur. @ .050 Cam Lift		Deg. Adv. Dur.		Deg. Lobe Center Line	Run'g. Clearance -HOT-		Gross Valve Lift		
				Int.	Exh.	Int.	Exh.		Int.	Exh.	Int.	Exh.	
Roller—Rough idle. perfor. usage. good mid & upper R.P.M. torque & H.P. incr. comp. ratio req., oval track, bracket racing w/auto trans.	4200 -8000	11931ʰ	Inverted-Roller IR-268/4168-2S-6	268	276	304	312	106	010	014	625	625	

*R.P.M. range shown is for average usage. These cam profiles with RPM higher, depending upon application.

ᵢRequires cam button spacer.

ʰRequires cam button spacer and 11990-1 (.489" I.D.) or 11989-1 (.500" I.D. Accel.) aluminum-bronze distributor drive gear.

CROWER CAMS

Chevrolet
262-267-382-302-305-307-327-350-400

Description	C.I.D. Group	Part Center	Grind Lobe Number	Advertised Duration		Duration at .050"		Gross Lift	
				Intake	Exhaust	Intake	Exhaust	Intake	Exhaust
Hydraulic Lifter Camshafts									
Mileage Beast—Smooth idle. Squeezes maximum mileage from you engine. RPM power range idle to 3500/redline 4500+.	350	00902	246H 112°	246°	252°	193°	198°	400"	.402"
Baja Beast—Exhibits stump-pulling broad power and torque. RPM power range 1200 to 3800/ redline 5200+.	350	00915	258H 112°	258°	264°	202°	208°	.414"	.422"
Hot Street Beast—Delivers impressive mid range and top end power. RPM power range 2000 to 4800/redline 6200+.	350	00903	278H 112°	278°	284°	218°	224°	.455"	.464"
Mileage Compu-Pro—These cams enhance throttle response and low end torque in vans, trucks, and passenger cars while delivering fuel efficient motoring. RPM power range idle to 3500/redline 4500+.	262 283 302	00236	236HDP 112° 246HDP	236°	246°	181°	186°	.372"	.377"
	327	00237	112° 250HDP	246°	253°	186°	192°	.377"	.396"
	350	00238	112° 260HDP	250°	256°	192°	196°	.398"	.401"
	400	00239	112°	260°	266°	204°	210°	.417"	.420"
Power Compu-Pro—These cams provide excellent low end and mid-range power with extended RPM range for spirited street and off-road driving. A perfect combination mileage and power profile. RPM power range 1500 to 4000/redline 5000+.	262 283 302	00238	250HDP 112° 260HDP	250°	258°	192°	196°	.398"	.401"
	327	00239	112° 270HDP	260°	266°	204°	210°	.417"	.420"
	350	00240	112° 276HDP	270°	276°	209°	218°	.421"	.444"
	400	00241	112°	274°	281°	211°	220°	.432"	.456"
High Performance Compu-Pro—Intended for the hot street and marine application, these cams offer extended RPM range with emphasis on upper bottom to top end power with strong mid-range. RPM power range 1800 to 4500/redline 6000+.	262 283 302	00240	270HDP 112° 276HDP	270°	276°	209°	218°	.421"	.444"
	327	00241	112° 280HDP	274°	281°	211°	220°	.432"	.456"
	350	00242	112° 284HDP	280°	286°	220°	225°	.456"	.466"
	400	00243	112°	284°	290°	226°	230°	.480"	.455"

continued

Description	C.I.D. Group	Part Center	Grind Lobe Number	Advertised Duration Intake	Advertised Duration Exhaust	Duration at .050" Intake	Duration at .050" Exhaust	Gross Lift Intake	Gross Lift Exhaust
Ultra-Performance Compu-Pro—Dual purpose hot street/drag profile. These cams deliver strong mid-range to top end torque and horsepower. RPM power range 2000 to 6000/redline 7000+.	262 283 302	00242	280HDP 112°	280°	286°	220°	225°	.456″	.466″
	327	00243	284HDP 112°	284°	290°	226°	230°	.480″	.455″
	350	00244	297DHP 112°	297°	308°	236°	242°	.504″	.502″
Solid Lifter Camshafts	400	00245	311HDP 112°	311°	316°	244°	252°	.510″	.526″
Pro-Street—High torque mid-range and top end grind. RPM power range 2000 to 6500/redline 7500.	302 327	00320	264SF 112°	264°	270°	230°	235°	.457″	.470″
Pro-Street—High torque mid-range and top end grind. RPM power range 2000 to 6000/redline 7500.	350 400	00321	274SF 114°	274°	282°	240°	247°	.481″	.507″
Pro-Street—High revving, super mid-to-top end power. RPM power range 3000 to 7500/redline 8000+.	302 327	00322	282SF 112°	282°	292°	247°	252°	.507″	.528″
Pro-Street—High revving, super mid-to-top end power. RPM power range 3000 to 7500/redline 8000+.	350 400	00323	294SF 114°	294°	300°	256°	260°	.532″	.543″
Compu-Pro—Broad power band. Short oval profile. RPM power range 2000 to 6000/redline 7000+.	350 400	00350	268FDP 107°	268°	274°	236°	240°	.496″	.502″
Roller Lifter Camshafts									
Street Roller—RPM powe range 2500 to 6000/ redline 7500+.	350 400	00425	280R 112°	280°	288°	242°	248°	.549″	.565″
Street Roller—RPM power range 3000 to 7000/ redline 8000+.	350 400	00426	288R 112°	288°	290°	248°	254°	.565″	.583″
Street Roller—RPM power range 3200 to 7500/ redline 8000+.	350 400	00427	290R 112°	290°	296°	256°	256°	.583″	.597″

EDELBROCK CAMS

Performer-Plus Camshaft

Chevolet V-8's 1962 & later
For up to 350 c.i.d.

Duration at .006 Lift:	Intake 278°	Exhaust 288°
Duration at .050 Lift:	Intake 204°	Exhaust 214°
Lift at Cam:	Intake .280	Exhaust .295
Lift at Valve:	Intake .420	Exhaust .442
Timing at .050 Life:	Open	Close
Intake	5° ATDC	29° ABDC
Exhaust	44° BBDC	10° BTDC

Performer-Plus Camshaft

Chevrolet V-8's 1970 & later
For 400 c.i.d.

Duration at .006 Lift:	Intake 288°	Exhaust 288°
Duration at .050 Lift:	Intake 214°	Exhaust 214°
Lift at Cam:	Intake .295	Exhaust .295
Lift at Valve:	Intake .442	Exhaust .442
Timing at .050 Lift:	Open	Close
Intake	0° ATDC	34° ABDC
Exhaust	44° BBDC	10° BTDC

ENGLE CAMS

Chevrolet Small Block 265-400 V-8

Description	Part Number	Grind Number	Valve Lift	Advertised Duration	Cam Lift	Duration At .050"	Lobe Center
Hydraulic Lifter Camshafts							
Economy, low end power for stock, low compression cars, trucks, & RV's. Powerband 1000-4500 RPM.	1014H	EP-14/100HYD	IN .405" EX .420"	248° 260°	.270" .280"	204° 210°	112°
Low & midrange torque for street & tow truck. 8.0 to 9.0:1 compression. Powerband 1200-5000 RPM.	1016H	EP-16/18HYD	IN .440" EX .458"	256° 260°	.295" .305"	210° 216°	112°
Heavy street performance cars & vehicles. 9.0:1 compression. Powerband 1500-5500 RPM.	1018H	EP-18/20HYD	IN .458" EX .468"	260° 268°	.305" .310"	216° 226°	112°
Medium hot rod performance, street. 9.0 to 9.5:1 compression. Powerband 1800-5800 RPM.	1022H	EP-22HYD	IN .480" EX .480"	274° 274°	.320" .320"	230° 230°	110°
Hot street & strip performance. 9.5 to 10.0:1 compression. Powerband 2000-6000 RPM.	1025H	EP-25HYD	IN .494" EX .494"	282° 282°	.327" .327"	236° 236°	110°
Turbocharger Hydraulic Camshafts							
Street & strip, good idle, modified engines. 8.0:1 compression. Powerband 2000-6000 RPM.	1002H	TSC-2HYD	IN .458" EX .440"	260° 256°	.305" 2.95"	216° 210°	116°
Street & strip, jet boats, moderate idle. 8.0 to 8.5:1 compression. Powerband 2800-6500 RPM.	1005H	TSC-5HYD	IN .483" EX .468"	274° 266°	.320" .310"	230° 226°	114°
Solid Lifter Camshafts							
Medium hot rod, street & heavy tow service. 9 to 9.5:1 compression. Powerband 1800-5800 RPM.	1020	EP-20	IN .482" EX .482"	268° 268°	.321" .321°	232° 232°	112°
Street & strip, 4 speed or 2000 stall. 9.5 to 10.0:1 compression. Powerband 2000-6000 RPM.	1022	EP-22	IN .491" EX .491"	274° 274°	.327" .327"	238° 238°	110°
Street & strip, brackets, moderate built. 10 to 10.5:1 compression. Powerband 2500-6500 RPM	1025	EP-25	IN .507" EX .507"	280° 280°	.338" .338"	244° 244°	108°
Brackets circle track, light cars, 10 to 10.5:1 compression. Powerband 2800-6800 RPM.	1026	EP-26/28	IN .520" EX .536"	288° 292°	.346" .351"	249° 256°	108°
Turbocharger Solid Lifter Camshafts							
Street & strip racing, good idle, 8.0 to 8.5:1 compression. Powerband 2000-6000 RPM.	1005	TCS-5	IN .456" EX .444"	268° 264°	.304" .296"	230° 224°	*114°*
Serious street & strip, jet boats. 8.0 to 9.0:1 compression. Powerband 2800-6800 RPM.	1007	TCS-7	IN .496" EX .456"	284° 268°	.331" .304"	242° 230°	114°

Chevrolet Small Block 265-400

Description	Part Number	Grind Number	Valve Lift	Advertised Duration	Cam Lift	Duration At .050"	Lobe Center
Roller Tappet Camshafts							
Street roller. Power 2000-6500. Weekend hot rod.	1050	RK-26	IN .521" EX .521"	254° 254°	.347" .347"	214° 214°	112°
Street roller. Power 2200-6700. Street/strip.	1052	RK-27	IN .527" EX .527"	265° 265°	.351" .351"	225° 225°	112°
Bracket racing. Power 2500-7000.	1054	RK-48	IN .609" EX .609"	294° 294°	.406" .406"	254° 254°	108°

ERSON CAMS

Chevrolet V8 265-283-307-327-350-400
1.5 to 1 Rocker Arm Ratio

Grind Number	Cam Part Number	Timing	Valve Clearance	Valve Lift	Duration	Duration @ .050	General Characteristics
Hydraulic Hi Performance Cams/Proferal Billets							
SRC	110102	IO 14 IC 64 EO 63 EC 26	.000 .000	.390 .410	258 269	194 202	Specially selected duplicate of OEM cam. Restores vehicle's original perf. and emissions if all OEM internal parts and controls are used.
RV5H	110011	IO 30 IC 64 EO 72 EC 22	.000 .000	.410	274	202	The "commuter". More power through entire range. Stop and go traffic and expressway use. Good idle, throttle response, fuel efficiency.
RV10H	110101	IO 33 IC 67 EO 75 EC 25	.000 .000	.420	280	208	Broad power range. City and expressway driving, towing. Cars, wagons, P/U's, heavier rigs. Good idle, throttle response and high fuel efficiency.

continued

Grind Number	Cam Part Number	Timing	Valve Clearance	Valve Lift	Duration	Duration @ .050	General Characteristics
M/P 1	111011	IO 30 IC 70 EO 84 EC 28	.000 .000	.420 .449	280 292	208 214	Smaller engines. Allows high compression engines (10 to 1 and up) to operate on low octane fuel with reasonable fuel efficiency. Good idle.
RV15H	110201	IO 37 IC 71 EO 79 EC 29	.000 .000	 .429	 288	 214	Strong mid range power. City, fast expressway and open road towing. Delivers max mid range torque. Good idle, throttle response and fuel efficiency.
TURBO I	110001	IO 34 IC 78 EO 72 EC 28	.000 .000	.449 .420	292 280	214 208	Strong low and mid range power plus good high RPM performance. Use with up to 5 psi boost, good idle.
TQ20H	113121	IO 39 IC 73 EO 81 EC 31	.000 .000	 .449	 292	 214	The "performer". Super low and mid range power. Good idle, fuel efficiency and driveability. 4 barrel and headers recommended.
M/P 2	111021	IO 34 IC 74 EO 93 EC 37	.000 .000	.429 .462	288 310	214 226	Larger engines. Allows high compression engines (10 to 1 and up) to operate on low octane fuel with reasonable fuel efficiency. Good idle.
Viking 100H	112061	IO 37 IC 73 EO 73 EC 37	.000 .000	 .447	 290	 224	General purpose street and strip cam for 302 or larger engine. OK for Turbo hydro with low gears. Fair idle.
TURBO II	110011	IO 43 IC 87 EO 78 EC 34	.000 .000	.462 .449	310 292	226 214	Strong broad range cam for engines over 300C.I. and boost up to 7 psi. Good idle, OK for Turbo Hydro.
TQ30H	113221	IO 48 IC 82 EO 90 EC 40	.000 .000	 .462	 310	 226	Mid range and strong top end. Needs 4 barrel, headers and lower gears. OK with automatic with low gears. Fair idle and fuel efficiency.
Hi Flow IH	110421	IO 41 IC 77 EO 77 EC 41	.000 .000	 .470	 298	 229	High lift, short duration, delivers broad power range, strong top end. Hot street, brackets, etc., fair idle. Needs 4 barrel, headers, compression and gears.
Hi Flow IIH	110521	IO 45 IC 81 EO 81 EC 45	.000 .000	 .472	 306	 235	Runs strong 3500 to 7000 RPM. Stick or auto with gears. Needs good intake and headers, 9.5 to 1 or more compression. Lopey idle.
TURBO-III	110010	IO 46 IC 90 EO 85 EC 41	.000 .000	.477 .472	316 306	240 235	Mid range and top end cam for larger engine with high boost. Fair idle. Drag racing, fast ski boats.
Hi Flow IIIH	115911	IO 50 IC 86 EO 86 EC 50	.000 .000	 .477	 316	 240	Runs strong 4000 to 7500 RPM. Needs lower gears, 4 barrel, headers and compression for maximum performance. Rough idle.
500 HLH	111121	IO 51 IC 87 EO 87 EC 51	.000 .000	 .504	 318	 244	New high lift redesign of the 500H, strong upper mid range and top end. Needs headers and gears.
525 H	110621	IO 51 IC 87 EO 90 EC 54	.000 .000	.504 .502	318 324	244 252	Dual pattern, Hi lift cam. A winner in well prepared 327 or larger engine. Strong past 7500. Needs headers and gears, rough idle.

Flat Tappet Hi Performance Cams/Proferal Billets

Grind Number	Cam Part Number	Timing	Valve Clearance	Valve Lift	Duration	Duration @ .050	General Characteristics
TQ20M	113122	IO 23 IC 67 EO 67 EC 23	.022 .022	 .465	 270	 220	Short duration, fast action, high lift. Makes power over broad range. Smooth idle, good for Turbo Hydro.
Hi Flow IM	110721	IO 35 IC 71 EO 71 EC 35	.022 .022	 .510	 286	 242	Hi lift short duration design delivers extra power through the entire R.P.M. range. The ideal street strip cam for the smaller engine.
Hi Flow IIM	110821	IO 39 IC 75 EO 75 EC 39	.022 .022	 .510	 294	 246	Hi lift street and strip cam. Super mid range and top end power, fair idle. Needs 4 barrel, headers and gears for best performance.
Hi R M2	111611	IO 50 IC 86 EO 86 EC 50	.022 .022	 .498	 316	 253	Strong performer mid range and top end, for 302 or larger. Stick shift, gears, 4 barrel and headers recommended.
Hi Flow IIIM	110831	IO 45 IC 81 EO 81 EC 45	.022 .022	 .510	 306	 254	Mid range and top end cam for the larger engine, must have good breathing intake headers and gears, fair idle.
320 HLM	110921	IO 52 IC 88 EO 88 EC 52	.022 .022	 .534	 320	 256	Mid range and top end performer. Needs headers, good intake and lower gears for best results.

continued

Grind Number	Cam Part Number	Timing	Valve Clearance	Valve Lift	Duration	Duration @ .050	General Characteristics
Flat Tappet Racing Cams/Proferal Billets							
TURBO IIM	111001	IO 35 IC 79	.022	.510	294	246	Strong broad range cam for engines over
		EO 75 EC 31	.022	.510	286	242	300C.I. Runs hard past 7000. OK for Turbo Hydro with low gears.
TURBO IIIM	111002	IO 41 IC 85	.022	.510	306	254	Upper mid range and top end cam for the larger
		EO 79 EC 35	.022	.510	294	246	engine, high boost. Valve train stable past 7500.
990 AH	111031	IO 48 IC 84	.028				New design, strong through broad range, pulls
		EO 84 EC 48	.030	.575	312	268	hard from 4000 up. Hot street, strip or bracket racer. For the built engine only.
990 SB	118631	IO 51 IC 87	.028				Strong mid range and top end cam, pulls hard
		EO 87 EC 51	.030	.550	318	278	past 7000 in well set up engine. Bracket racers favorite.
999 XX	113231	IO 52 IC 88	.028				Broad power range cam for 302-327 engines,
		EO 88 EC 52	.030	.575	320	276	tunnel ram or injectors. Will pull heavy chassis or bracket racing.
2450X	111009	IO 47 IC 83	.024	.565	310	276	Single carb applications with Turbo-Hydro—also
		EO 88 EC 52	.026	.565	320	286	good for heavy stick shift drag cars.
3010 D.P.-1	111008	IO 58 IC 94	.024	.592	332	290	Big cubic inch engines only. Can be used with
		EO 98 EC 62	.026	.592	340	311	nitrous oxide type tunnel ram manifolds.
Roller Tappet Cams/Steel Billets/Street Rollers							
RH-282-1	119811	IO 31 IC 71	.000				Mild hydraulic roller. Perfect for all around
		EO 71 EC 31	.000	.480	282	214	performance driving. Works well in small trucks.
RH-282-2	119812	IO 31 IC 71	.000	.480	282	214	Good performance increase over stock hi-perf.
		EO 74 EC 34	.000	.480	288	219	cams. Still idles well but has plenty of low and mid range power.
RH-288-1	119813	Io 36 IC 72	.000				Strong mid range power when used with 4
		EO 72 EC 36	.000	.480	288	219	barrel. Slightly rough idle. Pulls hard to 6500.
R-278-1	119800	IO 31 IC 67	.025	.555	278	238	Street roller cam with excellent low and mid
		EO 71 EC 35	.025	.555	286	246	range power. Needs 4 barrel and good exhaust.
R-294-1	119801	IO 39 IC 75	.025	.555	294	254	All out street roller cam. Also works well with 4
		EO 79 EC 43	.025	.555	302	260	barrel bracket cars. Not recommended for street use with auto trans.
R-296-1	119802	IO 40 IC 76	.032	.600	296	266	Maximum cam for street use. Must have
		EO 82 EC 46	.032	.600	308	278	4-speed, low gears and good intake. Can be used with tunnel ram manifold.
R-308-1A	119803	IO 46 IC 82	.032				Good mid range and top end for bracket racer
		EO 82 EC 46	.032	.600	308	278	or super stock with low stall speed atuo trans. Needs tunnel ram for best results.
Roller Tappet Cams/Steel Billets/Drag Racing							
R-314-1	119900	IO 52 IC 82	.032				283 cu. in. stick shift super stocks, 327-350 cu.
		EO 82 EC 52	.032	.667	314	283	in. bracket racers with auto trans.
R-314-2	119901	IO 51 IC 83	.032	.667	314	283	327 cu. in. super stock stick shift, 350 cu. in.
		EO 87 EC 55	.032	.667	322	288	auto trans. in super stock. Great also for 350 engine in brackets with heavy car.
R-314-3	119902	IO 51 IC 83	.032	.667	314	283	350 cu. in. stick shift in super stockers. Good
		EO 89 EC 57	.032	.645	326	292	single 4 barrel bracket cam in a light car.
R-320-2	119903	IO 52 IC 88	.032	.712	320	289	For small cu. in. modified engine with tunnel
		EO 93 EC 57	.032	.645	330	298	ram and modified cylinder heads.
R-324-2	119904	Io 53 IC 91	.032	.667	324	291	327 to 350 cu. in. modified engine with tunnel
		EO 95 EC 57	.032	.645	332	301	ram and good cylinder heads. Should use 1.6 ratio rockers on the intake side.
R-326-2A	119905	IO 53 IC 93	.032	.712	326	293	350 cu. in. and larger AHRA nitrous engines.
		EO 97 EC 57	.032	.645	334	302	Will also work well in big cu. in. non-nitrous modified engines. Needs big volume heads to work best.

HERBERT CAMS

Grind	IN Dur	EX Dur	IN Dur .050	EX Dur .050	1.5 IN Lift	1.5 EX Lift	1.6 IN Lift	1.6 EX Lift	1.7 IN Lift	1.7 EX Lift
C	285	295	235	245	500	500	534	534	570	570
C	310	320	260	270	550	550	585	585	625	625

ISKY MEGA-CAMS™

V-8 Engines

Part #	Application	Grind	Type	Lift	Running Duration	Duration @ .050"	Lobe Center
201271		270-Mega-cam	Hyd.	.465"	270°	221°	108°
201281	Small Block	280-Mega-cam	Hyd.	.485"	280°	232°	108°
201292	Chevy V8	292-Mega-cam	Hyd.	.505"	292°	244°	108°
201304		304-Mega-cam	Hyd.	.525"	304°	256°	108°

Chevrolet Small Block V-8
265-283-302-305-307-350-400 cu. in. Engines

Part No. Cam Only	Part No. Cam & Kit	Grind	RPM Range	Intake	Exhaust	Lift	Valve Lash Hot	Duration
Hydraulic Series/Cast Iron Billet								
201256	200256	256 Supercam	1500-4800	22-54	66-10	.425	.000	256°
+201258	200258	256 Supercam	1500-4800	26-50	62-14	.425	.000	256°
201262	200262	262 Supercam	2000-5500	23-59	59-23	.435	.000	262°
201270	200270	270 HL HYD	2000-6000	24-66	60-30	.445	.000	270°
201280	200280	280 HL HYD	2500-6500	29-71	65-35	.465	.000	280°
201300	200300	300 HL HYD	3000-7000	42-78	78-42	.485	.000	300°
201310	200310	310 HL HYD	3500-7000	47-83	83-47	.505	.000	310°
+For 305 Chevy V-8 only								
Hi-Rev Series/Flat Tappet Cast Iron Billet								
201020	200020	Z-20	2000-6000	22-65	66-22	.448	.018	268°
201025	200025	Z-25	2500-6500	31-67	67-31	.480	.018	278°
201030	200030	Z-30	3000-7000	37-73	73-37	.480	.030	290°
201040	200040	Z-40	3500-7500	47-83	83-47	.511	.026	310°
201050	200050	Z-50	3500-7500	42-78	78-42	.507	.028	300°
201065	200065	Z-65	4000-8000	49-85	85-49	.560	.028	314°
201070	200070	Z-70	3500-7500	44-80	80-44	.548	.028	304°
201075	200075	Z-75	4000-8000	52-88	88-52	.570	.028	320°
201085	200085	Z-85	4500-8500	57-93	93-57	.585	.030	330°
201506	200506	505-T	3000-7000	37-73	73-37	.505	.030	290°
Drags Roller Series/Genuine 8620 Steel Billet								
201570	200570	570-T	3000-7000	37-73	73-37	.570	.028	290°
201600	200600	600	4500-8500	52-88	88-52	.588	.028	320°
201602	200602	602	3500-7500	42-78	78-42	.602	.028	300°
201630	200630	630	4000-8000	49-85	85-49	.630	.028	314°
201660	200660	660	4500-8500	54-90	90-54	.660	.028	324°
201662	200662	662	5000-9000	58-94	94-58	.662	.028	332°

Lunati
The Bracket Master camshaft

		Lift		Intake Duration		Exhaust Duration		Valve lash		
Part no.	Grind no.	Intake	Exhaust	0.050 in.	Adv.	Adv.	0.050 in.	Intake	Exhaust	Kit no.
283-400 Chevrolet										
00101	BM-501	0.501	0.501	267	310	310	267	0.030	0.030	65075

The Bracket Master II camshaft

		Lift		Intake Duration		Exhaust Duration		Valve lash		
Part no.	Intake	Exhaust	0.050 in.	Adv.	Adv.	0.050 in.	Intake	Exhaust	Kit no.
Chevrolet 283-400 ci									
00010	0.480	0.480	230	292	292	230	0.000	0.000	65002
00011	0.455	0.455	230	285	285	230	0.000	0.000	65002
00012	0.515	0.515	246	300	300	246	0.000	0.000	65002
00013	0.500	0.515	256	300	310	270	0.028	0.030	65075
00014	0.485	0.485	252	315	315	252	0.028	0.030	65026

continued

Dual Purpose cams

Part no.	Grind no.	Lift Intake	Lift Exhaust	Duration Intake 0.050 in.	Intake Adv.	Exhaust Adv.	Exhaust 0.050 in.	Valve lash Intake	Valve lash Exhaust	Kit no.
Chevrolet 265-400 ci										
10101	DPA1-280	0.440	0.440	222	280	280	222	0.000	0.000	65002
10102	DPA1-300	0.450	0.450	230	300	300	230	0.000	0.000	65002
10103	DPA1-310	0.507	0.507	246	310	310	246	0.000	0.000	65002
20104	DPA2-300	0.450	0.450	248	300	300	248	0.016	0.018	65026
20105	DPA2-310	0.485	0.485	254	310	310	254	0.028	0.030	65026
20106	DPA2-320	0.492	0.510	257	304	320	270	0.028	0.030	65026

High Efficiency series

Part no.	Grind no.	Lift Intake	Lift Exhaust	Duration Intake 0.050 in.	Intake Adv.	Exhaust Adv.	Exhaust 0.050 in.	Valve lash Intake	Valve lash Exhaust	Kit no.
Chevrolet 283-400 ci										
06101	HI-262	0.393	0.393	201	262	262	201	0.000	0.000	65002
06102	HI-256	0.369	0.405	188	246	266	204	0.000	0.000	65002
06103	HI-270	0.420	0.442	204	270	280	214	0.000	0.000	65002
06104	HI-268	0.390	0.390	212	268	268	212	0.000	0.000	65002
06105	HI-258	0.440	0.440	208	258	258	208	0.000	0.000	65002
06106	HI-280	0.444	0.444	218	280	280	218	0.000	0.000	65002

Flat tappet grinds
Chevrolet 265, 283, 302, 307, 327, 350, 400 ci

Part no.	Grind no.	Lift Intake	Lift Exhaust	Duration Intake 0.050 in.	Intake Adv.	Exhaust Adv.	Exhaust 0.050 in.	Valve lash Intake	Valve lash Exhaust	Kit no.
30103	SPA1-276-290	0.402	0.436	212	276	290	220	0.000	0.000	65002
30104	SPA1-280	0.438	0.438	216	280	280	216	0.000	0.000	65002
30105	SPA1-290	0.465	0.465	228	290	290	228	0.000	0.000	65002
30106	SPA1-296	0.493	0.493	234	296	296	234	0.000	0.000	65002
30107	SPA1-300	0.465	0.465	235	300	300	235	0.000	0.000	65002
30108	SPA1-310	0.485	0.485	242	310	310	242	0.000	0.000	65002
30109	SPA1-320	0.510	0.530	245	315	325	255	0.000	0.000	65002
30110	SPA1-285-300	0.465	0.465	230	285	300	235	0.000	0.000	65002
40111	SPA2-285	0.501	0.508	240	280	290	249	0.028	0.030	65075
40112	SPA2-290	0.507	0.507	249	290	290	249	0.030	0.030	65075
40113	SPA2-295	0.507	0.519	249	290	300	258	0.030	0.030	65075
40114	SPA2-300	0.519	0.519	258	300	300	258	0.030	0.030	65075
40115	SPA2-305	0.519	0.531	258	300	310	267	0.300	0.030	65075
40116	SPA2-310	0.531	0.531	267	310	310	267	0.300	0.030	65075
40117	SPA2-315	0.531	0.536	267	310	320	279	0.300	0.030	65075
40118	SPA2-292	0.550	0.550	256	292	292	256	0.024	0.026	65075
40119	SPA2-292-302	0.550	0.571	256	292	302	268	0.024	0.026	65075
40120	SPA2-296-306	0.495	0.518	242	296	306	249	0.020	0.022	65075
40133	SPA2-297-304	0.549	0.567	260	297	304	268	0.026	0.028	65075
40131	SPA2-301	0.555	0.555	264	301	301	264	0.024	0.026	65075
40132	SPA2-302	0.571	0.571	268	302	302	268	0.024	0.026	65075
40121	SPA2-302-312	0.571	0.580	268	302	312	275	0.026	0.028	65075
40122	SPA2-306-316	0.518	0.540	249	306	316	261	0.020	0.022	65075
40123	SPA2-312-322	0.580	0.600	275	312	322	289	0.026	0.028	65075

continued

Flat tappet grinds
Chevrolet 265, 283, 302, 307, 327, 350, 400 ci

		Lift		Duration Intake 0.050 in.	Intake Adv.	Exhaust Adv.	Exhaust 0.050 in.	Valve lash Intake	Exhaust	Kit no.
Part no.	Grind no.	Intake	Exhaust							
40124	SPA2-316-326	0.540	0.563	261	316	326	271	0.020	0.022	65075
40125	SPA2-326-336	0.563	0.585	271	326	336	281	0.020	0.022	65075
40126	SPA2-286-292	0.528	0.550	246	286	292	256	0.024	0.026	65075
40129	SPA2-294-304	0.585	0.600	252	294	304	260	0.018	0.020	
40130	SPA2-304-312	0.600	0.621	260	304	312	270	0.018	0.020	

Roller tappet grinds

		Lift		Duration Intake 0.050 in.	Intake Adv.	Exhaust Adv.	Exhaust 0.050 in.	Valve lash Intake	Exhaust
Part no.	Grind no.	Intake	Exhaust						
50142	RRAH-270-279	0.417	0.447	209	270	279	213	0.000	0.000
50143	RRAH-284-292	0.468	0.477	218	284	292	226	0.000	0.000
50139	RRA-282-290	0.502	0.502	224	282	290	232	0.022	0.024
50101	RRA-304	0.528	0.528	244	304	304	244	0.030	0.030
50103	RRA-288-296	0.590	0.600	248	288	296	254	0.018	0.020
50104	RRA-400	0.600	0.600	266	300	300	266	0.018	0.020
50105	RRA-296-306	0.600	0.600	254	296	306	266	0.018	0.020
50106	RRA-306-314	0.600	0.605	266	306	314	268	0.018	0.020
50107	RRA-314-318	0.605	0.605	268	314	318	275	0.018	0.020
50108	RRA-318-324	0.605	0.609	275	318	324	280	0.018	0.020
50110	RRA-318-328	0.640	0.651	279	318	328	282	0.026	0.028
50111	RRA-320-322	0.655	0.620	273	320	322	282	0.018	0.020
50112	RRA-320-332	0.675	0.669	282	320	332	290	0.026	0.028
50114	RRA-663-669	0.663	0.669	280	322	332	290	0.026	0.028
50120	RRA-292-302	0.585	0.585	250	292	302	260	0.026	0.028
50121	RRA-258-268	0.600	0.618	258	308	318	268	0.022	0.024
50122	RRA-331-334	0.682	0.626	288	331	334	292	0.026	0.028
50124	RRA-262-271	0.622	0.624	262	300	310	271	0.022	0.024
50125	RRA-271-281	0.645	0.645	271	308	318	281	0.022	0.024
50126	RRA-281-281	0.645	0.645	281	318	318	281	0.022	0.024
50127	RRA-326-334	0.703	0.626	285	326	334	292	0.026	0.028
50128	RRA-288-294	0.690	0.660	288	332	336	294	0.025	0.027
50129	RRA-271-271	0.645	0.645	271	308	308	271	0.022	0.024
50130	RRA-271-416	0.624	0.624	271	310	310	271	0.025	0.027
50131	RRA-272-425	0.637	0.637	272	308	308	272	0.022	0.024
50132	RRA-317-334	0.672	0.628	283	317	334	292	0.025	0.028
50133	RRA-282-420	0.630	0.630	282	326	326	282	0.036	0.032
50134	RRA-286-288	0.702	0.667	286	324	327	288	0.032	0.030
50135	RRA-275-605	0.605	0.605	275	318	318	275	0.018	0.020
51036	RRA-274-278	0.630	0.630	274	318	322	278	0.028	0.030
50137	RRA-285	0.630	0.630	285	330	330	285	0.036	0.032
50138	RRA-283-284	0.672	0.646	283	317	318	284	0.028	0.030
50140	RRA-276-284	0.636	0.636	276	312	316	284	0.026	0.028
50141	RRA-284-285	0.702	0.630	284	324	285	326	0.035	0.030

TRW
PRODUCTS

Camshafts

Stock Number	Engine Type	Net Valve Lift		Duration @ .050 Cam Lift		Overlap @ .006 Cam Lift	Lobe Centers	Timing Event @ .050 Cam Lift				Rocker Arm Ratio (to 1)	Lash	
		Int.	Exh.	Int.	Exh.			Intake		Exhaust			Int.	Exh.
								Open	Close	Open	Close			
TP112N	Chev OEP & CP	.460	.460	232°	232°	75°	109° Int. 119° Exh.	BTDC 7°	ABDC 45°	BBDC 55°	BTDC 3°	1.5	Hyd.	Hyd.
TP113	Chev EP OEP & CP	.382	.382	228°	230°	49°	108½° Int. 112½° Exh.	BTDC 5½°	ABDC 42½°	BBDC 47½°	ATDC 2½°	1.5	.012 Hot	.018 Hot
TP118	Chev OEP & CP	.455	.455	254°	254°	67°	110° Int. 118° Exh.	BTDC 16°	ABDC 58°	BBDC 64°	ATDC 10°	1.5	.030 Hot	.030 Hot
TP146	Chev CP	.434	.434	244°	244°	96°	106½° Int. 109½° Exh.	BTDC 15½°	ABDC 48½°	BBDC 51½°	ATDC 12½°	1.5	Hyd.	Hyd.
TP147	Chev CP	.471	.488	257°	270°	84°	108° Int. 116° Exh.	BTDC 19°	ABDC 58°	BBDC 70°	ATDC 20°	1.5	.022 Hot	.024 Hot
TP150	Chev CP	.475	.475	250°	250°	70°	109° Int. 119° Exh.	BTDC 16°	ABDC 54°	BBDC 64°	ATDC 6°	1.5	.018 Hot	.018 Hot
TP168	Chev EP & CP	.480	.480	230°	230°	69°	107° Int. 111° Exh.	BTDC 8°	ABDC 42°	BBDC 46°	ATDC 4°	1.5	Hyd.	Hyd.
TP174	Chev EP & OEP	.442	.465	214°	224°	69°	107° Int. 117° Exh.	TDC 0°	ABDC 34°	BBDC 49°	BTDC 5°	1.5	Hyd.	Hyd.
TP178	Chev CP	.473	.496	244°	254°	82°	102° Int. 110° Exh.	BTDC 20°	ABDC 44°	BBDC 57°	ATDC 17°	1.5	.022 Hot	.022 Hot
TP179	Chev CP	.496	.518	254°	264°	92°	102° Int. 110° Exh.	BTDC 25°	ABDC 49°	BBDC 62°	ATDC 22°	1.5	.022 Hot	.022 Hot
TP180	Chev CP	.518	.541	264°	274°	98°	104° Int. 112° Exh.	BTDC 28°	ABDC 56°	BBDC 69°	ATDC 25°	1.5	.022 Hot	.022 Hot
TP187	Chev EP	.420	.443	204°	214°	59°	107° Int. 117° Exh.	ATDC 5°	ABDC 29°	BBDC 44°	BTDC 10°	1.5	Hyd.	Hyd.
TP191	Chev CP	.443	.465	214°	224°	69°	107° Int. 117° Exh.	TDC 0°	ABDC 34°	BBDC 49°	BTDC 5°	1.5	Hyd.	Hyd.
TP197	Chev EP	.398	.420	194°	204°	45°	109° Int. 119° Exh.	ATDC 12°	ABDC 26°	BBDC 41°	BTDC 17°	1.5	Hyd.	Hyd.
TP200	Chev CP	.458	.458	238°	238°	60°	107° Int. 117° Exh.	BTDC 12°	ABDC 46°	BBDC 56°	ATDC 7°	1.5	.022 Hot	.022 Hot
TP207	Chev EP	.420	.443	204°	214°	59°	107° Int. 117° Exh.	ATDC 5°	ABDC 29°	BBDC 44°	BTDC 10°	1.5	Hyd.	Hyd.
TP208	Chev EP	.443	.465	214°	224°	69°	107° Int. 117° Exh.	TDC 0°	ABDC 34°	BBDC 49°	BTDC 5°	1.5	Hyd.	Hyd.
TM274	Chev EP & OEP	.391	.410	194°	205°	43°	108° Int. 116° Exh.	ATDC 11°	ABDC 25°	BBDC 37°	BTDC 14°	1.5	Hyd.	Hyd.
TM628	Chev EP	.373	.410	189°	202°	40°	102° Int. 116° Exh.	ATDC 9°	ABDC 18°	BBDC 37°	BTDC 15°	1.5	Hyd.	Hyd.

Manifolds

7

Intake manifolds

All Chevrolet intake manifolds interchange. The choice you make will depend on how much fuel you want delivered and in what rpm range you want your power developed.

For the purposes of keeping a car original, remember that manifolds are cast parts and as such bear casting identification and the date of manufacture. If, for example, you have gone to the trouble of restoring a 1971 Chevrolet Impala convertible to original and the date on your intake manifold clearly reads E 21 72, you could be embarrassed—especially if you are running a two-barrel because you wanted to keep the car original.

Intake manifolds are designed to help regulate flow velocity by passage and port size. The car-

This manifold is from a 1968 210 hp 327 ci engine. The front oil filter tube was a standard 1968 feature. Extremely small throttle bore diameters came stock on the 307 ci as well. This choke mount remained the same until the 1971 model year.

This two-barrel large-throttle-bore manifold is typical of what was available on 1973 and later 350 ci engines. Notice the EGR valve and choke mounting pads.

When the production date information of February 6, 1975, is combined with extremely small mixture passages, the trained parts person may well recognize this as a 262 ci manifold. The first year of the choke-heat-tube appliance (notice the access mounting hole) was 1975. This manifold should not be used on a larger engine unless low-speed mixture velocity through the manifold is important to vehicle performance.

buretor base plate size usually reflects the size of the carburetor throttle bore on the manifold.

In 1968-69, low-performance 200 hp, 307 ci and 210 hp, 327 ci engines came equipped with small two-barrel intake manifolds. The idea behind small throttle bores in the manifold was to help keep velocity high through the carburetor. The design worked because the throttle response and low-rpm power of the engines were terrific.

As vehicle weights increased, the intermediate-performance 235 hp, 327 ci engine of the 1969

This is a Quadrajet four-barrel carburetor installed on a 1969 intake manifold bolted onto a 1980 small-block 400 ci engine from a van. The whole assembly has just been installed in a 1977 Camaro. Chevy interchangeability is a real bargain!

model year and the 245 hp, 350 ci engine of the 1970 model year came equipped with larger-diameter throttle bores on two-barrel intake manifolds. The large-two-barrel-equipped cars were usually full-size or station wagon models. The theory behind the large two-barrel was that the vehicle weight and final drive ratio may not allow enough engine vacuum under load to open secondary air dams of a Quadrajet at low- and mid-rpm range.

Few people are interested in the two-barrel manifolds or two-barrel Rochester carburetors. If you must run a two-barrel, use a non-EGR (Exhaust Gas Recirculation) 1970, 1971 or 1972 station wagon or pickup truck large-throttle-bore unit. Some of these manifolds were cast in Canada and say so. The flow of these manifolds is good. Pre-1973 manifolds are not equipped with an EGR valve. Without this valve, exhaust is not used to dilute the incoming mixture, so make sure the mixture stays rich enough to keep cylinder temperatures low.

When more upper-rpm horsepower is desired, a spread-bore manifold is used. The term spread-bore refers to a manifold or carburetor design in which the secondary throttle plate diameters are quite a bit larger than the primary throttle plate diameters.

Chevrolet uses Rochester carburetors, and Rochester builds a good performance/economy four-barrel model in its Quadrajet, which is a spread-bore-type carburetor. Quadrajet carburetors have mechanical secondary throttle plate linkage. The rate at which the secondary operation occurs is governed by a spring-pressure-regulated air dam. As vacuum pressure builds during engine acceleration, the spring pressure is overcome and air is allowed to rush into the venturi to be mixed with fuel.

This system has been used since the mid-sixties. Its small primary bores and two large secondary bores create the best combination as long as

If your car has air conditioning and you want an intake manifold for your Quadrajet without an EGR passage, make sure that these threaded holes are present, as on this 1971-72 manifold. Otherwise you won't be able to mount the rear compressor support bracket.

engine load is not too severe and rpm remains above 3000 when secondary operation is desired. (The primary throttle bores are slightly smaller than those of early two-barrel manifolds used on low-performance engines, and the secondary bore diameters are huge at 2⁵⁄₁₆ in.) Engines equipped with the four-barrel Quadrajet manifolds were considered performance engines and had horsepower ratings of up to 350.

Through the seventies, large two-barrel carburetors were used on the 262, 305 and 350 ci engines. The 1975 and later 305 engines used the same style of intake manifold as the 350 engines. The 262 ci engine had a special intake manifold with small intake passages. The small restrictive passages helped keep vacuum higher, improving low-rpm power development. Do not use a 262 ci engine manifold on any larger small-block. If you do, you will limit the engine's performance drastically.

In the 1979-81 model years, the 267 ci engine was used. This engine had a special intake manifold made of aluminum with a bolt pattern that fit a Rochester Dualjet. (The Dualjet is simply the front primary half of a Rochester Quadrajet.) This carburetor and manifold type should not be used on any engine larger than 305 ci. The aluminum construction is lightweight and disposes of heat well, but the carburetor does not allow enough air into the engine to create horsepower. However, if your goal is exclusively fuel economy, this carburetor has a smooth operation on a V-8 and conserves fuel nicely.

Chevrolet also uses Holley carburetors. Holley builds several square-bore, four-barrel-design models used on small-blocks. These carburetors are of the 4150 and 4160 type, and most have vacuum-operated secondaries. The secondaries are governed by a spring-loaded vacuum diaphragm assembly. Vacuum pressure overcomes the diaphragm and spring cup so that the secondary throttle plate will open.

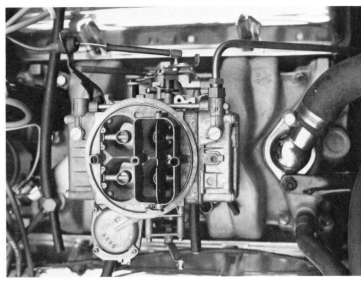

This early Z28 manifold is one of the best ever produced for the small-block. It is easily recognized by the cast-over oil filter tube hole and W casting mark. In the rear the casting number and firing order are present. A 1968-70 choke-spring mounting boss is also visible.

Carburetors with vacuum secondaries have one accelerator pump for the primary half. Holley also builds a double accelerator pump version of these carburetors. When a carburetor has two accelerator pumps, a fuel shot is delivered upon the throttle plate opening for both primary and secondary halves of the carburetor. These double

This is an EGR-equipped Quadrajet manifold with the choke appliance access hole. These manifolds were standard on all four-barrel 1975 and later passenger cars.

This 350 ci engine with its early Z28 manifold would probably run better with a larger Holley carburetor. The divided-plenum dual-plane features of this manifold allowed for a 780 cfm to 830 cfm carburetor from the factory.

This is the factory replacement bow-tie manifold that only accepts a square-bore Holley carburetor. It was designed for the 1968-69 302 ci Z28 Camaro and 1970 LT1 350 ci engine. It is part number 14044836.

pumpers also have mechanical secondary throttle plate operation, which is why the secondary fuel shot is necessary. Holley has no air dam to gradually activate secondary operation.

Some 1969 and 1970 LT1 small-blocks came with an 830 cfm (cubic feet per minute) double pumper that was also used on L88 and LS6 big-block engines. The part number issued by GM is 3965736 and it appeared on the air horn; the list number is 4830. This carburetor is no longer available at the Chevrolet parts counter, but you may see one at a swap meet. If you find one of these off-road carburetors, grab it because these work well.

Special high-performance 302 ci and 350 ci engines came equipped with what is considered the best performance manifold ever built for the small-block. This aluminum, performance four-barrel manifold has throttle bores of equal size to fit a square-bore Holley carburetor. It is the Z28 mani-

If you consider the expense of an LT1-Z28 manifold (part number 14044836) prohibitive, the next best choice is probably this Edelbrock Performer. A Quadrajet, spread-bore Holley or square-bore Holley will bolt on. Another nice feature is that two different choke styles will fit.

fold, sometimes called the LT1 manifold, and it is still available as an off-road part. The current part number is 14044836.

The Quadrajet cast-iron manifold (part number 1409011), Quadrajet aluminum manifold (part number 14007377) and aluminum high-rise Z28/LT1 manifold are the best choices for the street-driven performance engine, and they are all available at your Chevy parts counter.

If the cost of a new intake manifold is out of your reach, the local auto wrecking yard should have some good choices. If you can, buy a manifold *and* carburetor setup as an original assembly. The reason for this is that carburetor and choke relationships and designs are periodically changed.

The 1968 and 1969 combinations of thermostatic choke spring and carburetor linkage are interchangeable. From the 1971 to 1974 production years, thermostatic springs mounted differently on the manifold. The linkages worked according to which way the springs were wound. In 1975, the manifold mount was eliminated. A choke housing, mounted on the carburetor, used a heat exchanger tube. The appliance was mounted through the manifold into the head. This method of cold-start choke control was used until the onboard computer system was installed in the 1981 model year.

The same type of design changes apply to air conditioning and alternator mounting brackets. Study the problems of interchange carefully, because everything will fit—all you need is the right combination for your application.

Dual-plane manifolds

Whether two-barrel, four-barrel, cast-iron or aluminum, all factory street production manifolds are of the dual-plane 180 degree design. Dual-plane means that both left and right sides of the intake manifold flow through different chambers—one mounted above the other, resulting in two different levels. This creates less turbulence during engine operation.

The Holley 300-36 high-rise, dual-plane aluminum manifold for 1955-73 small-blocks.

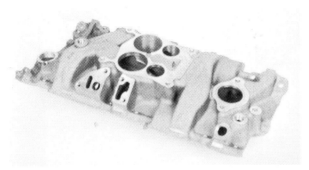

If you like the late-model Quadrajet manifold, this aluminum version of the production iron unit is available. It was standard issue on 1978-79 Corvettes and can be ordered using part number 14007377.

A cast-iron manifold that accepts both Quadrajet and Holley square-bore carburetors is available under part number 14096011.

A divided-plenum, dual-plane manifold is best for maintaining high velocity of flow at low- and mid-rpm-range engine speeds. (The plenum area is the manifold entry chamber located just under the carburetor.) The cylinders alternately pull mixture from each side of the carburetor and manifold. This is because one side of the carburetor feeds every other cylinder, 1-4-6-7, while the opposite side of the carburetor feeds cylinders 8-3-5-2. Thus, the sequence of operation is 1-8-4-3-6-5-7-2.

The design technique of dividing the left and right sides of the carburetor and channeling the mixture through long narrow runners makes the performance engine very drivable even with a large carburetor.

Quadrajet and Holley equipment with flow rates of 700 cfm through 800 cfm were standard on performance engines. Small-blocks are able to use larger carburetors because of their efficient manifold design. Years of factory research have gone into the development of these manifolds, so your money is well spent on the stock, four-barrel system. The rate of flow or velocity of air and fuel mixture to the cylinders is kept high by the restrictive nature of the manifold's smaller passages. Normally, performance would be impeded because of this type of design, but the large carburetor is able to feed the engine at higher speeds so that performance in the upper-rpm range does not suffer.

All regular production factory manifolds have a divided plenum. The plenum divider between the two manifold planes (upper and lower) should remain intact. Do not modify this area in any way.

Some articles in speed magazines suggest that an inch or so of the divider should be removed to improve upper-rpm performance. Don't do it! If you wish to experiment with opening the plenum area, use a 1 in. carburetor spacer and leave the manifold alone. Chances are that any high-rpm gain in performance will be so overshadowed by

the loss of low- and mid-rpm power that you won't want the spacer installed for long. (Think how unhappy you would be if you had ruined your manifold.)

When you combine the two planes and open up the plenum area, there is less throttle response because the velocity or speed of mixture flow is reduced by the increase in the chamber size. Vacuum is reduced, and the car accelerates more slowly at low rpm, because the mixture is less agitated when the undercarburetor area is essentially doubled.

Ideally, you want to build your engine to have low- and mid-range performance. If the engine revs up to only 5500 rpm and falls flat on its face, fine. Consider how often you drive at rpm above 5000: hardly ever. If this is your everyday transportation, be conservative!

Another point is that the carburetor design should match the manifold exactly. This means that

A single-plane, open-plenum, aluminum bow-tie manifold with raised runners to fit the bow-tie head is available under part number 10051103. It has an air gap under the plenum to insulate the carburetor from engine heat. Part number 10051102 will fit stock heads.

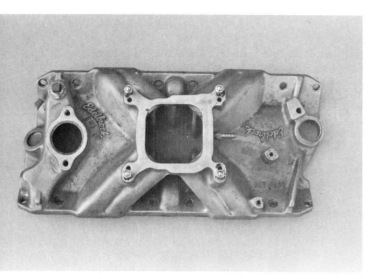

Another example of an open-plenum single-plane 360 manifold is the Edelbrock Torker. This low-rise manifold, when installed with a long-duration camshaft, delivers sluggish performance until about 4000 rpm.

no adapter plates of any kind should be used between the carburetor and manifold. Typically, adapter plates are used to place a square-bore Holley carburetor onto an intake manifold designed for a Rochester Quadrajet. Don't do this, however, because adapters seriously disrupt airflow to the cylinders. This condition usually causes weird cylinder-to-cylinder, air-fuel mixture differences. Adapters may also reduce the carburetor's cfm flow capacity because of flow disruption or funneling.

I like Rochester Quadrajets for economy and smooth operation. If you don't, Holley's double pumper, spread-bore carburetor bolts right onto a Quadrajet manifold. Holley spread-bores are available in 650 and 800 cfm sizes that pack the same fuel delivery wallop as the Holley square-bore units.

If you feel you need larger primaries and want to install an 800 cfm square-bore double pumper, use a square-pattern Z28/LT1 GM 180 degree manifold or equivalent.

Single-plane manifolds

Above 4000 rpm, a single-plane, open-plenum, 360 degree intake manifold will create more horsepower. Your effective power range will be changed to between 4000 and 7000 rpm.

If high-rpm operation and horsepower are what you are looking for, Chevrolet parts are available. Chevrolet has two styles of an open-plenum, straight-runner, bow-tie manifold. Part number 10051102 fits stock cylinder head ports, and part number 10051103 fits taller bow-tie head ports. These manifolds use Holley carburetors of up to 850 cfm with double accelerator pumps.

Aftermarket Edelbrock Torker manifolds and Torker II manifolds, which are single plane and

open plenum, will bolt onto the small-block. The earlier Torker manifold ran well from 4000 to 7500 rpm, but driving a car with one of these was work. The manifold would cause the engine to falter and pop back through the carburetor until it reached about 3500 rpm. Once the rpm came up, the engine revved quickly to 7000 rpm.

The Torker II is an improvement because the runners are longer and narrower. The operation of this manifold is more realistic at about 2500 to 6500 rpm. Neither of the Torkers or any other open-plenum, single-plane manifold will work well on the street with a large camshaft. (Holley, Edelbrock, Weiand and others also offer manifolds that exhibit the same running characteristics with similar camshafts installed.)

A cure for some of these open-plenum, single-plane woes is a smaller carburetor. The vacuum and velocity in the manifold are low, so an increased carburetor venturi speed will help. Remember, too, that each cylinder draws off the entire mass under the carburetor, so fewer total cfm are acceptable. Somewhere around 600 to 750 cfm should work well. If low vacuum or too much camshaft is a problem, go with a double pumper.

Velocity is important. The speed of flow must be kept up to ensure a fully charged air-fuel mass. When the mixture is kept moving, less fuel dropout occurs. (Dropout is when fuel mist that is suspended in manifold air falls out of that air onto the floor of the intake manifold.)

Tunnel ram

Mixture flow velocity can be kept higher and less fuel dropout will occur at low rpm if the length of the intake manifold runners is increased. The tunnel ram intake manifold is an example of an extended high-rise system. When the runners of the manifold are longer and straighter, turbulence is reduced. With less change of direction, a ramming takes place directly from a high suspended plenum down long runners into the head's intake ports.

Tunnel ram manifolds are available in many styles: single four-barrel, dual four-barrel, divided runners, combined runners, large plenum and small plenum. These manifolds are produced by a number of manufacturers and have a wide variety of construction characteristics, with the only common denominator being that all are of a 360 degree design.

Chevrolet does not offer a tunnel ram manifold. This may be because many states do not allow vision obstructions of more than a few inches off the normal hood height. Chevrolet could offer a tunnel ram as an easily installed off-road part, but the setup requires hood modifications that alter the vehicle's appearance.

Many enthusiasts feel that the tunnel ram should not be used on the street. Normally, they are correct. A single four-barrel is the way to go for the conservative hot rodder who is concerned with economy but wants an occasional thrill.

But not everyone is conservative. Often hobbyists build into their small-blocks compression ratios that are too high, install carburetors that are too large, use camshafts with too much duration and use an open-plenum, 360 degree manifold. This combination will probably run well from 4500 rpm, up. To make the car streetable, sometimes a tunnel ram with small carburetors will help keep the mixture velocity high enough to tame the beast at lower rpm. In fact, a pair of 390 cfm—and certainly no larger than 450 cfm—Holleys on a tunnel ram often works better than does an 800 cfm Holley on a standard-height, open-plenum, straight-runner manifold in lower rpm ranges.

Fuel injection

Fuel injection is the most efficient way to feed an engine. Injectors work to atomize fuel much more effectively than do carburetors. This is because fuel is sprayed into the engine in much smaller, equally sized droplets. As a result of the finer fuel mist, intake air surrounds the fuel more evenly.

Tremendous power can be developed when fuel burns more efficiently. Unfortunately, General Motors engineers didn't fully develop the performance benefits. The concern at the factory was the federal fuel economy and emission standards effective in the 1981 model year.

Electronic fuel injection (EFI) was first introduced to the small-block as a production item in 1981. The electronic control system (C4) provided the control to electronically monitor emissions by adjusting injector pulse length and air-fuel ratios.

Two basic systems are used on the small-block: the throttle body injection (TBI) system and the tuned port injection (TPI) system. To use either system, an onboard computer must be installed. The electronic control module (ECM) with the system's programmable read-only memory (PROM) can be installed in any vehicle. Aftermarket wire harnesses and computers are available for any car.

Throttle body injection first became available on 1981, 1982 and 1984 Corvettes and on 1983-84 Z28 Camaros. This system consists of an injector mounted above a throttle plate, the throttle plate being a structure resembling a carburetor base without float bowl, venturi area, air horn and choke assembly. The fuel spray is electronically controlled by a solenoid which controls a needle and seat and is activated by the computer in pulses. These pulses occur more and more rapidly, and steadily increase in duration, as engine speeds increase.

The Chevrolet Crossfire injection system uses two throttle body plates, one for each side of the engine. Cylinders 1, 3, 5 and 7 have one setup, while cylinders 2, 4, 6 and 8 have another identical setup.

An electric fuel pump, usually mounted in the tank, keeps up a constant 10 to 13 lb. of fuel pressure to maintain uniform injector pulses. A pressure regulator valve adjusted by engine vacuum controls fuel pressure, and any excess fuel returns to the tank through a bleed-off fuel return line.

The injector nozzle sprays directly at the throttle plate. The regulated pulses are cone-shaped at about a sixty-degree spread.

Each throttle body injection control PROM is programmed specifically for its application; thus, for example, the Corvette program is different from the Camaro program. The computer relies on many input signals to regulate fuel. Manifold vacuum, engine speed, air temperature, barometric pressure and throttle position all help control engine function. The programming in the computer places emphasis on emission and economy rather than on performance.

The Crossfire system has been replaced by tuned port injection in performance vehicles and

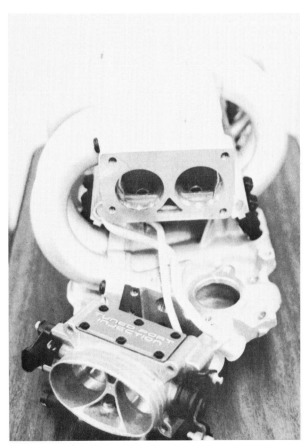

The tuned-port injection plenum and manifold can be completely disassembled. Aftermarket throttle bodies with larger throttle bores are available but test results don't show much improvement as compared with the stock unit.

When installed on the 5.7 liter Corvette engine, the tuned-port system with the correct computer program delivers exceptional performance.

by model 220 throttle body injection elsewhere. Model 220 looks much like a two-barrel throttle body with dual nozzles, one mounted above each throttle plate. The control of this system is much like that of the Crossfire TBI system it replaces. The good news is that model 220 is much less complicated than Crossfire injection and provides more reliable operation.

The tuned port injection system is best because only air flows through the manifold area. No fuel dropout can occur because each port is injected just behind the intake valve. The injection point is programmed after the intake valve is open, when only vacuum pressure is present. This feature is especially good because fuel cannot back up into the manifold area as a result of reversion pressure that occurs just as the intake valve opens. Fuel delivery is exact because each cylinder has its own injector. (You can keep injectors clean with GM tank additive, part number 12345104.)

Air first enters the tuned port injector system through a device that monitors airflow called a mass airflow sensor (MAF). This sensor contains a screen and a suspended platinum wire. The wire is energized by the twelve-volt auto system that keeps this wire at a temperature of 212 degrees Fahrenheit. The air rushing into the system blows across the wire, cooling it and thus creating a demand for more voltage. The voltage needed to keep the wire temperature constant is monitored. From that information, the air mass being used is determined. From air mass information, fuel pulse length is calculated by the ECM.

The Corvette TPI system is interchangeable onto all other small-blocks. The only special re-

quirements for installation are the aforementioned wire harness and the computer.

One problem with the system is that it will supply enough airflow for only 380 ci. A 0.250 in. stroked, 350 ci (now 383 ci) engine should work well with this system, which flows about 600 cfm. However, larger camshafts, more compression and headers will tax this system and limit the size of the engine it can supply. Modifying the system, and changing the computer PROM, will help. Check aftermarket part suppliers and study test results before deciding what to do.

Nitrous oxide

Properly used, nitrous oxide can add considerable horsepower to your small-block. Improperly used, nitrous oxide can ruin your engine.

The chemical make-up of nitrous oxide is as its name suggests: two parts nitrogen and one part oxygen. By itself, nitrous oxide won't burn. It only supports combustion because of its great oxygen content, about sixty percent higher than the oxygen content of the air in the earth's atmosphere.

Nitrous oxide injection kits are available from a variety of manufacturers in many styles. Usually, the more expensive the kit, the safer and more effective the power gain.

The problems with using this system begin when inexpensive under-carburetor plate kits are used without adding fuel. Without more fuel, the use of nitrous oxide will so radically lean a fuel mixture that huge secondary jets must be installed or the cylinder temperatures will get so high that the pistons distort.

The use of nitrous oxide on a stock engine is also a risk. Forged pistons and other heavy-duty parts will help your engine last longer when creating power using nitrous oxide injection.

For the cost, a good direct injection system with a fuel nozzle and a nitrous nozzle for each cylinder is hard to beat. An expensive system will come with a 10 to 35 lb. aluminum tank, two sets of solenoids, two sets of injection lines (gasoline and nitrous) for each cylinder, two distribution blocks, some steel braided line and a switch.

The throttle should be wide open when the solenoids are activated. The fuel and nitrous oxide shots simultaneously enter the intake manifold runners where the nozzles have been mounted. The gasoline side should run its own separate electric fuel pump, while the nitrous side is already in liquid form under high pressure in the tank. Gasoline enters as a spray, and the liquid nitrous oxide, when injected, vaporizes into a gas and cools to approximately negative 145 degrees Fahrenheit.

The cold vapor and fuel are dense enough to add another ten to fifteen percent to your engine's combustion pressure. Try not to build more than a 9:1 compression into an engine intended for nitrous injection.

Chevrolet does not offer a nitrous oxide injection kit, and it probably never will because of the federal emission laws.

Some states that do not permit engine modifications may not renew registration at inspection time if nitrous systems have been installed. If you want to keep your kit a secret, you can easily hide nitrous plumbing on the underside of the intake manifold, and several companies offer California kits, cheater kits and so on.

Turbochargers

General Motors currently offers a turbocharger option on the 3.8 liter V-6 and the 1.8 liter L4. The turbocharger is an air-drive system. It uses exhaust gas pressure exiting the exhaust port to pressure-drive air into the engine. The system consists of an exhaust funneling chamber that directs the outgoing exhaust against a turbine wheel. The spinning turbine wheel is connected by a common shaft to an impeller compressing wheel that spins in another chamber, inducting air. While the exhaust pressure builds and spins the turbine faster, the impeller side draws and compresses more air, forcing it into the engine. This system can work through a carburetor or with fuel injection.

When turbochargers work with carburetors, they can be of the draw-through or the blow-through type. GM uses a blow-through type with the carburetor downstream from the turbo. An airbox is usually installed over the air horn to force the additional compressed air through the carburetor.

At slow cruise or idling, there is not much exhaust pressure. Under these conditions the turbocharger is not compressing air nor providing a boost. At low rpm, upon hard throttle pressure, the engine will rev to as much as 3000 rpm before a boost is felt. This lag time upon depressing the accelerator is normal. It is almost the same as that experienced when carburetor secondaries open.

The turbocharger takes some time to work because it is driven by exhaust gas pressure instead of by drive belts and pulleys. Time is needed to spin the impeller up to as much as 100,000 rpm to achieve total boost. Enough boost pressure is not a problem because eventually pressure builds up to an overboost condition: overboost will raise cylinder pressures beyond engine capabilities. Operating with too much combustion pressure will cause detonation and engine failure. For such conditions, a wastegate is installed. The wastegate is controlled by an electrically operated solenoid that is activated by the ECM in the GM system. The program in the ECM opens the wastegate at about 9 lb. of boost.

When air is compressed by the turbocharger, it heats up. This heating, plus exhaust heat, can cause a less dense, hot airstream into the carburetor. This excessive heat can also cause detonation. To reduce

the air temperature before it enters the intake manifold, engineers developed the intercooler. The intercooler is an air-to-air heat exchanger that works much like a radiator.

Aftermarket turbochargers are available from many manufacturers. They are complicated and hard to install; when you consider all the potential problems it may be better to wait for a factory system.

I had hoped that eventually the Corvette small-block would have a turbo option so that we could wait for the factory system. Unfortunately, with Chevrolet's release of the ZR1 Corvette and the LT-5 optional aluminum V-8, that dream may never be realized. I wonder how many other small-block enthusiasts felt betrayed when they heard that news. The new non-small-block-powered Corvette is impressive but GM should have remained loyal to us and released the LT-5 into another car line. It's not too late—I hope they are listening.

Another GM model may someday be the receiver of a turbo small-block. Can you imagine a turbo 5.7 liter small-block IROC Z-28? I'd stand in line for that one!

GMC superchargers

Unlike the turbocharger, with its lag time and weak exhaust drive, the supercharger, or blower, gives a power boost immediately. This is because the drive system uses a belt with pulleys to turn the air induction rotors.

Originally, the General Motors positive-displacement supercharger was designed to scavenge the cylinders of two-stroke diesel engines used in trucks. These old GM diesels of the thirties had modular cylinders that displaced 71 ci each. The engines could have four, six or eight cylinders, with a larger blower unit for each combination; this is where the model names 4-71, 6-71 and 8-71 came from.

In the fifties, when the small-block came on the scene, hot rodders quickly adapted these GMC blowers to their custom cars for use as draw-through power boosters. Drag racers usually used port fuel injection compressing air only. Some injected engines split the fuel delivery, usually with fifty percent injected ahead of the rotors and fifty percent injected at the port, but the ratio was changeable. The fuel mist drawn through the rotors lubricated and cooled the rotors while the fuel amount injected at the port was adjusted to balance out horsepower in each cylinder. Power balance adjustment is necessary because the rotors in the 71 series GMC blower are built in a spiral pattern to create a continuous draft. Whenever air and fuel are drawn through the system, rapid quarter-mile acceleration causes fuel to be pushed back to the rear of the blower. With the split delivery system, this condition can be corrected by the use of larger injector nozzles in the front cylinders.

How fast to drive the blower is a problem. For the street, I use a 9:1 compression ratio and underdrive the blower by twenty percent to be conservative. Very often the engine on which the blower is installed revs up to 7000 rpm and creates 12 lb. of boost even when underdriven. To run the blower at an even 1:1 ratio would cause too much combustion pressure at that rpm using the 9:1 base compression ratio. Using a base compression ratio of 8:1 or lower, and spinning the blower faster (even overdriving it), will give more boost and create more upper-rpm power, but the low-rpm performance will be sluggish. Furthermore, changing drive ratios is expensive.

GM superchargers never came as stock parts on small-blocks, and the debate goes on as to whether the GM units are the best or not. I'm sure later designs offer some advantages over units designed more than fifty years ago, but there is some kind of nostalgia associated with the old GMC blower.

Exhaust manifolds

Before rushing out to buy a set of tubular exhaust headers, consider that your exhaust system must complement your intake system. For example, installing a set of 2 in. diameter header pipes onto an otherwise factory stock engine will probably slow your car down and increase your fuel consumption. When the headers are installed, normal back pressure that holds some of the exhaust in the cylinder is gone. The header over-scavenges the cylinder, creating a power and fuel loss by drawing some of the incoming fuel charge right through the cylinder before it is even compressed or burned. The fuel charge, now less dense, develops fewer horsepower than before. The problem is that the headers are too free-flowing for the rest of the engine.

For open-exhaust competition, headers are a must. Again, headers must complement the application. For high-rpm horsepower and torque development, large-diameter pipes with short, large-diameter collectors work well. If low-rpm torque and mid-range power are a must, the header pipes should be smaller in diameter and the collector should be longer as well as smaller in diameter to promote a greater low-speed velocity.

The tuning qualities of headers can be used to create more horsepower. To obtain the maximum header effect, the diameters, lengths and curves of the pipes must create the best possible scavenge of the cylinders in the desired rpm range. Lengths and diameters affect the pulse pressure inside the pipe. The exhaust pulse pressure travels down the pipe, and when it reaches the collector it expands into the remaining portion of the system. This sudden expansion creates a vacuum condition that helps to evacuate exhaust completely and to densely charge

the cylinder with combustible mixture. At least this is what should happen if the selections of diameter and length are correct for the engine. This is called the desired scavenge effect.

The first dimension, diameter, is the most important. Most racers who use small-blocks will install a 1¾ in. pipe with a 3 in. collector. These diameters are fairly standard. The pipe diameter for the street should be 1½ to 1⅝ in. and should match the exhaust valve diameter.

The second dimension is length. When headers are open, the pipes must be of equal length. The lengths cannot be just close—they *must* be equal. Each pipe must be at least 30 in. long (the closer they are to 36 in., the better).

The disadvantages of running headers on the street are that headers are noisy, create engine compartment heat, can scrape on the ground, leak, make spark plugs difficult to change, and rust out and need to be replaced. These problems are easily avoidable if you sacrifice the possible 10 hp gain and don't use headers on the street. (A 10 hp gain is the average gain when headers are installed on a car that had the stock muffler system connected to the collectors.)

If you have already installed a larger carburetor on a taller intake manifold, used a high-performance camshaft and recurved your distributor, the next step would be an exhaust header system. If you are unsure what diameter pipes to use, be conservative and use 1⅝ in. if you have 1.600 exhaust valves, and 1½ in. if you have 1.500 valves.

All the systems of the engine work together. If you have used a stock induction system or have only slightly modified the factory setup, leave your manifolds in place and use a dual exhaust system with a less restrictive muffler. I didn't say louder, I said less restrictive. A larger muffler will often keep the noise level down and handle a greater exhaust mass with less restriction. Use large 2¼ in. pipes to the muffler or mufflers, and install 2¼ in. tailpipes.

To further dampen noise and reduce back pressure, a balance pipe, of a diameter at least equal to the exhaust pipe diameter, should be installed. Connecting the two exhaust sides will change the frequency of the exhaust pulses and allow a crossover of pressure between halves. The pipe can be located ahead of the oil pan sump, or just behind the transmission, to ensure ground clearance.

Chevrolet exhaust manifolds

Chevrolet offers three basic styles of exhaust manifolds. They are center exiting (ram's-horn type), rear exit (sweep-back style) and the late-model manifold with an exit just ahead of the last exhaust port at the rear of the engine.

The late-model design is used in Camaros. On the left side, it closely resembles the many common early-model manifolds. On the right side, it looks like a sweep-back but has a rear mounting hole ½ in. closer to the rear. (This right-side manifold is common in a few models beginning in the 1979 production year.) This manifold will only interchange onto a head that has the extra ⅜ in. mounting hole for the number 8 exhaust port. All other exhaust manifolds interchange.

Some exhaust manifolds feature Air Injection Reactor (AIR) tube holes and mount heat riser valves of either thermostatic spring or vacuum control type. If these systems are necessary for your vehicle, headers can be fitted with AIR system holes, but not with heat riser system valves. Without a heat riser valve, the engine will take longer to reach operating temperature.

Dual-exhaust manifold systems are less expensive, quieter and produce less undercar heat than their header counterparts. Most street-driven cars run better with the dual-exhaust manifold system.

Since almost all exhaust manifolds interchange, the only consideration left to influence your choice is whether or not the manifold exit will permit pipe mounting in the chassis you have selected.

The exhaust manifold design with the best flow characteristics is the ram's-horn style. Some Corvette manifolds of this type have large 3 in. exit passages. Even the stock exit size of this style flows better than does the sweep-back design. With 1968-79 Novas, you can remove the sweep-back manifolds and install the ram's-horn style that came stock on the 1968-69 full-size models. These manifolds with the dual-exhaust pipes, originally intended for big cars, work beautifully on these Novas. Be sure to install the transverse, big-block model muffler, or two turbo Corvair units and tailpipes for a great system.

Dual-exhaust installations are sometimes easier if you use earlier-model transmission cross-

This LH exhaust manifold represents another special part for the V-8 Monza.

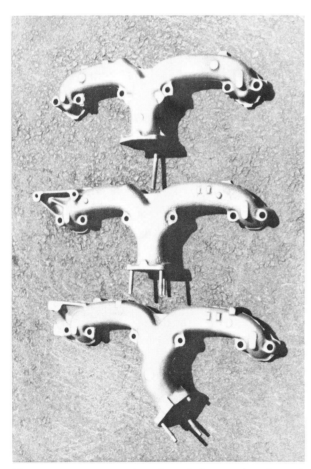

Here are some examples of ram's horn exhaust manifolds. The RH has no mounting boss. The LH, with alternator mounting, has two styles.

Typical exhaust manifolds for B, A and X bodies. These can come with or without air injection holes. Similar styles can have only two pipe mounting studs.

members designed with dual-exhaust clearance. For example, the 1973-74 Monte Carlo, Chevelle and El Camino transmission cross-members will fit perfectly into similar-model 1975-77 cars. (The late-model catalytic-style cross-member will interfere with the left-side pipe, but when the earlier part is substituted, there is no problem.) However, 1978-88 Malibus, Monte Carlos and El Caminos have cross-members that do not interchange with earlier

models. Dual-exhaust installations here will require some custom work on the cross-member or exhaust pipes for clearance.

Be careful. The 1975 and up models all came with catalytic converters. It is illegal to remove these devices from your cars, so you may modify these later-model cars only if they are exclusively off-road vehicles.

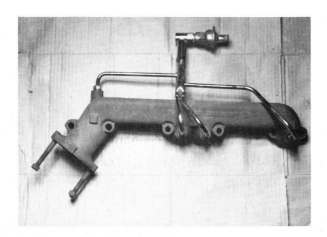

These F body manifolds only have two studs and will fit other chassis. They have air injection tubes and a computer oxygen-sensor.

The sweptback design of this manifold requires moving the mounting hole. Caution: these manifolds will only fit heads with the third exhaust port mounting hole on the end.

Ignition

8

Distributors built for Chevrolet by Delco-Remy are some of the finest ignition systems in the world. Their simple construction and reliable performance make them suitable for any application. With little or no alteration, these distributors, when equipped with heavy-duty Delco parts, are ready to be used for racing.

Breaker-point ignition

Originally, the small-block was equipped with a conventional breaker-point ignition system. This system used a variety of point styles. The standard-issue Delco points were numbered D106P and were accompanied by a condenser numbered D204. The D106P contact set will operate without point bounce until approximately 5500 crankshaft rpm (2750 distributor rpm).

If a higher rpm is required, contact set D112P heavy-duty points are available that will work to as much as 8000 rpm without bounce. The D112P contact set uses the same D204 condenser, and all other distributor parts remain unchanged when these heavy-duty parts are used.

Chevrolet also offers a uniset. This breaker point set has the condenser attached and is not considered a performance item. The number to avoid is D1007.

To further improve point control, the distributor cam can be changed to the 1968-69 302 ci unit (part number 1969763). Use of this cam permits higher engine speeds because the points open and close more smoothly.

A word of caution: When using heavy-duty points, the rubbing block may show additional wear if it is not lubricated well with the wick and holder assembly that comes stock from the factory. The point gap will decrease and retard ignition timing. To avoid unnecessary wear, be sure that the lubricator kit is installed. This kit (part number 1852935) snaps into a square hole on the point plate. When the holder is put in place, make sure the lubricated end of the wick makes good contact with the distributor cam.

A dual-point plate (part number 1953752) will fit onto stock single-point distributors. Two sets of breaker points increase the duration of voltage flow, and that has a desirable effect at high rpm. A stock dual-point distributor (part number

This is a 1968 327 ci ignition system. This small single-point unit and remote-mounted coil remained in use until the end of the 1974 production year. Except for the change to an aluminum housing, small-block base ignitions changed little during the first 20 years.

1110985) is available at your Chevrolet parts counter. This Chevrolet dual-point also has a tach drive but no vacuum advance.

Here is the Chevy high-performance dual-point distributor with tachometer drive and a cast-iron housing. It is available under part number 1110985.

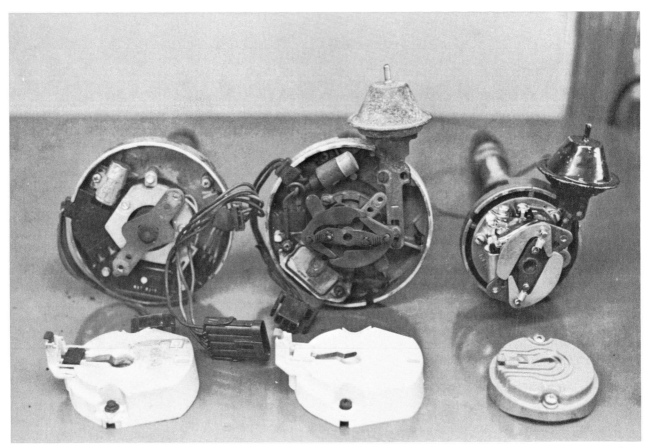

These three distributors are the most widely used. Rotors have been removed so that the centrifugal advance mechanisms can be more easily observed. On the right is the single breaker-point type with vacuum and centrifugal advance systems. In the center is the 1975-80 electronic HEI with similar systems. On the left is the 1981 and later C4 computer-controlled unit. This distributor relies on computer commands to advance or retard ignition timing—note the absence of devices used for advance.

HEI electronic ignition distributors have a larger diameter cap that provides greater separation of the high voltage and enough space for coil mounting. There are no adjustable air gaps on the HEI so the access door for distributor point-dwell adjustment is no longer needed.

Electronic ignition

Transistorized ignition systems are available from Chevrolet, but they are complex and I have never seen one in operation on the street. They are available in two styles: a bronze bushing assembly (part number 1111267), and a ball bearing assembly for use with a gear-drive cam (part number 1111263). The ball bearing distributor can be used with a chain-drive cam if the lower gear (part number 1958599) is changed. Both of these transistorized ignition systems must be used with the ignition kit (part number 3997782). The ignition kit includes the following parts: ignition amplifier (part number 3955511); ignition coil (part number 1111507); connector (part number 6288704); harness (part number 6297688); and wires (part numbers 6297793 and 8901973).

I prefer the electronic ignition equipment used from 1975 to 1980. These distributors, sometimes referred to as high-energy ignition (HEI) systems, have a vacuum advance. They also have a changeable mechanical advance system, which means that different weights and springs can be used to alter the rate at which mechanical advance occurs. Many of these weight and spring kits are available from aftermarket suppliers; GM hesitates to encourage changes in the advance curve because of its effect on emission levels.

Conventional versus electronic ignition parts comparison

The distributor cap, rotor, mechanical advance and vacuum advance systems are similar on both conventional and electronic distributors. Parts that differ are as follows:

Conventional point ignition	High-energy ignition
1. Distributor cam (eight lobes)	1. Timer core (eight projections)
2. Breaker point set	2. Pole piece and permanent magnet
3. Condenser	3. Pickup coil
	4. Power (ignition amplifier) module
	5. Condenser

Replacement parts

Conventional point ignition		Electronic ignition	
Part	Part number	Part	Part number
Coil	1152207	Coil	1985473
Distributor cap	1971244	Distributor cap	1974408
Rotor	1852722	Rotor	1977026
Points	1966289 (D106P)	Pole piece	1875981
Heavy-duty points	1966294 (D112P)	Power module	1875990
Uniset	1876600 (D1007)	Pickup coil	1875981 (D1907)
Condenser	1932004 (D204)	Condenser	1876154 (D211)
Distributor cam	1969763	Timer core (must buy shaft)	
Lubricator kit	1852935	Silicone dielectric grease	(U1921)
Wire set	12043785 (508U)	Wire set	12043741 (608U)

Ignition advance

Mechanical advance is governed by engine speed. Centrifugal force created by the spinning distributor shaft expels weights outward. The weights overcome spring pressure and change the relationship of the spinning rotor to the distributor cap, making the spark occur earlier.

The spark will also be affected by changing the vacuum-sensitive diaphragm that is connected to the point plate in a conventional system or to the pole piece in the HEI system. The factory dia-

These distributors have the rotors installed. All have similar lower design and camshaft drive. The distributor shaft also drives the oil pump shaft. In the foreground is a 1970 distributor body and modified shaft that is used to prelube a new engine when turned by an electric drill.

phragm cup has a degree number on the attaching arm. This number (10, 12, 15, 18, 20 or 24) represents how many crankshaft degrees the cup will advance the timing. For example, if your distributor has sixteen degrees of mechanical advance and your advance cup has ten degrees, that is a total advance of twenty-six crankshaft degrees. Another ten degrees of static timing at the harmonic balancer, created by rotating the entire distributor, will give a thirty-six-degree total advance.

Vacuum advance will not affect engine performance during periods of low engine vacuum. Engines encounter low vacuum during wide-open-throttle operation. Whether during acceleration or during top-speed running, total advance is less without vacuum action on the diaphragm. Engines encounter the highest vacuum conditions during part-throttle cruising or while idling. Remember

The high-performance electronic HEI distributor does not come with tachometer drive or vacuum advance but it has a Tufftrided shaft, precision advance cam and reinforced weight pins. The standard electronic cap and rotor will also fit.

that during lower-rpm operation, less centrifugal (mechanical) advance takes place. This is the way a balance is achieved—with some mechanical advance and some vacuum advance. The total advance can be corrected to fit the engine's requirements by adjusting basic distributor timing.

Total advance can be confusing. Remember that the distributor is driven one-to-one by the camshaft, and the camshaft turns at only half the crankshaft speed. This means that when figuring distributor advance, those numbers must be doubled to figure crankshaft advance. Remember too that the harmonic balancer is directly connected to the crankshaft. Any advance dialed in here, by rotating the distributor, counts as crankshaft advance.

The distributor rotates once for every two rotations of the crankshaft. If you are speaking of degrees of distributor advance only, and your distributor has a combined centrifugal and vacuum advance of fourteen degrees at high rpm, wide-open throttle, the crankshaft rotates twenty-eight degrees. If another twelve degrees is dialed in by rotating the distributor, that makes a total advance of forty degrees at high rpm, wide-open throttle.

Most performance distributor advance curves are designed to have all degrees of advance by 3000 rpm. If vacuum advance is installed and in operation, the advance can start at as little as 500 crankshaft rpm, continuing until all vacuum, as well as mechanical advance systems, have the full amount of advance by 3000 rpm. When no vacuum advance system is installed, only mechanical advance that relies on engine speed comes into play. This system begins advancing the timing at between 1000 and 1500 crankshaft rpm, so considerably more dialed-in advance can be used.

The whole idea of variable ignition advance systems is to ensure that the spark is delivered to the cylinders at the best time (the best time is the point during operation at which maximum cylinder pressures can be obtained). By burning the fuel charge at the correct time, the most horsepower can be gained.

Combustion in the cylinders can occur only at a certain rate; in other words, gasoline vapor will burn at only one speed. When engine components move more and more quickly, the burning process has to begin earlier to ensure smooth and efficient engine operation. This is what ignition advance is all about. When the initial advance is set, this is the point before top dead center (BTDC) where the distributor is placed. Whether eight degrees or more is dialed in at the harmonic balancer will partially depend on idle speed. At an idle speed of 750 crankshaft rpm, the eight degrees of initial lead on the balancer will usually be accompanied by as much as six additional crankshaft degrees of vacuum advance from the distributor vacuum cup. This idle speed total of fourteen crankshaft degrees will provide good idle operation.

As internal engine speeds increase, the pistons move more and more quickly. Keep in mind that combustion can happen only at a fixed rate. As the piston moves in and out of the combustion area more quickly, advance has to be increased relative to crankshaft speed. For example, if the engine is at a cruise rpm of 2600, the advance mechanisms will provide as much as thirty-two degrees of advance to accommodate the combustion rate within that rpm range. At top engine speeds, as much as forty-two degrees of advance can be built into the ignition system.

Be careful not to advance the ignition timing beyond what is absolutely required. Too much advance can cause detonation (pinging), and that will cause severe engine damage. To help avoid detonation, use only the best fuel available. At least a 91 octane rating is required for any engine with up to a 9:1 compression ratio. More than a 9.5:1 compression ratio will require special fuel or maybe less ignition advance.

Voltages

Advance mechanisms are common between the conventional point-type and electronic HEI systems. Voltages are different.

The conventional ignition system can produce only a maximum of approximately 18,000 volts to fire the spark plug. With this system, spark plug life is at best only about 12,000 miles. Spark plug life is further shortened when an engine is modified to create more horsepower. This happens when the engine is used as a racer and is also asked to perform as everyday street transportation. Because of the normal street driving, too-lean carburetor jetting may be left in place. When the engine is pushed hard, the too-lean jetting causes cylinder

The 1968-70 regular production, and some later factory replacement high-performance heads, all had flat spark plug seats. These represent common $^{13}/_{16}$ in. socket gasketed spark plugs that were usually gapped at 0.035 in.

temperatures to rise to a level detrimental to spark plugs.

Electronic HEI systems can produce as many as 60,000 volts to fire spark plugs. With these systems, spark plugs last much longer because they fire more easily with the increased voltage. Carburetor jetting is not as much of a problem because larger spark plug gaps, which will accommodate leaner mixtures, can be used.

Structurally, the electronic HEI ignition is much larger in diameter than the conventional point-type ignition. The HEI has four spring-loaded cap latches, instead of two. The reason for the larger-diameter cap is to place the wire mounting posts farther apart. This greater separation reduces the possibility of the high voltage crossfiring under the cap. The larger cap also provides enough space for coil mounting, which makes the HEI system self-contained.

The HEI system requires no maintenance because Chevrolet electronic ignitions have no adjustable air gaps. Conventional point-type ignitions have a point gap adjustment of 0.017 in. or a dwell angle adjustment of twenty-eight to thirty-two degrees.

Spark plugs

A hot-heat-range spark plug is used in a stock low-performance, usually two-barrel, carbureted engine. A cold-heat-range spark plug is used in a high-performance modified four-barrel engine. All other combinations of engines using medium-heat-range spark plugs fall in between.

When referring to spark plugs, the terms hot and cold mean the opposite of what some people may think. These terms simply explain a spark plug's thermal characteristics or ability to dispose of heat at the firing tip into the cylinder head and then into the coolant. The heat range rating has no effect on the way a spark plug is fired by the ignition system.

A cold spark plug transfers heat quickly from the firing tip. These plugs usually have a short firing end. A hot spark plug transfers heat slowly from the firing tip to the cylinder head. These plugs often have extended firing tips, which are more exposed to the flame. As a result, the heat has a longer path to follow before cooling can take place, and the plugs hold heat longer.

When you modify your engine, changing ignition timing, installing a larger camshaft, adding more carburetor or increasing compression will make it necessary to install colder plugs. If you plan to street drive your modified engine, you may want to use a cold plug with an extended firing tip. An example would be an AC R 43TS. When not exposed to too much compression or cylinder heat, this spark plug works well in a high-performance street engine.

These are some of the tapered-seat plugs used in the small-block. The 1971 and later heads had a tapered-seat spark plug hole. These ⅝ in. socket plugs are much more easily installed when tool clearance is a problem. These plugs are gapped at 0.035, 0.045, 0.060 or 0.080 in. depending upon which ignition system is used. The best street performance plugs are 43T or R43T, not shown.

General Motor's AC spark plug division uses a number for heat range and code letters for any additional description. For example, 42-43 means colder, 44 means medium, 45-46 means hotter, R means resistor, S means extended tip, T means tapered seat and X means wide gap. So, R 44 TSX translates to resistor, medium-heat, tapered-seat, extended-tip, wide-gap AC spark plug.

Testing

To check your spark plugs, first make sure they have been gapped properly. Point-type ignitions usually have spark plug gaps of 0.035 in. In 1975, when the high-energy ignition system was introduced, spark plug gaps of 0.060 in. were common for Chevy small-blocks. In later years, spark plug gaps closed slightly in some applications, to as small as 0.045 in. The smaller gap enabled the HEI system to exhibit less spark fade at high rpm.

Once the plugs are properly gapped, and when you are sure the carburetor jetting or the injector size you have selected is correct, the plugs should turn a dark tan after being run hard. Be sure to run the engine long enough to get the plugs colored. To determine if all the choices you have made are correct, test all the types of driving or racing you intend on doing.

Temperature and humidity will have an effect on your test results, so be sure to repeat your test loop and driving style under several different weather conditions. Keep in mind that once your driving loop is finished, the engine must be shut off immediately because idle time will alter spark plug coloring.

Ignition wire

When selecting spark plug wires, you are faced again with almost limitless choices. Always choose wires that are silicone insulated. Internally, wires that are copper core, steel core, soft graphite or carbon core are available. My favorites include the Moroso Blue Max wires for custom-length applications and precut, premeasured GM wires.

Keep the wires secure and separated from each other. Use the stock wire looms or well-insulated aftermarket looms wherever possible. I cannot overstress this point. If wires are loose, and are allowed to burn and arc out on header pipes, all the work that has been done on advance curves and distributor total advance will be wasted. Keep everything neat, and keep the wires free of grease and oil.

Computer Command Control system

In the 1981 model year, Chevrolet small-blocks lost mechanical and vacuum advance adjustments at the distributor. Since then, the distributor advance has been controlled by an onboard computer. The Computer Command Control (CCC) system monitors complete engine function.

When the engine with this control system is first started, static and programmed distributor timing is in effect. No advance-retard action is calculated or relayed to the distributor from the computer until the engine is up to full operating tem-perature in what is called a closed-loop computer mode.

This system is excellent for fuel economy and low emission levels, but it is slow to react to radical driving techniques and, because of this, limits performance.

With the CCC system, distributor advance is increased again and again in increments of one. As the distributor advance is increased, pinging knock is sensed at a block sensor. When knock occurs, the computer retards the distributor timing by three degrees. The cycle then begins again: up one degree, up one degree, up one degree, until a ping activates the knock sensor voltage and computer control retards the timing. The cycle continues during the entire time the car is running. The computer corrects the timing continually based on the input of engine and other sensors, at varying engine speeds and workloads.

The CCC system can allow as much as sixty degrees of advance into the distributor. This is extreme and unnecessary. Many times when I have stepped on the throttle of a CCC-equipped car, I have heard the engine knock. The knock occurs for less than one second before the timing is retarded, but this situation should be avoided when the car is being driven in competition.

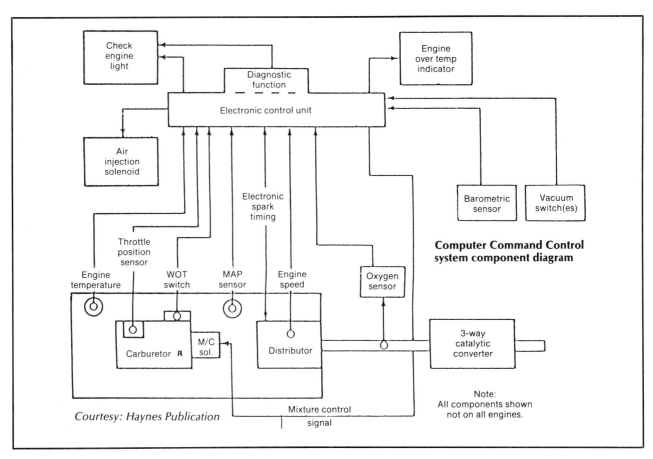

Computer Command Control system component diagram

Courtesy: Haynes Publication

Note:
All components shown
not on all engines.

The onboard computer is equipped with the programmable read-only memory. Whatever the program calls for, the computer will do. General Motors also offers improved program kits (in part group 3.670) that are federally regulated to comply with motor vehicle emission requirements. Aftermarket control PROMs, or chips as they are sometimes called, are better able to give the desired advance curve and fuel metering than are on-road GM parts. These off-road performance PROMs will cost some of your fuel economy, but can improve the performance characteristics of computer-controlled engine functions and computer-controlled automatic transmissions.

Whatever performance level PROM comes with the small-block-powered Chevrolet, it can be improved upon. For example, a 1986 Chevrolet Camaro with a 305 V-8 tuned port injection and 700 R4 automatic transmission will get slightly improved performance when the Chevrolet improved MEM CAL PROM (part number 1228291) is installed. When the same car is equipped with a 350 engine, use one of the many export calibrator PROMs intended for use in the Corvette.

On occasion I have unplugged the CCC-style distributor and removed it from the engine. In its place I have installed a calibrated 1975-80 style HEI. The only modifications required are to neatly run a fourteen-gauge wire from the positive ignition-on power supply pin at the fuse box to the positive bat connector on the distributor cap. The only work left to do is to start the engine and dial in a static timing of between eight and twelve degrees at the balancer. (This advance is dependent upon what total wide-open-throttle advance you wish to run.) The last thing to do is to install a T-connector to connect the manifold vacuum and hose to the vacuum cup.

This method of off-road distributor modification has helped quarter-mile elapsed time figures considerably and seems to have no harmful effect on the computer. Information is still gathered and signals are still sent from the computer to control the air-fuel ratio, but distributor signals are never received.

When the late-model CCC distributor is reinstalled, it will be necessary to temporarily disconnect the orange power lead to the computer so that static timing can be reset. After resetting the timing, reconnect the orange power lead with the ignition turned off. Within about twenty minutes, the computer should relearn how to control your car's systems, and performance should return to normal.

If you believe that an aftermarket ignition system and high-voltage coil are the key to your car's high-performance success, then be prepared to spend a lot of time and money selecting the system that will be best for you. The different brands available seem endless, and it can be difficult to separate a good system from a bad one. Capacitor discharge, crankshaft trigger, light-emitting diode and other electronic pulse systems require special accessories. The expense of this equipment may help you decide that the stock system, perhaps with a high-voltage coil and brass inserts in an aftermarket distributor cap, is the way to go.

Keep in mind that all small-block distributors interchange. My favorite stock point unit is the 1969 302 ci Z28 distributor, and my favorite electronic unit is the 1976 big-car or truck 350 ci distributor.

Distributorless ignition

At this time, Chevrolet does not offer a distributorless ignition for the small-block, although GM does offer the system on the 3.8 liter Buick V-6. It is clearly a performance ignition system and it is my hope that it may someday be a factory option.

The reason this system works is that it eliminates moving parts. Moving parts wear out and must be replaced; moving parts also limit the rpm that can be attained due to structural designs limiting performance while in motion. For example, although I like the electronic GM HEI ignition, it does exhibit spark fade at high rpm with large spark plug gaps, tired magnets or corroded spark-receiving terminals under the distributor cap. All these conditions are avoidable when these parts are not used.

The distributorless system works with the onboard computer. It consists of a crankshaft position sensor, a camshaft position sensor, ignition wires and four dual-terminal modular coils mounted on a control block. With the crankshaft in motion, the crankshaft and camshaft position sensors signal the computer that a cylinder is in firing position. The control block and modular coils each fire two cylinders, so four coils are required on a small-block system. The ignition voltage travels in a loop between the two terminals on each coil. Each terminal is connected to a spark plug by an electronic ignition wire that is much like the HEI wire used with distributors. When the position sensors signal the computer to fire a cylinder, the voltage travels from the coil's first terminal through the terminal wire to the spark plug, firing the cylinder. The voltage then travels through the engine block, reverse-fires the spark plug attached to the second terminal on the coil and returns through that wire to the coil. Each coil fires two cylinders at the same time—even though one is on the exhaust stroke. Electronic circuits in the coil's mounting block receive computer impulses that control when each coil is activated.

These systems are available from aftermarket suppliers. Be careful, as they are tricky to install and need computer control. The cost may be more than your budget will allow.

Emission controls

9

Every few years, the state and federal exhaust emission standards get more stringent. Emission devices get more complex every production year to keep pace with the changing requirements of the federal government's Environmental Protection Agency (EPA).

Many engine enthusiasts hear the word emissions and immediately have negative feelings about these requirements. However, if everyone eliminated emission control devices, or disconnected them, we would have a more serious problem with air pollution than already exists. Furthermore,

improperly disconnecting—or connecting—these devices may cause faulty distributor timing. This could result in a too-lean air-fuel ratio that can seriously damage an engine.

This chapter is designed to help you decide which parts to interchange by describing what each device does and then asking you to use your common sense. Always keep in mind the requirements of the EPA, and what is and is not legal in your state.

Everything you do to your engine affects its emission levels. For example, if you interchange cylinder heads and by doing so increase the com-

This picture hangs in the GM Tarrytown, New York, training facility. Emission devices are attached and labeled. Anyone with an AC-Delco parts supplier recommendation can attend the classes for a further explanation of emission systems.

pression ratio, the air-fuel ratio also has to change. When the air-fuel ratio changes, so do the hydrocarbon (HC) and carbon monoxide (CO) levels. These levels usually increase because more compression requires a richer mixture.

For another example, if you advance the distributor timing from eight degrees static to twelve degrees static, the oxides of nitrogen (NO_x) emissions will increase. And so on with each emission device discussed here.

Emission controls

The Positive Crankcase Ventilation system, or PCV valve as it is more commonly known, has been in use since the early sixties. This device has been installed in many different locations on the top of the engine, but in 1968, with a redesign of the valve covers, it found a home in the valve cover above cylinders 1 and 3.

The PCV valve eliminates blow-by gases from the crankcase. Vacuum pressure is used to pull filtered air from the air cleaner, down the breather pipe, into the crankcase. From here the fresh air mixes with the blow-by gases and is routed to the carburetor base to be reburned by the engine. The action of the PCV system keeps down the sludge level inside the engine and reduces hydrocarbon emissions.

In 1968, Chevrolet introduced one of the most effective emission control systems to date. This sys-

A sure way to keep pollution down is by keeping engine temperature up: never run less than a 180 degree Fahrenheit thermostat. Shown here is a 195 degree Fahrenheit thermostat. When the engine is operated at a constant temperature, tune-up adjustments made at that temperature are an effective way to control emissions.

tem is still in use today and is called the Air Injection Reactor system. The AIR system is simply an air pump and delivery system. The air pump, driven by the fan and alternator belt, pumps fresh air directly into the exhaust system. As the burning exhaust exits the engine through the exhaust manifold, the newly injected fresh, combustible air keeps the mass burning. With the extra burning time comes a

Emission requirements (grams/mile) (passenger cars)

MODEL YEAR	HYDROCARBON (HC) CALIFORNIA	FEDERAL	CARBON MONOXIDE (CO) CALIFORNIA	FEDERAL	OXIDES OF NITROGEN (NOx) CALIFORNIA	FEDERAL
1978	0.41	1.5	9.0	15.0	1.5	2.0
1979	0.41	0.41	9.0	15.0	1.5	2.0
1980	0.39	0.41	9.0	7.0	1.0	2.0
1981	0.39	0.41	7.0	3.4	0.7	1.0
1982	0.39	0.41	7.0	3.4	0.4	1.0
1983	0.39	0.41	7.0	3.4	0.4	1.0
1984	0.39	0.41	7.0	3.4	0.4	1.0
1985	0.39	0.41	7.0	3.4	0.7	1.0
1986	0.39	0.41	7.0	3.4	0.7	1.0
1960 (No Control)		10.6		84		4.1

One of the simplest devices to help keep the air clean is the PCV valve. Here are the valves that have been used during the past 20 years. The best one to use for the hot street machine is the CV774C. A nice benefit from the PCV is that it also keeps your oil cleaner.

cleaner exhaust because the additional hydrocarbons, which otherwise would have been released into the outside air, have been burned up while still in the exhaust system.

The following figure shows the air-fuel ratio cycle of operation resulting from information received and processed by computer emission controls. The oxygen sensor monitors the amount of oxygen present in the exhaust and sends a voltage signal to the electronic control module. A voltage signal to the mixture control solenoid allows the ECM to adjust the rich or lean setting of the carburetor using metering rods. These adjustments occur at a rate of ten times each second to ensure the leanest possible operating condition.

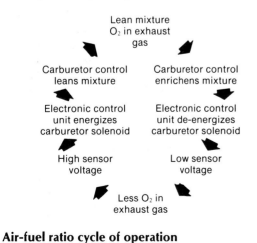

Air-fuel ratio cycle of operation

The AIR pump may cost a few horsepower to run, but it may also be a required device in your state. The good news is that it works without changing the running characteristics of your engine. It is especially designed to work at all times other than during high-speed deceleration. If air were added in this case, severe backfire and exhaust system damage would result.

During the twenty years of AIR system service, the injection point of air has changed little. Some models have the air injected into the end of the Y-pipe, but most models still inject at the base of each exhaust port in the exhaust manifold.

Another feature of the AIR system that has changed little is its location on the engine. From the system's introduction in 1968, the pump mounting has remained under the alternator on the front left lower section, with the one exception being the mounts on the Corvette engine.

In 1969, another beneficial device was introduced. It was the anti-diesel solenoid, or idle stop solenoid, which was designed to prevent run-on after the ignition is shut off. The solenoid is attached to the right side of the carburetor and is electrically operated. When the ignition is turned on, a plunger extends to hold the throttle valve partially open to maintain idle speed. When the ignition is turned off, the throttle completely closes down, preventing any incoming mixture from entering the cylinders.

This device does not change the way an engine operates and should be left in place. If your car doesn't have an anti-diesel solenoid, consider getting one.

In 1970, a system was introduced to reduce oxides of nitrogen in the exhaust. The Transmission Control Spark (TCS) system is composed of three main components: the electric solenoid that controls vacuum from the carburetor to the distributor; the relay box that controls the electric signal from the transmission switch to the solenoid; and the transmission switch itself. In some cases, the system also uses a temperature control to delay operation when the engine is started.

If the TCS system is not installed, the result is a smoother idle, good throttle response and more efficient engine operation. This is because the TCS system was designed to eliminate the vacuum advance at the distributor until the transmission is shifted into drive gear. The elimination of nitrogen oxides during the critical development of horsepower may increase fuel consumption dramatically.

In 1973, another device to limit the production of oxides of nitrogen was introduced. The Exhaust Gas Recirculation (EGR) system was designed to cool combustion temperatures by using the exhaust to dilute the intake charge. Oxides of nitrogen are produced when cylinder and combustion temperatures are high. If a noncombustible exhaust gas is introduced, less burning occurs and cooling results.

If the horsepower of former Chevrolet engines is your goal, use an intake manifold from 1972 or earlier (all Chevrolet small-block intake manifolds are interchangeable). Or use an aftermarket manifold such as the Edelbrock Performer.

If you elect to use the EGR valve because you have to meet certain standards, use a vacuum temperature switch labeled HRD. This switch delays EGR function until the engine reaches operating temperature. If the delay system is not used, the engine may stall repeatedly when started from dead cold.

The EGR valve is vacuum-operated. To use the HRD switch, a vacuum line is run from the carburetor base to the unmarked port on the switch. Another line is then run from the port marked EGR to the valve.

In 1975, an exhaust system emission device was introduced. It was called the catalytic converter. Even though it is an exhaust system part, it has a great effect on the engine.

The catalytic converter is designed to reduce the hydrocarbon and carbon monoxide emissions. It is a chamber holding ceramic pellets that are coated with a metallic catalyst that usually contains a platinum alloy. Leaded gasoline will clog the coated pellets and prevent the engine's exhaust from flowing.

When a catalytic converter is part of your vehicle's engine, only unleaded fuel can be used in that engine. This is important because unless you plan to use octane booster additives, your highest available octane level at the pump is 93.5. At a 93.5 octane level, your compression ratio should not exceed 9.5:1. (Not all gasoline companies offer this ultra-high-rated unleaded gasoline: the average is around 92 octane, regular leaded fuel is 89 octane and Cam 2 racing gasoline is as much as 106 octane. All 1975 and later vehicles are prohibited by law from using any leaded fuel.)

Computer Command Control system

The Computer Command Control (CCC) system, also known as the C4 system, first became available on 1980 models. This system controls exhaust emissions while retaining drivability by maintaining a continuous interaction between all emissions systems. Any malfunction in the Computer Command Control system is signaled by a Check Engine light on the dash, which goes on and remains lit until the malfunction is corrected.

The Computer Command Control system requires special tools for maintenance and repair, so any work on it should be left to a dealer or a qualified technician. Although it is complicated,

One of my least favorite emission devices is the EGR valve. If you must run one to comply with regulations, use a water neck with this temperature-sensitive control valve. This valve allows the EGR valve to operate only when the engine is up to temperature. As you can see by the picture, carburetor vacuum enters at the bottom port. It is then relayed via the top port (labeled EGR) to the valve.

the system can be understood by examining each component and its function.

The electronic control module (ECM) is essentially a small onboard computer, located under the dash on most vehicles. It monitors up to fifteen engine and vehicle functions, and controls as many as nine different operations.

The ECM contains a programmable read-only memory calibration unit that tailors each ECM's performance to conform to the vehicle. The PROM is programmed with the vehicle's particular design, weight, axle ratio and so on, and cannot be used in another ECM in a car that differs in any way.

The ECM receives continuous information from the Computer Command Control system and processes it in accordance with PROM instructions. It then sends out electronic signals to the system components, modifying their performance.

The oxygen sensor (OS) is mounted in the exhaust pipe, upstream of the catalytic converter. It monitors the exhaust stream and sends information to the ECM on how much oxygen is present. The oxygen level is determined by how rich or lean the fuel mixture exiting the carburetor is.

The mixture control solenoid controls the fuel flow through the carburetor idle and main metering circuits. The solenoid cycles ten times each second, constantly adjusting the air-fuel mixture.

The ECM energizes the solenoid based on information it receives from the oxygen sensor to keep emissions within limits.

The ECM uses the information from various pressure sensors to adjust engine performance. Those sensors are the coolant sensor, barometric pressure sensor, manifold absolute pressure sensor and throttle position sensor.

The coolant sensor in the coolant stream sends information to the ECM on engine temperature. The ECM can then vary the air-fuel ratio for conditions such as cold start. The ECM can also perform various switching functions on the EGR and AIR management systems, depending on engine temperature. This feedback from the coolant sensor can also activate the hot temperature light.

Located in the engine compartment, the barometric pressure (BARO) sensor provides a voltage to the ECM indicating ambient air pressure, which varies with altitude. Not all vehicles are equipped with this sensor.

Also located in the engine compartment, the manifold absolute pressure sensor (MAPS) senses engine vacuum (manifold) pressure. The ECM uses this information to adjust air-fuel mixture and spark timing in accordance with driving conditions.

Mounted in the carburetor body, the throttle position sensor (TPS) is moved by the accelerator. It sends a low-voltage signal to the ECM when the throttle is closed and a high-voltage signal when the throttle is opened. The ECM uses the voltage feed to recognize throttle position.

The idle speed control (ISC) maintains low idle without stalling under changing local conditions. The ECM controls the idle speed control motor on the carburetor to adjust the idle.

The high-energy ignition (HEI) distributor used with this system has no provision for centrifugal or vacuum advance of spark timing. Instead, it uses electronic spark timing (EST), in which the spark is controlled electronically by the ECM, except under certain conditions such as when cranking the engine.

The Air Injection Reactor is also controlled by the ECM. When the engine is cold, the ECM energizes an air switching valve, which allows air to flow to the exhaust ports to lower carbon monoxide and hydrocarbon levels in the exhaust.

The ECM controls the ported vacuum to the Exhaust Gas Recirculation system with a solenoid valve. When the engine is cold, the solenoid is energized to block vacuum to the EGR valve until the engine is warm.

Using the proper equipment, the Computer Command Control system can be used to diagnose malfunctions within itself. The Check Engine light can flash trouble codes stored in the ECM Trouble Code Memory. This diagnosis should be left to your dealer or qualified technician because of the tools required and because ECM programming varies from one model of vehicle to another.

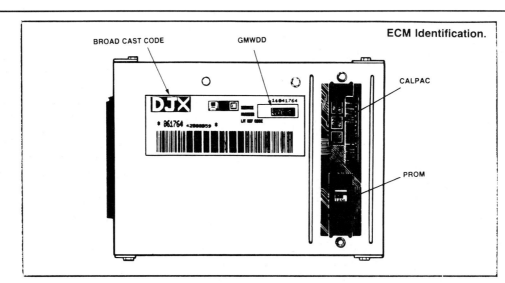

ECM PROM Calpac Identification

The ECM is identified by a service number located at the upper right corner of the identification label

The upper 8-digit number is the **Delco Electronics Parts Number.**

The 7-digit (boxed in) number located on the label is the GMWDD "Parts Service Number."

The "broadcast code" located in the upper left corner of the identification label, should match the code located on the PROM.

The calibration pack (Calpac) has its own 8-digit ID number.

Lubrication and cooling

10

It is almost impossible to improve on the stock Chevrolet lubrication system. The stock wet-sump system, usually consisting of four quarts of oil in the pan and one additional quart of oil in the filter, can effectively service an engine creating up to 600 hp.

The small-block oiling system is simple. Advantages are that the oil pump is submerged inside the oil pan and the pump has a cast-iron housing. The wet pump feature allows for a short pickup tube. If you think about it, there are few oil-related failures associated with the small-block. Unlike the Buick V-8 engines and especially the 231 ci, 3.8 liter Buick V-6 with its external pump mounting, aluminum housing and a pump that is constantly losing prime, the small Chevy is equipped with the best system ever designed.

The Chevy's pump, mounted on the rear main bearing cap, sucks oil past a screened shield designed to prevent a whirlpool that may allow air into the system. The oil is then pumped to the filter,

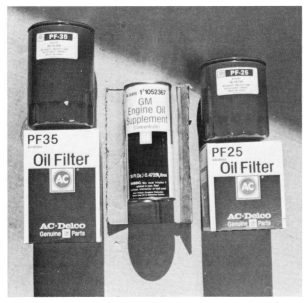

Do your engine a favor and only use AC-Delco filters. The best high-performance deep filter is the PF 35. Aftermarket double oil filters are too restrictive and therefore hold the bypass valve open at all times. GM also supplies an oil supplement that is recommended for new assemblies.

often bypassing it. Once past the filter area, it enters the crankshaft, to the bearings and main lifter oil galleries flowing from back to front. There is no oil passage from the block to the heads. Oil in the main galleries flows through the lifters, through the pushrods, then to the pivot ball rocker arms on the heads.

After lubricating the moving cylinder head parts, oil drains back through holes at each end of the heads to the lifter valley. From the lifter area, the oil returns to the pan through lifter valley holes or past the timing chain in the front and past the distributor shaft drive in the rear. If you intend to run the engine at high rpm often, the lifter valley return holes should be threaded and plugged. This is done to prevent returning oil from splashing on and being picked up by the crankshaft weights. Oil will still return through the front or back openings.

Filters

Early small-blocks had cartridge-type oil filters that provided nearly 100 percent oil filtration. These housing and cartridge design filters required additional maintenance and because of this were unpopular. Some racers prefer this older system and use adapters on late-model blocks to use it again. In 1968 the rear block filter-pad area was redesigned to accept a spin-on filter. The oil filters manufactured by AC, and provided by GM as original equipment, were the PF-25, PF-35 and PF-932. The PF-25 is designed for light-duty passenger car use and holds one quart of oil. The PF-35 is for heavy-duty and street-performance applications. The PF-35 is slightly longer and holds almost 1½ quarts of oil.

Unfortunately, the PF-25, PF-35 and most spin-on filters will not handle total oil filtration. For this reason, an oil filter bypass system is built into the oil filter appliance (part number 3952301) because these filters cannot handle the output of the pump. The bypass is nothing more than a flat spring-loaded disc. Normal small-block oil pressure is 30 to 45 lb. and the spring pressure of the bypass valve is held open at 12 to 15 lb. As a result, much of the oil being pumped into the engine from the pan is unfiltered.

Chevrolet truck division has a PF-932 spin-on filter with a two-quart capacity that can filter nearly

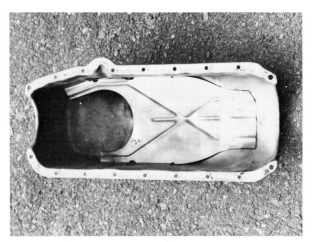

From the 1968-77 production years, this oil pan (part number 465221) was installed in just about every model. Driver's side dipstick location was changed as the factory began to down-size cars.

all of the oil pump volume as before. Some engine builders use this filter with the bypass hole in the adapter appliance threaded and plugged to force 100 percent filter flow.

A better solution is to increase the spring tension on the bypass valve. This can be done by shimming the spring with washers or replacing the stock spring with a stronger custom one.

If you insist on forcing the 100 percent solution, be prepared to blow apart a filter. This does not always occur but when bypass valves are eliminated, a small relief hole is sometimes necessary in the plumbing plug that replaced the bypass valve in the filter appliance. I have drilled holes as large as ¼ in., depending on pump pressure. The relief hole does allow unfiltered oil back through the system but in a reduced volume compared with the open relief valve. Remember, only experiment with

bypass elimination if the PF-932 filter is used. Use of any other filter will result in filter failure or blow-out.

The PF-932 is long and may not fit directly onto the engine because of exhaust system clearance problems. It is possible to use an aftermarket remote mounting system if the large filter is what you want but clearance problems prohibit stock mounting.

If you wish to use an oil cooler, block adapters are available from Chevrolet that allow use of stock filters. Corvette adapter (part number 340258 or 14088848) has forward outlets, optional adapter (part number 326098) has side outlets and both require two bolts (part number 3951644) for installation. These adapters fit nicely between the block filter pad and the filter. They allow oil out to the cooler and back to the filter of the engine. Both adapters use stock-type pressure relief systems.

When installing the adapter, a connector (part number 3853870) may be needed. The connector is for reconnecting the oil filter below the adapter. The connector and seals (part numbers 326100 and 14015353) sometimes are not included with the kit.

Oil pans

Oil pans from 1968-74 changed little. There were two basic styles, standard with nonremovable baffle and high performance. The standard pan (part number 465221) does not permit the use of a windage tray or removable baffle (part number 3927136). To use the windage tray, the high-performance Z28 pan (part number 465220) must be used. When the removable windage tray baffle is installed, five mounting studs (part number 3960312) are needed.

The sump design on this common 465221 oil pan clears the frame on all 1968-77 A, B, X and F models. It is the most easily interchanged oil pan of all Chevy pans.

One of the few GM custom-design oil pans is the 1975-77 Chevrolet Monza 262 through 305 ci unit. This will fit Vega models if the subframe member is changed. This 305 ci engine was completely rebuilt in our shop and replaced a 196 ci 3.2 liter Buick Skylark engine. A short water pump and fuel pump block-off had to be used for additional clearance.

Wherever the oil pan is built closely to the crankshaft as in the forward section of the stock unit, oil attempting to return to the sump area often becomes trapped and bounces back up into the spinning crankshaft.

What happens to crankshaft action because of the oil is much like what occurs when a stone is thrown into a pond. The velocity of the stone is cut down by the resistance of the water. It doesn't happen as drastically as in the example but when the crankshaft has to spin through gobs of flying oil, speed is reduced because power is expended.

As much as 10 hp can be saved on a stock L82 Corvette assembly when the windage tray is used. For the purpose of dividing the crankshaft windage area from the sump area these trays are great. They prevent oil sloshing around below the crankshaft from being picked up by the turbulence above. Unfortunately, this wraparound tray also prevents some of the returning oil from getting back to the sump area. This results in the same condition that occurs in the front section of the pan: oil bounces back off the tray into the spinning crank weights.

When all is considered, you are still better off with the windage tray. I have tried to remedy the oil return problem by cutting ⅛ in. wide, 5 in. long slots directly below the spinning crank weights to speed the return of trapped oil to the sump area.

A similar result may be obtained by cutting louver slots in the same areas. Position the louver humps upward toward the crank weights to create small scoops. Upon acceleration the scoops will trap the oil running toward the back of the tray and return it to the pan.

These parts and modifications may be more than is needed for the average street machine but these additions and changes help performance *and* fuel economy. Z28 oil pans and associated oil control hardware can be used beyond the 1974 model year if the dipstick exit of your block is on the left side at deck height.

Early Corvette oil pans had an extended front sump area. These and many heavy-duty truck pans, although interchangeable onto other blocks, will not fit most car chassis. Therefore, the only way to increase oil pan volume and isolate the sump area farther from the crankshaft is to extend the sump area downward. Increasing the depth of the pan will mean extending the pickup tube length. Do not extend the tube more than 2 in. downward. If more than 2 in. are required to bring your pickup within ⅜ in. of the bottom of the pan, aftermarket pump extension mounts are available from Moroso or Milodon.

Some 1978 and later intermediate-sized Chevrolet V-8 equipped cars came with dipstick mounting in the pan. A triangular patch, with a dipstick entry point soldered into place on the oil pan (part number 464607), is for the 305 ci engine installed in A body cars.

The 1980 and later blocks, with dipstick exits on the right side of the engine, used an oil pan (part number 14082348) with the dipstick clearance bulge on the right.

The 1986-88 Camaro pans (part number 14088506) and Corvette pans (part number 14087077) are made so that they fit the chassis clearance requirements and the newly designed rear block area.

Consider where your block has the dipstick located and what chassis you intend using before selecting the pan. An example of a special oil pan would be the 1975-77 pan designed for the Chevy Monza 2+2. These 262 ci and 305 ci equipped cars had to use oil pans and pickups specially designed for the framing of the vehicles.

Oil pumps

The key to the entire small-block oiling system is the pump, and Chevrolet currently offers three basic pump types: the standard pump (part number 14057041) available in the Corvette, the high-performance Z28 pump (part number 3848907) that will handle most anything, and the heavy-duty off-road high-volume pump (part number 14044872).

The new oil pump pickup is about to be installed on an HM 55 HV replacement pump. This small-block unit is similar to the GM 3764547 pump.

119

Many articles and performance books suggest milling pressure relief slots on the gear side of the pump cover to reduce gear chatter. Gear chatter, they say, may cause erratic spark timing because of vibration through the shaft driving the pump. I can believe that this condition may occur at high engine speeds. The small-block pump is a simple light-duty design, probably never meant for extreme rpm use. The pump gears run roughly because the gear teeth are spaced so far apart. For average passenger car and mild performance use, the stock Z28 pump is fine without any modification.

If you intend to race your small-block, or even thrash it on the street, eliminate any modifications to the stock oil pump and use a big-block pump. The big-block pump doesn't move more oil but it does pump with more even pressure. Further, the big-block oil pump has twelve-tooth gears instead of the seven-tooth gears used in the small-block. The big-block pump gear teeth mesh more smoothly because they are closer together. As a result of the smoother operation, less chatter and vibration is transferred to the distributor. The stock LS-6 pump (part number 475908) has standard components and is superior to the small-block pump design. The best big-block pump available is (part number 3969870) intended for ZL-1 Corvette use and has optional 1.3 gears.

Both listed big-block oil pumps come with pickup tube and screen assemblies. The tubes have been spot arc-welded to the pump body. Installing the big-block pump into a small-block pan will require tilting the pickup. Keep the pickup about ⅜ in. from the bottom of the pan, and modify the assembly as little as possible. The stock big-block pump will give 45 to 60 lb. of hot oil pressure. When the engine is at operating temperature, oil pressure should never exceed 65 lb.

If the small-block oil pump is all you think you need, remember that the pickup tube and screen assembly must be installed on the pump. Pickup screen (part number 3830080 or 3855152) can be installed with Kent-Moore tool J 8369. I have not had access to one of these tools for ten years, and have had to use a ⅝ in. open-end wrench cushioned by a ¼ in. diameter strip of lead solder wound around the tube in front of the raised lip. When the pump is secured into a soft lined vise, gently tap the ⅝ in. wrench handle forcing the lubricated tube end into the pump body. The solder is crushed but it saves the raised lip portion of the pickup tube from being damaged by the hardened wrench.

Once in place, spot arc-weld the tube to the pump body: a ¼ in. spot is all it takes. Have a wet shop rag ready to place onto the weld. Do not heat the pump body by brazing the tube all the way around as the heat may distort the body and ruin the pump. I have heard horror stories about oil pressure bypass pistons and springs blowing right out of the pump body. This has never happened to me, even when I reinstalled the same roll pin I removed.

If any part of the pump or the entire pump is disassembled, take all precautions to make sure it doesn't come apart while in service. Be sure to use Loctite on the threads of the pump cover bolts if you have opened it to check gear clearance. If you plan to install the white-stripe high-pressure spring (part number 3848911), use new hardware for reassembly. The bypass piston roll pin retainer can be replaced by a screw-in plug if you thread the hole and shorten the plug to only go as far in as the roll pin did.

All these modifications are a pain in the neck so if you decide against the small-block pump in favor of the big-block unit, be aware that the big-block pump requires more power to drive. Extra drag and the possible modification of the pickup tube are a small price to pay for the smooth operation and reliable performance at high rpm.

This shot of a 1968 327 ci short water pump shows that it is driven by the inner crankshaft pulley groove, as 1969 and later pumps are. Earlier pumps were driven by the outer crankshaft pulley groove. Notice how close the pump is to the timing chain cover.

Remember, if you increase the depth of your sump area, make sure, when your front suspension is completely bottomed out, that your deep pan does not hit the ground. Also keep the length of the pickup tube within 2 in. of stock in a vertical direction. Too much tube length may cause the pump to starve for oil or lose prime.

Aftermarket pans from Moroso or Milodon also offer increased sump area without depth increase. The sump section has been widened to accommodate a larger oil volume. Special one-way doors are installed to keep the oil around the pump even when cornering. Don't get carried away—these are expensive pieces.

Late-model engines from the factory come with Goodwrench oil. This is said to be as thin as 5W30. If clearances are set to factory specs and unmodified parts are used, 15W40 Valvoline Turbo oil is all you will ever need. You can install a big-block oil pump and average 55 lb. of hot oil pressure. Three thousand miles is just about right between oil and filter changes to give the engine a chance at a long life. Stay away from oil with a high parafin content. Unless you are experiencing bad oil pollution or dilution problems, because of blowby or fuel, you shouldn't need oil as heavy as 20W50.

If you have installed an oil cooler, use a gauge and regulate oil flow to keep oil temp at 220 to 240 degrees Fahrenheit. This oil temperature will boil off any coolant or condensed water that may be in the crankcase. Install enough crankcase venting to vacuum in order to keep the internal pressure low enough so that blowby or oil fumes will not enter the combustion chamber past the rings.

Water pumps

The 1968 water pump had short mounting legs and was the same basic unit that was used on all

The short pump, on the right, is like the bow-tie aluminum in that it does not have the mounting bosses necessary to use 1969 and later accessory mounting brackets.

earlier small-blocks. Original equipment pre-1969 pumps have a small 1¾ in. pulley mounting bolt pattern. When using the early-style pump, small pattern pulleys and compatible accessory mounting brackets must also be installed. Rebuilt or new replacement water pumps, intended for early models, have the small- *and* late-model, large 2⅛ in. pulley mounting bolt pattern.

The Chevrolet bow-tie water pump (part number 14011012) has both bolt patterns, an aluminum body and a cast-iron high-performance rotor and is intended for early-model-style installations. The bow-tie pump can be used for 1969 and later installations if Moroso spacers (Moroso number 63500) are used. The spacers allow the use of late-model passenger car pulleys because they

Here are the two basic water pump styles. These are late-model pumps that share the 2⅛ in. pulley bolt pattern. The short pump on the left has the larger diameter Corvette impeller shaft and, therefore, will only accept the Corvette pulley. The long pump on the right has the same dimensions as every other 1969 and later model.

Both of these long pumps will interchange; the dimensions are the same. Compare the 1969-70 long pump on the left to the new style on the right to see the long pump's evolution. Note the small diammeter of the housing where the impeller bearing is mounted, the weep hole location and lack of case reinforcement as compared with the 1974 unit on the right. (Studs are for clutch fan mounting.)

Another view of the pair of long pumps shows casting number ID and the bearing support reinforcement of the case on the right. Notice that all of the mounting bosses are identical.

These are long water pump drive pulleys. The large diameter 7⅛ in. unit will underdrive the pump slightly. The double-groove 1978 and later pulley uses the inner groove for power steering drive.

duplicate the block distance that the 1969 and later long-leg pumps have. Understand that although the distance is duplicated, and late-model pulley drives will align, late-model bracket mounting bosses and threaded holes are absent. The absence of mounting bosses will make it necessary to design and build custom mounting.

The long water pump, first used on 1969 models, has changed little during the past twenty years. The pump body was originally extended to accommodate a larger impeller shaft bearing and to gain greater clearance for the timing cover and accessory mounting. Minor changes were made to the pump housing as years passed but it is still recognized as a long-leg, late design. In 1974, the upper alternator mounting bracket boss was moved, and the power steering pump mounting hole had to be threaded in 1975 because of a change in the pump's hanging and pivot bracket.

The 1985 production year produced another style of water pump for the small-block. Sport models, Corvettes and Camaros came equipped with serpentine belts. This new belt style required mounting a much wider pulley and a reverse-rotation impeller to accommodate the direction of belt travel. The latest pump also has an aluminum housing but internally it is very like all other original equipment pumps.

The stock, standard-duty water pump has a press-fitted, six-blade steel impeller that unfortunately is not as efficient as it could be. As with many base production GM parts, there is always room for improvement. Stock unmodified pumps waste considerable energy because of too much internal clearance. The problem primarily exists because the impeller is often too far from the back cover. The extra clearance causes the impeller to force some of the water back against the cover instead of directing it into the engine. This internal leakage also causes impeller cavitation at high rpm that further cuts efficiency.

The pump can be improved by reducing the clearance between the impeller and the cover,

Crankshaft pulleys of single, double and triple grooves all have equally spaced water pump outer drive grooves. The most common diameter is 6⅞ in. The only exception is the three-groove AC pulley with an 8 in. diameter water pump drive. These designs will only work with long pump hardware.

This view of drive and driven pulleys illustrates the radical differences in size.

accomplished by riveting a $\frac{3}{32}$ in. thick steel disc to the back of the impeller. The diameter of the disc should not exceed the greatest diameter of the impeller vanes. This modification is currently being used by various aftermarket water pump rebuilders, and is said to increase pump efficiency by as much as thirty percent.

A more efficient water pump will allow you to reduce pump speed while still moving the same volume of water. Speed reduction will save horsepower that is normally expended by pumping inefficiently. It has been said that an average of 18 hp is required to drive the water pump at 6000 rpm. If the pump efficiency is increased by thirty percent, the improved pump can now be slowed by one-third without the danger of overheating. This can mean saving almost 6 hp while running at this high rpm.

Water pump speed can be changed by the use of stock production pulleys. The most common crankshaft pulleys measure 20 in. in circumference in one- or two-groove styles and 23 in. in circumference in the three-groove style. The outer pulley groove always drives the water pump. Changes in the size of the outer crankshaft drive pulley and changes in the pump pulley diameter will increase or decrease pump speed. The most common water pump pulleys measure 21, 20 and 18 in. in circumference in a single groove style. There is a two-groove pulley that also measures 18 in. in circumference.

Some of these pulleys, once manufactured by GM, are no longer available from Chevrolet dealer parts counters. The good news is that auto wrecking yards are full of what you might need to change ratios and that the pulleys have part numbers stamped on them for easy identification.

Aftermarket Moroso pulleys are available for the short water pump, bracket arrangement. Combinations of twenty-five percent, thirty percent and fifty percent speed reductions (underdrive) are possible.

Late-model long water pump pulleys from GM, unlike stock 1:1 ratio short pump pulleys, provide different ratios when installed in combinations.

Ratios of late-model pulley combinations

Crank pulley drive size (in.)	Pump pulley driven size (in.)	Drive
23	21	Overdrives 10 percent
23	18	Overdrives 20 percent
20	18	Overdrives 10 percent
20	21	Underdrives 5 percent

Most of the production pulley arrangements overdrive the water pump relative to crankshaft speed. This is done because most of the work demanded of the small-block is performed in low- and mid-rpm ranges. When the engine is worked hard at slower speeds, the water pump, in most cases attached to the fan, must spin faster to accomplish cooling relative to engine load. When the engine is run at high speeds and vehicle speed is also high, the cooling process is more easily accomplished because of the wind velocity through the radiator.

Horsepower creates heat and often, when the engine is built to produce more than the stock power rating, the standard efficiency cooling system proves inadequate. Larger radiators are often the answer but if radiator surface area is limited because of space, water pump output is the only

Late-model long-leg pump pulley numbers and dimensions

Stamped no. on crank pulleys	Grooves	Circumference (in.)	Diameter (in.)	New part no.	Availability
3956664	1	20	$6\frac{7}{8}$	None	Auto wrecker; discontinued
3956666	2	20	$6\frac{7}{8}$	14023147	Chevy parts or auto wrecker
3972180	3	23	8	14023148	Chevy parts or auto wrecker

Stamped no. on pump pulleys	Grooves	Circumference (in.)	Diameter (in.)	New part no.	Availability
3995631	1	18	$6\frac{3}{16}$	None	Auto wrecker; discontinued
3989305	1	21	$7\frac{1}{8}$	None	Auto wrecker; discontinued
351680	2	18	$6\frac{3}{16}$	None	Chevy parts or auto wrecker

solution to the problem. Building in more efficiency by modifying pump parts, or speeding up pump rotation to handle difficult cooling tasks, will only work if the design limitations of the pump are not exceeded.

Aftermarket water pumps with computer-designed impellers are available if the factory system still can't handle the job even after modification.

Velocity of the pumped coolant is important; never run the engine without a thermostat.

Rate of flow, pressure and temperature of coolant are regulated by the opening and closing of the thermostat. The AC Delco division of General Motors makes 195, 180 and 160 degree Fahrenheit rated thermostats. Most factory-installed thermostats are rated at 195 degrees; some enthusiasts install the 160 degree thermostat. The 160 degree base temperature is too cool and the 195 degree base is too hot. In fact, a heavy traffic situation may allow the coolant temperature to climb an additional 30 degrees. When a 195 degree base temperature thermostat is installed, the resulting temperature of almost 230 degrees is unacceptable.

Cylinder temperatures as a result are excessive to the point of detonating the fuel. For this reason, I prefer a base temperature thermostat of 180 degrees. A 180 degree base temperature will reduce the possibility of detonation because the cylinder temperatures remain lower. If the cooling system is working properly, the coolant temperature, even under trying circumstances, will not exceed 210 degrees.

I have been told not to, but I use straight antifreeze. I think that the cooling system stays corrosion free if water is not used.

Interchanges

11

The small-block engine is an engine-swapper's dream. Transverse mounting is limited because the ninety-degree design is too wide and spark plug access against a firewall is nearly impossible. Yet, when equipped with stock exhaust manifolds the engine is so compact that it should fit into any rear-wheel-drive vehicle.

Interchanges

Some work is required to construct and install receiving pads for motor mounts that the engine can sit on but this is usually easy to do. Several exhaust manifold styles are available that make exhaust routing simple. There are multiple accessory mounting combinations that eliminate most clearance problems, and wiring is no problem. The only obstacle to overcome is cooling.

Radiator capacity has to be increased relative to horsepower created if the vehicle is to be driven more than a few minutes at a time. Simply put, the cooling system capacity and the radiator surface area have to be large enough to cool the horsepower the engine produces. On the average, the front of the vehicle must have enough space to mount a radiator with at least a twenty-two-quart capacity, including the fluid in the block.

The next concern is to make sure the oil pan does not interfere with steering linkage or the vehi-

This close-up view of the frame shows the steel receiver that accepts the rubberized 229 ci V-6 engine mount. Notice the extra holes in the frame.

This engine compartment view shows the mount receivers (to be removed) and the Turbo Hydra-matic 350 transmission that was installed a year earlier. The wiring hanging around the compartment will plug into the 305 ci engine we are installing.

Here is the 229 ci engine as installed from the factory in our 1979 Malibu. Notice that the accessories and all the front water pump area accessory mounts will bolt onto the small-block.

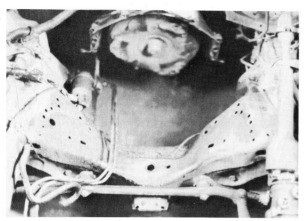

With the V-6 mounting hardware removed, look at the profusion of holes. Every GM motor mount for the A body line will fit onto this frame.

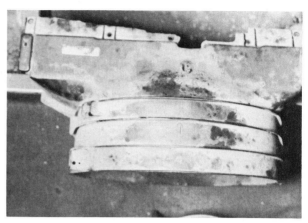

The Chevrolet V-6 fan shroud is very deep. The arrow on the top center of the circular section indicates a separation line.

When the small-block mounts are installed, bolt all the V-6 accessories onto the V-8 and drop it in.

cle frame. Several sump designs from the factory can be modified for clearance. If you can't make a factory pan work, custom aftermarket oil pans for a wet-sump or shallow-pan, dry-sump system are available.

When fabricating engine mounting pads or locating the engine in a chassis, use an empty block. The block can be bolted to an empty transmission case to check length and an oil pan can be added to check depth and clearance under the block.

Installing the small-block in any rear-wheel-drive GM car is easy. Most Oldsmobile, Pontiac or Buick models have a Chevrolet counterpart. GM bodies and frames are products of the Fisher Coach Division of General Motors and all Fisher Body frames are drilled to accept any GM motor mount appliance. This means that any engine produced

A close-up view of the V-8 mount shows how much farther forward it sits than the V-6 steel receiver. When finished, even the six-cylinder flywheel and starter will be reused.

At the separation line of the shroud are staples that hold the two sections together. When the staples are removed, the fan shroud is perfect for V-8 installation. The fan, pulleys, all accessories, front mounts and even the radiator will work for the small-block.

for that particular model line will interchange. GM Fisher bodies are given letter identification: A body, B body, G body, F body, and so on, are all rear-wheel-drive GM cars.

The A body cars of a few years ago included the Oldsmobile Cutlass, Pontiac Grand Prix, Buick Regal, Chevrolet Monte Carlo and Malibu. Recently some of these models have been given G body identification but the point is that they share a frame that accepts a small-block engine as a bolt-in. The Grand Prix, for example, has Monte Carlo engine mount holes in the frame, and it is simple to bolt in the frame mount that accepts the Chevy engine mounting appliance.

The B body full-size Oldsmobile 98 or 88, Pontiac Bonneville, Buick Electra (when these were rear-wheel-drive cars) all used the same frame engine cradle as the Chevrolet Caprice and Impala.

The F body includes the Pontiac Firebird and Chevrolet Camaro which share drivetrain combinations today but years ago came with their own motor division engines. The engine mount holes are there; mount the Chevy engine and change the front springs accordingly.

The X body cars 1968-79 all had identical front sub-frames. The X models include the Chevrolet Nova, Oldsmobile Omega, Pontiac Ventura and Buick Appolo. (In fact, the Chevy Nova was the first X body, and that is probably why the others bear the names they do. Nova, Omega, Ventura, Appolo: the first letter of each model name spells Nova.) Enough examples and trivia. It is sufficient to know that every X body car will accept a bolt-in small-block.

This is the Cutlass installation when the 305 ci engine had been in for its first maintenance. The only dilemma when a diesel engine is removed concerns the front springs, which are intended for the heavier diesel engine and now support the lighter small-block. These heavy-duty springs raise the front end of the car by an inch or more.

The engine exchange will involve changing frame mounts, rerouting exhaust pipes, perhaps rerouting fuel lines and certainly wiring, and most important, the transmission. Unfortunately, Chevrolet engines have a dissimilar bolt pattern as compared with the Oldsmobile, Pontiac and Buick engines. Also, depending upon which GM body is used, there are three possible transmission lengths.

When the 229 ci V-6 engine was replaced by a V-8, the front end springs sagged so much under the increased load that they had to be replaced. This should be done when the engine weights differ by more than 200 lb.

This 1982 Grand Prix has a 231 ci 3.8 liter engine that was knocking loudly; the computer-controlled transmission was also slipping. We purchased a totaled 1978 Malibu wagon that had an engine with less than 70,000 miles on it and combined the two cars.

B body wagons in the early and mid-seventies had Turbo Hydramatic 350, 375 and 400 series transmissions that were 36 in. long. Two- and four-door B body sedans of the same time period had Turbo Hydramatic 350 transmissions that were 31½ in. long. Mid-sized A bodies of the late sixties and early to mid-seventies had Turbo Hydramatic 350 and sometimes 400 series transmissions 28 in. long.

When installing a small-block, it will be necessary to use the Chevrolet bolt pattern automatic transmission of the correct length for the vehicle. When using a manual transmission, the bellhousing, and certainly the flywheel, pressure plate and clutch plate for the Chevy engine you are installing, must be used. Manual transmission and bellhousings combined usually measure 28 in.

Wiring

I have replaced GM diesel, Buick and Chevrolet V-6 and straight six-cylinder engines with the small-block Chevy. The only time-consuming part of the exchanges have been removing and replacing the motor mount frame appliances and the wiring. Before removing any engine, carefully disconnect and label the ignition wires, alternator wires, starter wires, oil pressure and temperature sending switch wires. If the vehicle is equipped with air conditioning, remove and label the fast idle solenoid and air-conditioning compressor wires. Your goal is to isolate the wires needed to install the small-block. In some cases there might be wires left over because the late-model V-6 Buick and the GM

diesel engines have electrically controlled solenoid and emission devices not present on the small-block. Note that when labeling GM diesel wiring, label the fuel injection pump wire Distributor Battery Positive. Change the wire's clipend and plug it into the distributor for ignition.

Once the small-block is installed, you will find that wires have to be lengthened or shortened because the accessories are often located on different sides from one engine to the other. Be sure to splice in the same gauge wire, being careful not to disturb the end connections installed at the factory that attach to the accessories. Do not try to stretch wires to fit and be sure all your work is wrapped with electrical tape and then put into factory-type plastic-flex wire covers.

Factory wire covers come in at least three different diameters and have snap-together connectors at the ends. Flex covers also have fasteners that clip to valve covers, inner fenderwells and firewalls. If you run short, miles of flex cover can be found at the junkyard.

Take your time and pay close attention to detail because when care is used the installation looks factory original.

The air-conditioning compressor installed on the old engine should be used again to avoid any minor system differences. The high-pressure hoses will probably have to be replaced because the lengths here are also different. Many large auto part dealers can make custom-length hoses if they

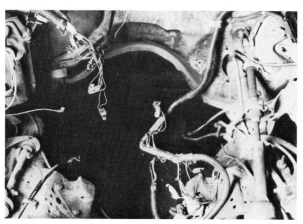

After the 231 ci V-6 was removed, the motor mounts were changed. The engine was installed with its transmission attached and all the accessories were moved from the Malibu to the Pontiac. Notice, on the left, the computer control wire harness. We insulated the connector ends and neatly tucked this mess between the inner fenderwell and outer fender. The wire harness draped on the frame has all the wires needed by the V-8 and its non-computer systems. The air-conditioning wires on the extreme left had to be lengthened to reach the small-block air-conditioning compressor mounted on the opposite side.

Notice the empty frontal cavity in this car's motor bay. All this room, and an examination of the wiring, make it obvious that a small-block swap wouldn't be too difficult here. It looks complicated but it isn't. Removing this blown 2.8 liter six-cylinder is easy. Be careful to label wiring, and vacuum and pressure hoses. A small-block costs less than one of these, so go for it. In this particular case, I was able to trade the V-6 transmission for a V-8 unit.

are given the ends you have. This will save you some cash because your original air-conditioning evaporator core can still be used. Unfortunately the simplest way to reconnect the air-conditioning system is by changing over to the stock Chevrolet motor division style hoses and evaporator which can probably be found at the junkyard.

Another junkyard item might be a throttle cable of the correct length and style for the carburetor your Chevy engine will be using.

Transmissions

The Chevrolet 200 ci, 229 ci and new 262 ci (4.3 liter) V-6 engines have transmissions with Chevy small-block V-8 bolt patterns. These Chevrolet six-cylinder engines also use accessory mounting that is the same as or similar to the V-8 engines. Many of these accessories and much of the mounting hardware will bolt directly onto the small-block. You should be aware that many V-6 equipped cars have metric 200 series transmissions that will not last long when driven aggressively.

Many late-model three-speed Turbo Hydramatic 350 and four-speed 200 R4 and 700 R4 transmissions have lock-up torque converters. These converters have an internal clutch device that usually does not take too much punishment before failing. Check the torque converter and transmission model to make sure they will accept the V-8 swap.

It is important to understand that 1981 and later transmissions are computer controlled and you may not wish to reconnect the C4 onboard computer system. If this is the case, and your 700 R4 transmission for example is 31½ in. long, ask your local automatic transmission rebuilder for an intermediate length Turbo Hydramatic 350 transmission that doesn't need computer control. This transmission change will eliminate lock-up and unfortu-

The engine's width in the same car is a different story. Still, the room is there for an easy engine swap.

nately overdrive but these automatics will take more punishment and if the worst happens, are less expensive to repair.

Computer controls

Some mid-year 1980 and later GM cars have computer-controlled distributor timing and carburetor fuel metering. If the onboard computer control is to be disconnected from the original engine, the small-block engine replacing it will require a new computer.

If the new computer and related distributor and carburetor are too expensive for you to consider, earlier pre-1980 type mechanically controlled distributors and carburetors can be used. Your fuel economy will be affected and your tune-ups will

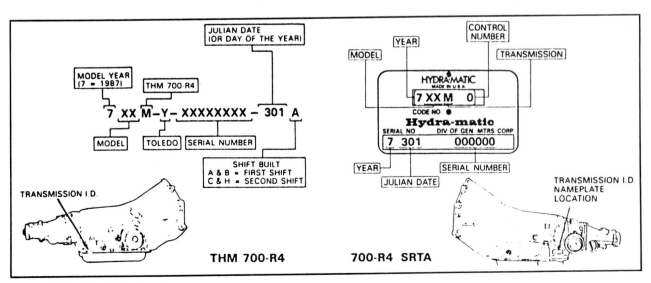

Transmission identification plate.

This 1970 Nova has the steel frame mount (LH PN 3955183, RH PN 3980938) and the rubberized engine mount (both sides are part number 3990918). In 1973 GM adopted a system of rubberized frame mount and steel engine mounts; the system is still used today.

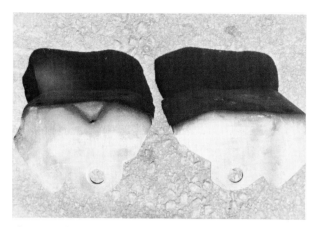

These steel engine mounts are the 1973-76 B body engine mount on the left (PN 334601) and the 1973 and later A, G, X and F body engine mount on the right (PN 334970). Notice the big car mount on the left is longer in reach from engine face to mounting hole than the mount on the right.

have to be more precise in order to meet federal emission requirements. The good news is that much of the engine's throttle response and behavior while driving aggressively will make up for a few lost miles per gallon. Of course when computer sensors are not connected, there are several more wires left over that will not be needed to run your newly installed non-computer small-block. Be sure to insulate these wires and leave them enclosed in their plastic-flex case. At this time, it would be wise to disconnect the computer power supply. It is illegal to remove emission devices from the vehicle: the onboard computer might be considered an emission device so leave it in the car.

Exhaust systems

The easiest exhaust system starts with the installation of exhaust manifolds that are intended for the small-block when it is installed in that particular chassis line. When stock manifolds are used, replacement single exhaust Y pipes and complete systems are available at the corner auto parts store. Dual systems are the way to go for good street performance. Installing these will require transmission cross-member modifications for lead pipe clearance on the driver's side.

Small-block installations in kit cars or custom street rods will have kit manufacturer header systems available or you can usually make one of the many styles of stock manifolds work.

The most popular exhaust manifolds produced are the special high-performance 1962-67 327 ci Corvette units (LH part number 3797901 and RH part number 3814970). These manifolds have a 2½ in.

Here are the two halves, foreground, and the combined mounts, background, that replaced the reverse arrangement in pre-1973 cars. These later mounts are resistant to failure unlike the earlier type.

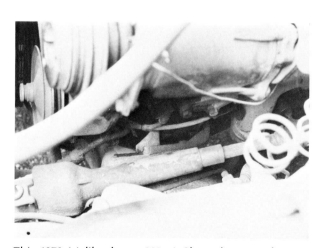

This 1979 Malibu has a 229 ci Chevrolet V-6. The V-6 mount has rubber on the engine received by this steel bolted to the frame.

exhaust outlet, and are compact enough to fit almost anywhere provided that the vehicle frame isn't in the way

Motor mounts

Changing the motor mount frame appliances or brackets was mentioned earlier in the chapter. This job requires patience and is better done by two people. There are usually three bolts on each mount and the engine cradle section of the frame has many access holes.

From 1968 to 1972 solid steel receiver brackets were bolted in place on the frame. The mount on the engine had rubberized construction that was prone to failure. For this reason, in 1973 Chevy engineers developed the steel engine appliance and rubberized frame mounts. These mounts (part number 459021) are universal throughout the Chevrolet car lines: the B, A, G, F and X small-block-equipped cars all have the same internally rubberized pieces bolted to the frame.

The steel brackets bolted to the engine from 1973 to 1988 differ slightly in length so it is important to get the correct pieces for the vehicle you have. The 1973-76 B body GM cars use the longer bracket (part number 334601); all other 1973 and later GM cars use the shorter bracket (part number 334970).

The 1982 and later Camaros can use the 459021 and 334970 combination of parts but GM suggests that you use frame mounts (part number 14039437) and a different right-side engine bracket (part number 14039436). I don't understand why the numbers are different as the parts look identical.

If you are ordering the parts new, use the latest GM replacement numbers. When working on the late-model Camaros that have five-speed transmissions, you must replace the bellhousing with the one intended for the V-8. The transmission is mounted on an angle, and straight-up bellhousings will not interchange except in the case of the four-speed nonoverdrive units. Use the Z28 front springs and struts after removing the V-6 2.8 liter or four-cylinder engine.

There are two different transmission lengths for the Camaro. The easiest V-8 swap involves using automatic transmissions. Manual clutch linkages will not directly adapt from the four- and six-cylinder engines to the V-8. The swaps that retain manual transmissions will need expensive replacement accessories.

When the small-block is installed, undercoat the new motor mount assembly to prevent it from rusting. This picture is actually from a 1979 Olds Cutlass where a 4.3 liter diesel was removed.

Body	Engine	Chevrolet	Pontiac	Oldsmobile	Buick	Cadillac
			1985 Models -- Body Styles and Nameplates			
A	Tr FWD	Celebrity	6000	Cutlass Ciera	Century	·
B	RWD	Impala/ Caprice Classic	Parisienne	Delta 88 Custom Cruiser	LeSabre / Electra Estate Wagon	·
C	FWD	·	·	98 Regency	Electra	De Ville Fleetwood
D	RWD	·	·	·	·	Fleetwood Brougham
E	FWD	·	·	Toronado	Riviera	Eldorado
F	RWD	Camaro	Firebird	·	·	·
G	RWD	Monte Carlo El Camino	Bonneville Grand Prix	Cutlass Supreme	Regal	·
J	Tr FWD	Cavalier	J2000	Firenza	Skyhawk	Cimarron
K	RWD	·	·	·	·	Seville
M	FWD	Sprint	·	·	·	·
GM20 (N)	FWD	·	Grand Am	Calais	Somerset Regal	·
P	RWD	·	Fiero	·	·	·
R	FWD	Spectrum	·	·	·	·
T	RWD	Chevette	T1000/ Acadian	·	·	·
X	Tr FWD	Citation II	·	·	Skylark	·
Y	RWD	Corvette	·	·	·	·

1986 General Motors Passenger Car
Vehicle Identification Numbering (VIN) System

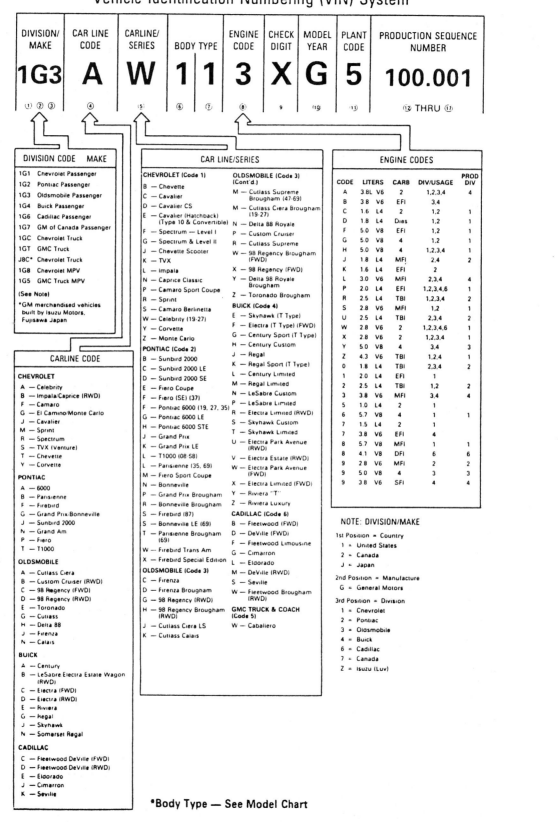

DIVISION/ MAKE	CAR LINE CODE	CARLINE/ SERIES	BODY TYPE	ENGINE CODE	CHECK DIGIT	MODEL YEAR	PLANT CODE	PRODUCTION SEQUENCE NUMBER
1G3	A	W	1 1	3	X	G	5	100.001
① ② ③	④	⑤	⑥ ⑦	⑧	9	⑩	⑪	⑫ THRU ⑰

DIVISION CODE — MAKE

1G1	Chevrolet Passenger
1G2	Pontiac Passenger
1G3	Oldsmobile Passenger
1G4	Buick Passenger
1G6	Cadillac Passenger
1G7	GM of Canada Passenger
1GC	Chevrolet Truck
1GT	GMC Truck
J8C*	Chevrolet Truck
1G8	Chevrolet MPV
1G5	GMC Truck MPV

(See Note)

*GM merchandised vehicles built by Isuzu Motors, Fujisawa Japan

CARLINE CODE

CHEVROLET
A — Celebrity
B — Impala/Caprice (RWD)
F — Camaro
G — El Camino/Monte Carlo
J — Cavalier
M — Sprint
R — Spectrum
S — TVX (Venture)
T — Chevette
Y — Corvette

PONTIAC
A — 6000
B — Parisienne
F — Firebird
G — Grand Prix/Bonneville
J — Sunbird 2000
N — Grand Am
P — Fiero
T — T1000

OLDSMOBILE
A — Cutlass Ciera
B — Custom Cruiser (RWD)
C — 98 Regency (FWD)
D — 98 Regency (RWD)
E — Toronado
G — Cutlass
H — Delta 88
J — Firenza
N — Calais

BUICK
A — Century
B — LeSabre Electra Estate Wagon (RWD)
C — Electra (FWD)
D — Electra (RWD)
E — Riviera
G — Regal
J — Skyhawk
N — Somerset Regal

CADILLAC
C — Fleetwood DeVille (FWD)
D — Fleetwood DeVille (RWD)
E — Eldorado
J — Cimarron
K — Seville

CAR LINE/SERIES

CHEVROLET (Code 1)
B — Chevette
C — Cavalier
D — Cavalier CS
E — Cavalier (Hatchback) (Type 10 & Convertible)
F — Spectrum — Level I
G — Spectrum & Level II
J — Chevette Scooter
K — TVX
L — Impala
N — Caprice Classic
P — Camaro Sport Coupe
R — Sprint
S — Camaro Berlinetta
W — Celebrity (19-27)
Y — Corvette
Z — Monte Carlo

PONTIAC (Code 2)
B — Sunbird 2000
C — Sunbird 2000 LE
D — Sunbird 2000 SE
E — Fiero Coupe
F — Fiero (SE) (37)
F — Pontiac 6000 (19, 27, 35)
G — Pontiac 6000 LE
H — Pontiac 6000 STE
J — Grand Prix
K — Grand Prix LE
L — T1000 (08-58)
L — Parisienne (35, 69)
M — Fiero Sport Coupe
N — Bonneville
P — Grand Prix Brougham
R — Bonneville Brougham
S — Firebird (87)
S — Bonneville LE (69)
T — Parisienne Brougham (69)
W — Firebird Trans Am
X — Firebird Special Edition

OLDSMOBILE (Code 3)
C — Firenza
D — Firenza Brougham
G — 98 Regency (RWD)
H — 98 Regency Brougham (RWD)
J — Cutlass Ciera LS
K — Cutlass Calais

OLDSMOBILE (Code 3) (Cont'd.)
M — Cutlass Supreme Brougham (47-69)
M — Cutlass Ciera Brougham (19-27)
N — Delta 88 Royale
P — Custom Cruiser
R — Cutlass Supreme
W — 98 Regency Brougham (FWD)
X — 98 Regency (FWD)
Y — Delta 98 Royale Brougham
Z — Toronado Brougham

BUICK (Code 4)
E — Skyhawk (T Type)
F — Electra (T Type) (FWD)
G — Century Sport (T Type)
H — Century Custom
J — Regal
K — Regal Sport (T Type)
L — Century Limited
M — Regal Limited
N — LeSabre Custom
P — LeSabre Limited
R — Electra Limited (RWD)
S — Skyhawk Custom
T — Skyhawk Limited
U — Electra Park Avenue (RWD)
V — Electra Estate (RWD)
W — Electra Park Avenue (FWD)
X — Electra Limited (FWD)
Y — Riviera "T"
Z — Riviera Luxury

CADILLAC (Code 6)
B — Fleetwood (FWD)
D — DeVille (FWD)
F — Fleetwood Limousine
G — Cimarron
L — Eldorado
M — DeVille (RWD)
S — Seville
W — Fleetwood Brougham (RWD)

GMC TRUCK & COACH (Code 5)
W — Caballero

ENGINE CODES

CODE	LITERS	CARB	DIV/USAGE	PROD DIV
A	3.8L V6	2	1,2,3,4	4
B	3.8 V6	EFI	3,4	
C	1.6 L4	2	1,2	1
D	1.8 L4	Dies	1,2	1
F	5.0 V8	EFI	1,2	1
G	5.0 V8	2	1,2	1
H	5.0 V8	4	1,2,3,4	1
J	1.8 L4	MFI	2,4	2
K	1.6 L4	EFI	2	
L	3.0 V6	MFI	2,3,4	4
P	2.0 L4	EFI	1,2,3,4,6	1
R	2.5 L4	TBI	1,2,3,4	2
S	2.8 V6	MFI	1,2	1
U	2.5 L4	TBI	2,3,4	2
W	2.8 V6	2	1,2,3,4,6	1
X	2.8 V6	2	1,2,3,4	1
Y	5.0 V8	4	3,4	3
Z	4.3 V6	TBI	1,2,4	1
0	1.8 L4	MFI	2,3,4	2
1	2.0 L4	EFI	1	
2	2.5 L4	TBI	1,2	2
3	3.8 V6	MFI	3,4	4
5	1.0 L4	2	1	
6	5.7 V8	4	1	1
7	1.5 L4	2	1	
7	3.8 V6	EFI	4	
8	5.7 V8	MFI	1	1
8	4.1 V8	DFI	6	6
9	2.8 V6	MFI	2	2
9	5.0 V8	4	3	3
9	3.8 V6	SFI	4	4

NOTE: DIVISION/MAKE

1st Position = Country
1 = United States
2 = Canada
J = Japan

2nd Position = Manufacture
G = General Motors

3rd Position = Division
1 = Chevrolet
2 = Pontiac
3 = Oldsmobile
4 = Buick
6 = Cadillac
7 = Canada
Z = Isuzu (Luv)

*Body Type — See Model Chart

Parts numbers

0.000 Engine assembly

1 10054575   Target Master replacement 305 ci engine. Less intake manifold, distributor, water pump, harmonic balancer, flywheel, 1976-80

1 10054560   Target Master replacement 305 ci engine. Less intake manifold, distributor, water pump, harmonic balancer, flywheel, 1980-85

1 10067353   Target Master replacement 350 ci engine. Less intake manifold, distributor, water pump, harmonic balancer, flywheel, 1973-85

1 10048971   Target Master replacement 1986 only. Truck use. Less intake manifold, distributor, water pump, harmonic balancer, flywheel

0.010 Gasket kit, engine

The engine gasket kits together with oil pan gasket kit (group 1.429) and cylinder head gasket kit (group 0.289) provide all necessary gaskets for complete engine overhaul.

1 14050646   1968-74 262 thru 400 ci small-block V-8 Chevy engines

1 14050645   1975-84 305 thru 400 ci small-block V-8 Chevy engines

0.033 Blocks and partial engines

1 366246   302, 327, 350 ci iron bare block, high tin alloy casting, 4 in. bore, four bolt nodular iron cap #2482 on intermediate mains, for 2.45 in. main journal crankshafts (casting #366245 or 14011064). This block is produced on production tooling and cylinder wall thicknesses are same as current-year production

1 366287   302, 327, 350 ci iron bare block with 3.980 in. semi-finished bore, four bolt nodular iron cap #2482 on intermediate mains, siamesed walls, blind head bolt holes, can be bored to 4.125 in. (casting #3666286), for 2.45 in. main journal crankshafts

1 366300   302, 327, 350 ci aluminum bare block, with 4 in. bore iron sleeves, splayed nodular, four bolt caps on intermediate mains for 2.45 in. mains journal crankshafts (casting #366299)

1 3966921   350 ci partial engine. Iron block with four bolt main, 1053 steel forged crank P/N 3941184 forged aluminum piston 11:1 compression ratio, camshaft mechanical street type P/N 3972178. For service components use 1970 350 W/S/H/P-RPO LT1 Corvette

0.056 Bolt stud, engine main bearing cap

6 3877669   Bolt all 302 thru 350 ci V-8 Chevy outer bolt (7/16-14 X 3 1/16)

10 3960312   Stud all 302 thru 350 ci V-8 Chevy outer stud for oil baffle tray attaching (7/16-14 X 5 5/8)

1 14011039   Stud kits all 302 thru 350 ci V-8 Chevy with four bolt main, includes ten long inner and six shorter outer stud only. Use flat washer 14011040 and nut 3942410 or 14044866

0.095 Main bearing caps

AR 3932482   Bearing cap, crankshaft 350 ci Chevy V-8 four bolt, production replacement type

1 3912030   Bearing kit, standard for rear main, all 302 thru 350 ci V-8 with 2.45 in. diameter main journals

4 3912038   Bearing kit, standard for front and intermediate mains on all 302 thru 350 ci with 2.45 in. diameter main journals

0.206 Engine cover, front

1 14011094   Front cover chrome 350 ci V-8 Chevy 1969-84 (same as 3991433 except for chrome). Use with timing pointer #14011095

0.219 Timing pointers, front covers

1 14011095   Pointer, engine front cover chrome 350 ci V-8 Chevy 1969-84 use with 6 in. damper (exc. S/H/P). Same as 3991435 except for chrome

1 14011096   Pointer, engine front cover chrome 350 ci V-8 Chevy 1969-84 use with 8 in. damper (W/S/H/P). Same as 3991436 except for chrome

0.253 Seat, cylinder head valve

8 14044818   Insert, exhaust valve seat, for 1.60 in. diameter, valve for 350 ci V-8 aluminum cylinder head #14011049, 14011050. Hardness Rockwell "C" 30-40, 1.65 in. OD

8 14044817   Insert, intake valve seat for 2.02 in. diameter, valve for 350 ci V-8 aluminum cylinder head #14011049, 14011050. Hardness Rockwell "C" 27-36, 2.10 in. OD

0.269 Cylinder head

2 10051101   Cylinder head V-8 aluminum, use with 2.02 in. intake and 1.60 ci exhaust (55 cc chambers), this cylinder head has valve guides and seats. It is the phase six racing head based on the 049 casting with angled spark plug entry. This and all aluminum heads should use the composition gasket (part number 14088948) that has stainless steel inserts

2 14088948   Gasket head V-8 Chevy 302 thru 350 ci stainless, O-ring design for aluminum head, 4 in. bore

2 10088115   Cylinder head V-8 aluminum use with 1.94 in. intake and 1.50 in. exhaust production 1988 L98 350 Corvette head sold as a complete assembly. Includes screw-in studs, guide plates, valve springs, retainers and keepers. Current list price, $319.33 each

2 14101127   Cylinder head V-8 aluminum use with 1.94 in. intake and 1.50 in. exhaust, angled spark plug, 58 cc chambers, production 1987 Corvette high-torque street head

2 14011049   Cylinder head V-8 aluminum use with 2.02 in. intake and 1.60 in. exhaust, 64 cc cham-

bers (this cylinder head has no valve seat or valve guides), angle spark plug design, casting #14011049 use with all 302 thru 350 ci Chevy V-8

2 14011050 Cylinder head V-8 aluminum use with 2.02 in. intake and 1.60 in. exhaust 64 cc chambers, with seat and guides, angle spark plug design, casting #14011049 made from T-356 aluminum with T-6 heat treat, use with all 302 thru 350 ci Chevy V-8

2 14011005 Cylinder head V-8 aluminum use with 2.02 in. intake and 1.60 in. exhaust, 64 cc chambers with seat and guides, solid cast head, no water passages, angle spark plug design, casting #14011049 use with all 302 thru 350 ci Chevy V-8

2 464045 Cylinder head V-8 cast iron use with 2.02 in. intake and 1.60 in. exhaust, 76 cc chambers, straight spark plug design. Light casted high-performance street head with screw-in studs and guide plates included

2 14011058 Cylinder head V-8 cast iron use with 2.02 in. intake and 1.60 in. exhaust, 64 cc chambers, angle spark plug design, casting #14011034, use with all 302 thru 350 ci Chevy V-8 (bow-tie design)

23958603 Cylinder head V-8 cast iron use with 1.94 in. intake and 1.50 in. exhaust valve, 65 cc chambers, straight spark plug design, all 302 thru 350 ci Chevy V-8

2 3987376 Cylinder head V-8 cast iron use with 2.02 in. intake and 1.60 in. exhaust, 65 cc chambers, straight spark plug design, casting #3991492

0.283 Guide, aluminum cylinder head valve

16 14011048 Guide, cylinder head intake and exhaust for aluminum 350 ci V-8 use W/P/N 14011004, 49, 50, 56 and 14044802-41 alloy cast iron, 2.24 in. length. Valve stem hole must be machined to size after installation

0.289 Gasket, engine cylinder head

2 462691 Gasket, head V-8 Chevy 302 thru 350 ci steel design, thickness is 0.0140 in. plus or minus 0.0025 in.

2 3916336 Gasket, head V-8 Chevy 302 thru 350 ci stainless steel, thickness is 0.0152 in. plus or minus 0.001 in.

2 3965790 Gasket head V-8 Chevy 302 thru 400 ci use with 4 in. through 4⅛ in. bore engines, composition material with stainless steel jacket with compressed thickness of 0.039 in.

2 14011041 Gasket head V-8 Chevy 302 thru 400 ci O-ring design for 4 in. through 4⅛ in. bore, this gasket is a composition type with solid O-ring around each bore, coated with Teflon. Compressed thickness is 0.040 in., no retorque required

0.293 Pin, stud, washer; engine cylinder

AR 585927 Pin, cylinder head dowel (⁵⁄₁₆ in. diameter X ⁹⁄₁₆ in.) V-8 283 thru 400 ci Chevy

16 3704796 Bolt, all 262 thru 400 ci V-8 (⁷⁄₁₆ - 14 X 1.75 in.)

14 3734594 Bolt, all 262 thru 400 ci V-8 (⁷⁄₁₆ - 14 X 3.75 in.)

4 3767468 Bolt, all 262 thru 400 ci V-8 (⁷⁄₁₆ - 14 X 3.00 in.)

AR 14014408 Stud kit, cylinder head 302 through 400 ci Chevy V-8, includes thirty-four studs only,

use with washer 14011040 and nut 3942410 or 14034866

16 14011035 Stud, (⁷⁄₁₆ - 14 X 2.69 in. OL) V-8 engines, part or unit 14014408

14 14011036 Stud, (⁷⁄₁₆ - 14 X 4.73 in. OL) V-8 engines, part or unit 14014408

4 14011037 Stud, (⁷⁄₁₆ - 14 X 3.99 in. OL V-8 engines, part of unit 14014408

AR 14011040 Washer, (0.45 in. ID - 0.78 in. OD) cylinder head use with stud kit 14014408, main bearing stud kit 14011039 or all aluminum V-8 cylinder heads. Special hardened washer

AR 3942410 Nut, cylinder head (⁷⁄₁₆ X 20) steel nut, 100 percent magnafluxed use with all Chevy stud kits (1038 steel)

AR 14044866 Nut, cylinder head heavy-duty off highway (⁷⁄₁₆ X 20) twelve-point (4037 steel), 100 percent magnafluxed, use with all Chevy stud kits

0.296 Valve, inlet

8 3989085 Inlet valve, 327, 350 ci standard stem (1.94 in. head)

8 3849814 Inlet valve, 327, 350 ci V-8 with aluminum head, standard stem (2.02 in. head)

8 361976 Inlet valve, 327, 350 ci V-8 standard stem (2.05 in. head)

8 366285 Inlet valve, 327, 350 ci V-8 standard stem (2.05 in. head) stainless steel

0.297 Exhaust valves

8 14025575 Exhaust valve, 262, 400 V-8 standard stem (1.50 in. head)

8 3849818 Exhaust valve, 327, 350 V-8 with aluminum head, standard stem (1.60 in. head)

0.303 Shim, spring; engine valve

Refer to Chevy Power Manual (catalog #CP5) for proper installation of valve springs.

AR 3731058 Shim (0.859 in. ID X 1.234 in. OD X 0.030 in. thick)

AR 3875916 Shim (0.703 ID X 1.484 in. OD X 0.015 in. thick)

AR 3891521 Shim (0.703 ID X 1.484 in. OD X 0.065 in. thick)

AR 3836755 Shield oil splash

AR 6263796 Valve spring and damper assembly, all 262 through 400 ci with rotator cap 6263794 only

AR 3911068 Valve spring and damper assembly, all 302 through 350 ci Chevy V-8 with special high performance, 1.241 in. OD valve spring (valve seal kit 14033547 recommended for this spring.) (spec.: 80 lb. at 1.70 in. installed height, 1.15 in. solid height, 267 lb. per in.)

AR 3927142 Valve spring and damper assembly, use with all 302 through 350 ci Chevy V-8 with moderate high lift cam (use with camshaft 3927140 or all stock high-performance production camshafts, 1.273 in. diameter spring (valve seal kit 14033547 recommended for this spring) (spec.: 110 lb. at 1.70 in. installed height, 1.16 in. solid height, 358 lb. per in.)

AR 330585 Dual valve spring, all 302 through 350 ci Chevy V-8 with moderate high lift cam (use with aluminum retainer 330586, use with camshaft 3927140, 3965754 or all stock high-performance cams, 1.379 in. OD outer spring, valve seal kit 14033547 recommended for this spring (spec.: 140 lb. at 1.75 in. installed height, 1.15 in. solid height, 325 lb. per in.)

AR 366282   Dual valve spring with damper, use with 302 through 350 ci Chevy V-8 with max high lift or roller cams, Chevy camshaft 366293 use with titanium valve retainer 366254, 1.525 in. OD outer spring, requires other than production type valve seals (spec.: 128 lb. at 1.70 in. installed height, 1.26 in. solid height, 406 lb. per in.)

0.308 Seal, shield; engine valve

1 14033547   Seal kit, valve stem oil (O-ring type) all 262 through 400 ci Chevy V-8

0.309 Cap, valve spring retainer

AR 6263794   Cap rotator valve spring, 262 through 400 ci V-8 (exhaust)

AR 14003974   Cap, valve spring steel, 262 through 400 ci Chevy V-8, 1.094 in. OD, stamped A, use with valve spring #3927142

AR 14003941   Cap valve spring steel, 262 through 400 ci, can be used with valve spring 3911068, stamped V

AR 330586   Cap, valve spring aluminum, all 262 through 400 ci Chevy V-8, use with valve spring 330585

AR 366254   Cap, valve spring titanium, all 262 through 400 ci Chevy V-8, use with valve spring 366282

0.310 Key, engine valve spring

AR 3947770   Key, valve keeper steel, all 262 through 400 ci Chevy V-8, with $^{11}/_{32}$ in. stem, color purple

0.333 Arm, engine valve rocker

AR 3974290   Rocker arm steel, all 262 through 400 ci Chevy V-8, includes rocker ball

0.386 Cover grommet, engine valve rocker arm

1 474207   Cover, rocker left hand aluminum used on Corvette 1969-77 350 ci V-8, aluminum die-cast buffed bright finish

1 474208   Cover, rocker right hand aluminum used on Corvette 1969-77 350 ci V-8, aluminum die-cast buffed bright finish

1 14025554   Cover rocker right hand black ribbed magnesium 1978-85

1 14025553   Cover rocker left hand black ribbed (same as right hand except for oil filler cap hole)

2 14044819   Cover, rocker no chrome, 262 through 400 ci V-8, tall cover will clear rocker arm stud girdles with gasket retainer (has Chevy bow-tie and word power embossed on top of cover). Ideal for competition engine

2 14044823   Cover, rocker chrome, 262 through 400 ci V-8, tall cover will clear rocker arm stud girdles (has Chevy bow-tie and word power embossed on top of cover)

2 14044824   Cover, rocker chrome 262 through 400 ci V-8, production height to clear all air-conditioning pumps (has Chevy bow-tie and word power embossed on top of cover)

AR 3894337   Grommet rubber (0.9375 in. ID X 1.21875 in. OD) for bow-tie rocker covers

0.413 Retainer, rocker cover

AR 14011078   Spring bar retainer, narrow design for tall or regular valve covers, special steel

AR 14044820   Spring bar retainer chrome, narrow design for tall or regular valve covers, special steel

8 14082320   Stud, rocker cover hold down special torx head (¼-20 X 1¼)

8 14051876   Nut rocker cover hold down (¼-20)

0.423 Gasket sealant, engine rocker cover

AR 1052366   Sealant, valve cover rocker (RTV)

2 3933964   Gasket, rocker all 262 through 400 ci V-8 (cork type)

0.426 Rod, engine valve push

16 366277   Push rod, all 262 through 400 ci V-8 engines (7.824 in. OD) hardened tip with 0.075 in. wall and 0.100 in. longer than production (0.3125 in. diameter tube)

0.429 Ball, nut, stud; engine valve adjusting

AR 3959142   Ball, valve rocker arm, all 262 through 400 ci V-8 engines (0.8125 in. diameter)

AR 3744341   Nut, valve rocker arm, all 262 through 400 ci V-8 engines (⅜-24) (0.625 in. across the flat X 0.500 in. thick)

AR 3973416   Stud, valve rocker arm, all 327, 350 ci with screw-in studs (0.375 in. diameter), for converting from press-in stud to screw-in type

AR 3921912   Stud, valve rocker arm (0.4375 in. diameter) (can be used for heavy-duty 350 V-8 valve-train by drilling stud boss to 0.4375 in. and retap)

0.429 Guide, engine valve push rod

AR 14011051   Guide plate, 350 ci V-8 engine, use eight per V-8 engine (cylinder head 14011049 and 14011050)

8 3973418   Guide, 327, 350 V-8 Chevy with screw-in studs, high-performance heads

0.459 Lifter, engine valve

16 5231585   Lifter, mechanical (edge orifice design, two-piece body, two holes in body, single groove around body) 327, 350 S/H/P V-8 engines stock valve springs, can be used with V-8 with production or similar light spring valve spring loads (use with roller rocker arms)

16 5232695   Lifter, mechanical with piddle valve design (2 in. OL X 0.844 in. OD) (use with 327, 350 ci V-8 Chevy with heavy-duty valve springs)

16 5232720   Lifter, hydraulic type all H/P, S/H/P 302 through 400 ci Chevy engines

16 366253   Lifter, mushroom mechanical type (with 0.960 in. diameter foot) use with cam 366293

AR 14044875   Lifter, bore repair sleeve kit. Drill defect lifter bore to 1.044 in. diameter and cool sleeve to minus 40 degrees Fahrenheit, insert in hole, bottom must be flush with camshaft cavity. Then drill 0.4375 in. hole through oil galley and finish drilling lifter hole to 0.8432 to 0.8442 in. diameter. You can predrill the oil galley hole to 0.500 in. before installing sleeve in block

0.519 Camshaft

1 14060653   Camshaft, 262 through 400 ci cam (hydraulic type) used in 305 high-torque and fuel economy (0.357 in. lift intake, 0.390 in. lift exhaust) with 1.5 rocker ratio

1 14060655   Camshaft, high-output 305 through 400 ci cam (hydraulic type) good torque and low-

end power (0.403 in. lift intake, 0.414 in. lift exhaust) with 1.5 rocker ratio

1 14060651 Camshaft, used in 307 through 400 ci (can be used in 305 ci). Good street cam (0.390 in. lift intake, 0.410 in. lift exhaust) old "929" cam with 1.5 rocker ratio

1 3863151 Camshaft, 302 through 400 ci V-8 Chevy (hydraulic type) used in S/H/P 327 ci RPO L79 engine, good torque, excellent power (0.447 in. lift intake, 0.447 in. lift exhaust with 1.5 rocker ratio) ident. #3863152

1 3896962 Camshaft, 302 through 400 ci Chevy V-8 (hydraulic type) used in 350 ci W/S/H/P with hydraulic lift, moderate torque, excellent power (0.450 in. intake lift, 0.460 in. exhaust lift with 1.5 rocker ratio) (ident. #3896964)

1 3736097 Camshaft, 262 through 305 ci V-8 (mechanical type) good small cube rpm cam (0.381 in. lift intake, 0.380 in. lift exhaust with 1.5 rocker ratio)

1 3972178 Camshaft, 302 through 400 ci Chevy V-8 (mechanical type) use in S/HP 327 ci and 350 ci W/S/HP RPO LTI, good all-around street mechanical cam (0.435 in. intake lift, 0.455 in. exhaust lift with 1.5 rocker ratio) (ident. #33972182) valve set at 0.024 in. intake, 0.030 in. exhaust

1 3927140 Camshaft, 302 through 400 ci Chevy V-8 (mechanical type) off-road racing first design, good short-track cam (0.469 in. intake lift, 0.486 in. exhaust lift with 1.5 rocker ratio) use with valve spring 3927142 (ident. #3927141) valve set at 0.024 in. intake, 0.026 in. exhaust

1 3965754 Camshaft, 302 through 400 ci Chevy V-8 (mechanical type) off-road racing 2nd design, good short track or road race cam (0.488 in. intake lift, 0.508 in. exhaust lift with 1.5 rocker ratio) (ident. #3965751) valve set at 0.024 in. intake, 0.026 in. exhaust

1 366293 Camshaft, 302 through 400 ci Chevy V-8 (mushroom type lifter) off-road racing 3rd design, good medium or long track cam (0.560 in. intake lift, 0.575 in. exhaust lift with 1.5 rocker ratio) use with valve spring 366282 (ident. #366293) valve set at 0.025 in. intake, 0.025 in. exhaust

0.539 Bearing, camshaft
1 474005 Bearing, all 262 through 400 ci V-8 (precision type) (stamped 1) (for position #1)

2 474006 Bearing, all 262 through 400 ci V-8 (precision type) (stamped 2) (for position #2 and RR)

AR 474007 Bearing, all 262 through 400 ci V-8 (precision type) (stamped 3 & 4) (for position #3 and 4 on V-8)

0.553 Plug, engine cam
1 3704158 Plug, all 262 through 400 ci Chevy V-8 (2.125 in. diameter steel)

0.603 Rod, engine piston
Engine must be rebalanced when using bow-tie design competition rod. Torque specifications use 30W oil then torque to 85 lb-ft or 0.0045 in. to 0.0047 in. stretch

AR 3946841 Rod, 302 ci V-8 Chevy 1968-69 with 2.100 in. diameter rod bearing and floating pin, 5.7 in. rod length, use on RPO Z28 (1038 steel forging), magnafluxed and shot peened (0.375 in. diameter bolts)

AR 14095071 Rod, 350 ci V-8 Chevy, 1970-80 W/H/P and S/H/P (2nd design service replacement), 5.7 in. rod length with pressed pin design with 2.100 in. rod bearing diameter (1038 steel forging) magnafluxed and shot peened (0.375 in. diameter bolts)

AR 14011090 Rod heavy-duty off-road (bow-tie design) 5.7 in. service only, 302 through 350 ci Chevy V-8 (with pressed pin, 2.100 in. diameter rod bearing) (4340 forged steel, magnafluxed, shot peened) cap screw design with 7/16 bolt P/N 14011092, washer #14011093

AR 14011091 Rod heavy-duty off-road (bow-tie design) 6.0 in. service only, 302 through 350 ci Chevy V-8 (with pressed pin, 2.100 in. diameter rod bearing) (4340 forged steel, magnafluxed, shot peened), cap screw design with 7/16 bolt P/N 14011092, washer P/N 14011093

0.616 Bearing kit, engine connecting rod
8 3910555 Bearing kit, connecting rod (standard) all 302 through 400 ci V-8 with 2.100 in. diameter rod journals (aluminum M-400)

0.623 Bolt, engine connecting rod cap
AR 461372 Bolt, all 302 through 350 ci W/S/H/P Chevy V-8, 3/8-24 × 1⁵⁹/₆₄

AR 14011092 Bolt, use with bow-tie rods P/N 14011090-91, 7/16 × 20 diameter, with twelve-point head, special hardened 8740 steel, use with washer 14011093

0.626 Nut, washer; connecting rod bolt
AR 225854 Nut, all 302 through 400 ci Chevy V-8, 3/8 × 24

0.629 Piston, engine
8 3946876 Piston assembly, standard 1968-69 302 ci Chevy V-8 (RPO Z28) 11:1 compression (forged aluminum), floating pin design (ID #3927173)

8 3946882 Piston assembly, 0.030 in. OS 1968-69 302 ci Chevy V-8 (RPO Z28) 11:1 compression ratio, (forged aluminum) floating pin design (ID #3927176)

8 3871208 Piston assembly, standard 1968-69 327 ci Chevy V-8 W/S/HP (RPO-L-79) 11:1 compression ratio, (forged aluminum) press pin design (ID #3871209)

8 3850139 Piston assembly, 0.030 in. OS 1968-69 327 ci Chevy V-8 W/S/H/P (RPO-L79) 11:1 compression ratio (forged aluminum) pressed pin design (ID #3850136)

8 3942541 Piston assembly, standard 350 ci Chevy V-8 W/S/H/P 1969, 11:1 compression ratio (forged aluminum), pressed pin design (ID #3942546)

8 3942543 Piston assembly, 0.030 in. OS 350 ci Chevy V-8 W/S/H/P 1969, 11:1 compression ratio (forged aluminum), pressed pin design (ID #3942548)

8 474190 Piston assembly, 1971-80 350 ci Chevy V-8 W/S/H/P (RPO L82), 9.0:1 compression

ratio, forged aluminum, pressed pin design (ID #336747, 464664 or 464692) Piston OD 3.998 in. to 3.999 in.

8 474191 Piston assembly, (standard high-limit), 1971-80 350 ci Chevy V-8 W/S/H/P (RPO L82) 9.0:1 compression ratio, forged aluminum, pressed pin design (ID #464693) Piston OD 3.999 in. to 4.000 in.

8 474192 Piston assembly, (0.030 in. OS), 1971-80 350 ci Chevy V-8 W/S/H/P (RPO L82) 9.0:1 compression ratio, forged aluminum, pressed pin design (#464695)

8 3989048 Piston assembly, standard 1970 350 ci Chevy W/S/H/P (RPO LT1-Z28) 1970, 11:1 compression ratio (forged aluminum) (use as pressed or floating pin design) (ID #3949456). Pin retainer #3946848 and floating pin rod for floating pin application required

8 3989051 Piston assembly, 0.030 in. OS 1970 350 ci Chevy W/S/H/P (RPO LT1-Z28) 1970, 11:1 compression ratio (forged aluminum) (use as pressed or floating pin design)(ID #3949464) Pin retainer #3946848 and floating pin rod for floating pin application required

4 14011020 Piston assembly, standard 350 ci Chevy (heavy-duty off-road with 5.7 in. rod length) 12.5:1 compression ratio, forged aluminum, use on cylinder numbers 2, 3, 6 and 7, pin retainer P/N 14011033 (ID 4 14011006) required

4 14011021 Piston assembly, standard 350 ci Chevy (heavy-duty off-road with 5.7 in. rod length) 12.5:1 compression ratio, forged aluminum, use on cylinder numbers 1, 4, 5 and 8, pin retainer P/N 14011033 (ID #14011007) required

4 14011022 Piston assembly, 0.030 in. OS 350 ci Chevy (heavy-duty off-road with 5.7 in. rod length) 12.5:1 compression ratio, forged aluminum, use on cylinder numbers 2, 3, 6 and 7, pin retainer P/N 14011033 (ID #14011008) required

4 14011023 Piston assembly, 0.030 in. OS 350 ci Chevy (heavy-duty off-road with 5.7 in. rod length) 12.5:1 compression ratio, forged aluminum, use on cylinder numbers 1, 4, 5 and 8, pin retainer P/N 14011033 (ID #14011009) required

4 14011024 Piston assembly, 0.060 in. OS 350 ci Chevy (heavy-duty off-road with 5.7 in. rod length) 12.5:1 compression ratio, forged aluminum, use on cylinder numbers 2, 3, 6 and 7, pin retainer P/N 14011033 (ID #14011010) required

4 14011025 Piston assembly, 0.060 in. OS 350 ci Chevy (heavy-duty off-road with 5.7 in. rod length) 12.5:1 compression ratio, forged aluminum, use on cylinder numbers 1, 4, 5 and 8, pin retainer P/N 14011033 (ID #14011011) required

0.639 Retainer, engine piston pin

AR 3946848 Retainer (Spirolox design) 1.013 in. OD × 0.042 in. THK used on 1968-69 302 ci can be used 1969-70 W/S/H/P 350 ci V-8 when converting to floating pin design

AR 366219 Retainer (Spirolox design) 1.013 in. OD × 0.072 in. THK use with 350 ci type piston (ring groove must be remachined for thicker retainer)

AR 14011033 Retainer (round wire design) 1.07 in. OD × 0.064 in. THK used on all 350 ci heavy-duty off-highway 12.5:1 pistons

0.643 Ring unit, piston

8 3995664 Piston ring unit, standard 350 ci Chevy V-8 with low tension, 0.0781 $\frac{5}{64}$ in. top and 2nd ring

8 3995667 Piston ring unit, 0.030 in. OS, 350 ci V-8 with low tension, 0.0781 in. top and 2nd ring

8 366289 Piston ring unit, standard 350 ci Chevy V-8, with moly faced 0.0625 ($\frac{1}{16}$) in. top and 2nd ring, 0.1875 in. low tension oil ring (use W/H/D off highway 12.5:1 compression ratio 350 ci piston), excellent competition ring

8 366291 Piston ring unit, 0.030 in. OS, 350 ci V-8, 0.0625 in. moly faced, 0.0625 in. top and 2nd ring, 0.1875 ($\frac{3}{16}$) in. low tension oil ring (use W/H/D off highway 12.5:1 compression ratio 350 ci piston), excellent competition ring

8 366292 Piston ring unit, 0.060 in. 350 ci V-8, with 0.0625 in. moly faced, 0.0625 in. top and 2nd ring, 0.1875 in. low tension oil ring (use W/H/D off-highway 12.5:1 compression ratio 350 ci piston), excellent competition ring

0.646 Crankshaft, engine

1 14011073 Raw crank forging, V-8 small-block, 5140 steel forging, can be machined from 2.7 in. to 3.10 in. stroke. This crank has "no" machining done (ID #14011073)

1 366280 Raw crank forging, V-8 small-block, 5140 steel forging, can be machined from 3.1 in. to 3.75 in. stroke. This crank has no machining done (ID #366280)

1 3932444 Crankshaft, 1968-85 350 ci Chevy V-8 (L48 engine) 3.48 in. stroke, cast-iron with 2.10 in. rod, 2.45 in. main diameter (ID #442)

1 3941180 Crankshaft, 350 ci Chevy V-8, 3.48 in. stroke, none nitrided, 1053 steel forging with 2.10 in. rod, 2.45 in. main diameter (ID #1182)

1 3941184 Crankshaft, 1970-80 350 ci Chevy V-8, W/S/H/P, 3.48 in. stroke, nitrade finish on journals, 1053 steel forging with 2.10 in. rod, 2.45 in. main diameter (ID #1182)

1 3951527 Crankshaft, 1970-80 400 ci Chevy V-8, 3.75 in. stroke, cast-iron with 2.10 in. rod, 2.65 in. main diameter

0.649 Bearing, engine crankshaft, clutch pilot

3752487 Bearing, all Chevy V-8 engines, bushing type 0.594 in. ID, 1.094 in. OD × 0.75 in.

0.659 Balancer, damper, pulley; engine crankshaft

1 3817173 Balancer, 1962-68 302, 327 ci Chevy V-8 W/S/H/P, 8 in. OD diameter, cast-iron, pre 1969 timing mark, (ID #7173)

1 3947708 Balancer, 1969 302 ci Chevy V-8, 8 in. OD diameter, cast-iron (ID #7173)

1 6262221 Balancer, 1969-84 305 through 350 ci Chevy V-8, all exc. H/P-SHP 6.75 in. OD diameter, cast-iron

1 6262224   Balancer, 1969-80 350 ci Chevy V-8, all W/S/H/P, 8 in. OD cast-iron (ID #2224)

1 364709   Balancer heavy-duty off-highway, 302 through 350 ci Chevy V-8, 8 in. OD nodular iron (ID #4709)

1 3858533   Pulley, crankshaft, 1968 302, 327 ci Chevy V-8, W/S/H/P, double-deep groove, 6.75 in. OD (ID #3766987) late model pulleys

0.662 Bolt, washer; engine crankshaft pulley and balancer
1 3815933   Bolt, all 302 through 350 Chevy V-8 ($7/16$ in. 20 $\times$ 2¼ in.)

1 14001829   Washer, all 302 through 350 Chevy V-8 (½ in. $\times$ 1¾ in. $\times$ $5/16$ in. thick)

0.666 Flywheel, engine crankshaft
1 361950   Flywheel with automatic transmission, 350 ci W/S/H/P Chevy off-highway, starter ring OD 14 in.

1 3991406   Flywheel with manual transmission, 302 ci (RPO Z28) W/HP (RPO L69) 13 lb. nodular iron, 10½ in. diameter clutch, starter ring OD 12¾ in. (ID #3856579)

1 3986394   Flywheel with manual transmission, all 400 ci type engines, use with 11 in. clutch, starter ring OD 14 in. (ID #3963540). This is an external balancer flywheel

0.669 Bolt, dowel; flywheel
6 839756   Bolt, all 262 through 400 ci V-8 Chevy, with manual transmission ($7/16$-20 $\times$ 1 in.)

6 3727207   Bolt, all 262 through 400 ci V-8 Chevy, with automatic transmission ($7/16$-20 $\times$ $27/32$ in.) 290 M steel

1 3701679   Dowel, all V-8 ($7/16$ in. $\times$ $7/8$ in.)

0.673 Gear, engine flywheel
1 460583   All with 12¾ in. diameter flywheel, ring gear only

1 3991407   All with 14 in. diameter flywheel, ring gear only

0.685 Dowel, engine clutch housing or transmission
2 1453658   Dowel, all V-8, 0.638 in. $\times$ 1.1875 in. diameter

0.724 Chain, engine timing
1 346261   Timing chain, link type, 262 through 400 ci V-8 W/S/H/P. Must be used with crank sprocket #464617 and cam sprocket #340235

1 3735411   Timing chain, double row roller link type, 262 through 400 ci Chevy V-8 for heavy-duty off-road usage. Must be used with crank gear P/N 3755413 and cam sprocket P/N 3735412

0.728 Sprocket, engine crank
1 464617   Crankshaft sprocket steel for link type chain, all 262 through 400 ci Chevy V-8 W/S/H/P heavy-duty. Must use chain 346261 and cam sprocket 340235

1 3735413   Crankshaft sprocket steel roller link type, 262 through 400 ci Chevy V-8, heavy-duty off-highway usage. Must be used with chain P/N 3735411 and sprocket P/N 3735412

0.736 Sprocket, camshaft
1 340235   Cam sprocket hardened iron for link type chain, all 262 through 400 ci Chevy V-8 W/S/H/P. Must be used with #346261 timing chain and #464617 crank sprocket

1 3735412   Cam sprocket iron roller link type, 262 through 400 ci Chevy V-8, heavy-duty off-highway usage. Must be used with chain P/N 3735411 and crank gear P/N 3735413

0.796 Stud, clutch fork
1 3729000   Stud ball, $13/16$ in. - 16 $\times$ 1.48 in. OL

1 3790556   Stud ball, $13/16$ in. - $\times$ 1.78 in. OL

0.859 Cover, engine clutch
1 6273958   Clutch cover, 1968-69, 1970-72 350 ci W/S/H/P (RPO LT1) single plate design, 10.4 in. OD

1 3884598   Clutch cover, all 350 ci W/S/H/P single plate design, 11 in. OD

0.862 Bolt, engine clutch cover to flywheel
6 838653   Bolt, $3/8$ - 16 $\times$ 1 in.

0.886 Plate, engine clutch driven
1 3886059   Clutch plate, 1968-70 350 ci W/S/H/P (RPO LT1) with woven facing, single plate design, 10.4 in. OD, ten tooth spline. Use for heavy-duty off-highway

1 3991428   Clutch plate, 1971-72 350 ci W/S/H/P (RPO L82) with woven facings, single plate design, 10.4 in. OD, twenty-six tooth spline. Use for heavy-duty off-highway

1 3908960   Clutch plate, 1968-70 327 through 400 ci W/HP-S/H/P Chevy with woven facings, single plate design, 11 in. OD, ten tooth spline

1 3989030   Clutch plate, 1971-74 350 ci W/HP-S/H/P with woven facings, single plate design, 11 in. OD, twenty-six tooth spline

1.062 Pulley, reinforcement, fan and coolant pump
1 3770245   Pulley, water pump, 1968 350 ci Corvette W/SP/HP, Camaro with 302 ci engine, two groove, deep groove, small hub 0.625 in. shaft, 7.125 in. OD

1 3720616   Reinforcement, water pump pulley, small hub 0.625 in. shaft

1 3942992   Pulley, water pump, deep two groove, fits large hub. Must be reworked for 0.750 in. diameter shaft

1.066 Belt, drive belts
1 9433722   Belt, fan and water pump, 34 in. $\times$ $3/8$ in., captured belt V-8 Chevy

1.069 Pump kit, engine coolant pump, rotor, seal, seats, bearing and shaft assembly, and gasket
1 3998270   Pump unit, 262 through 400 ci V-8 1968-70 Corvette with short mounting legs (with 0.625 in. diameter shaft) cast iron housing

1 6258551   Pump unit, 350, 305 ci V-8 1971-81 Corvette, with 0.750 in. diameter shaft and large 1.50 in. diameter bearing, cast iron housing

1 14011021   Pump unit, aluminum, 262 through 400 ci V-8 for heavy-duty off-highway usage, short legs, 0.0750 in. diameter shaft and large 1.50 in. diameter bearing, cast iron rotor

1 3923250   Rotor, water pump for V-8 350 ci cast iron, 0.625 in. shaft hole

1 908101   Bearing and shaft assembly for V-8 350 ci pump assembly #6258551 or 14011012 (1.50 in. bearing diameter, 0.750 in. diameter hub shaft, 0.625 in. diameter rotor shaft)

1 6263704   Seal, water pump, for V-8 350 ci pump assembly #6258551 or 14011012

1 6270079   Seal, water pump for V-8 350 ci pump assembly #6258551 or 14011012

1 3782611   Gasket, housing to rotor cover-water pump all V-8 water pumps

1.426 Pan, pan kit; engine oil

1 465220   Oil pan, 302 through 350 ci V-8 1968-79 W/S/H/P, 4 qt., use screen assembly #3855152

1 462221   Oil pan, 262 through 400 ci V-8 1968-79, 4 qt.

1 464607   Oil pan, 305 through 400 ci V-8 1978-80, dip stick mounted in pan, 4 qt.

1 14082348   Oil pan, 305 through 400 ci V-8 1980-85, dip stick mounted right side, 4 qt.

1.429 Gasket, oil pan

1 14050645   Gasket, oil pan, 262 through 400 ci 1968-74

1 14079398   Gasket, oil pan, 262 through 400 ci 1975-85

1 357159   Seal, front, oil pan, 262 through 400 ci

1 458625   Seal, rear oil pan, 262 through 400 ci

1 14088505   Rear seal, 1986-88

1 10051118   Adapter seal, 305 through 350 ci 1986-88, allows use of early two-piece seal crankshaft in late one-piece block

1.430 Baffle, oil pan

1 3927136   Baffle tray, 302 through 350 ci V-8, use with oil pan #465220, semi-circular (requires five #3960312 MTG. studs)

1.609 Spring, oil pressure regulator

1 3848911   Spring pressure regulator, 327, 350 W/S/H/P, oil pump #3848907, 70 psi, white stripe

1.652 Oil pump, engine

1 3848907   Pump assembly, all 327 through 400 ci V-8 H/P-S/H/P, does not include screen

1 14044872   Pump assembly, all 302 through 400 ci V-8, for heavy-duty off-highway usage, special high volume pump, does not include screen

1 3969870   Pump and screen assembly, 427, 454 ci (with RPO ZL1-LS7) (1.3 in. gear), distance from mounting surface to bottom of screen is 4.94 in.

1 475908   Pump and screen assembly, 396, 427, 454 ci W/S/H/P (RPO LS6) (distance from mounting surface to bottom of screen is 4.88 in.)

1 475902   Pump and screen assembly, 427 with heavy-duty 1967-69 (distance from mounting surface to bottom of screen is 4.94 in.)

1.656 Screen, oil pump

Weld screen and tube assembly to pump for heavy-duty off highway use.

1 3830080   Screen assembly, 305 through 350 ci V-8 Corvette 1968-75, 1980-82, use with oil pan 360866, 359942, 14067363 (with 3848907 pump, from plane parallel to oil pump attaching surface to lowest point of screen assembly is 4.50 in.)

1 3855152   Screen assembly, 262 through 350 ci V-8 1975-79 Corvette, 1968-84, use with oil pan 465220-465221 (with 3848907 pump, from plane parallel to oil pump attaching surface to lowest point of screen assembly is 5.12 in.)

1 3955283   screen asm 396/427/454 (from plane parallel to oil pump attaching surface to lowest point of screen asm is 6.05 in.)

1 3955281   screen asm 396/427/454 (from plane parallel to oil pump attaching surface to lowest point of screen asm is 4.88 in.)

1 6269895   screen asm 396/427/454 (from plane paral-

lel to oil pump attaching surface to lowest point of screen asm is 4.94 in.)

1.758 Cap breather, oil filter

1 6421868   oil cap and breather, push-in type for off-highway chrome covers, (breather not chromed)

1 3894337   grommet, rubber plug ($^{15}/_{16}$ ID $\times$ $^{7}/_{32}$ OD diameter) for rocker cover

1.840 Adapter, oil coolers

1 326098   adapter oil cooler and filter, allow installation of oil cooler lines, side outlets

1 340258   adapter oil cooler and filter, allow installation of oil cooler lines, forward outlets

2 3951644   bolt, adapter ($^{5}/_{16}$ in. 18 $\times$ 1$^{1}/_{8}$)

1.844 Gasket seal, oil filter

1 326100   gasket, oil cooler adapter and filter

1 14015353   seal, oil cooler adapter and filter

1.855 Connector, oil filter

1 3853870   connector, oil filter for screw-on filter (required with oil filter adapter and cooler)

2.041 Motor, starter

1 1108789   Starter motor, heavy-duty for all V-8 with 12$\frac{3}{4}$ in. overall diameter flywheel (use with flywheel 3963537 or 3991406)

1 1108400   Starter motor for all V-8 with 14 in. overall diameter flywheel (use with flywheel 361950-336717-3993827)

2.042 Bolt, brace; starter motor

1 14057099   Bolt, starter mounting, long special shoulder bolt ($\frac{3}{8}$ $\times$ 4$^{21}/_{32}$)

1 14057098   Bolt, starter mounting, short special shoulder bolt ($\frac{3}{8}$ $\times$ 1$^{27}/_{32}$)

1 3733289   Bolt, starter mounting, ($\frac{3}{8}$ - 16 $\times$ 3$\frac{5}{8}$)

1 354353   Brace, starter motor, front starter support

2.085 Housing, starter motor drive with bushing

1 1968122   Starter housing, use on starter motor #1108381, 1108789 for 12$\frac{3}{4}$ in. diameter flywheel ring

1 1984098   Starter housing, use on starter motor #1118400 for 14 in. diameter flywheel ring

2.170 Coil ignition

1 1115207   Coil, use with transistorized ignition (embossed 176-12V) (1.8 ohm wire) part of ignition kit 3997782, use with distributor P/N 1111263 or 1111267

1 10037380   Coil, use with heavy-duty off-road electronic distributor system. Use with distributor #10037373, control box #10037378. Coil has a top with an extra-tall high-tension wire tower to prevent arc over to the terminals. The high turns ratio provides extra voltage to the spark plugs. The coil is oil filled for better heat dissipation under high rpm operating conditions

2.240 Wire, spark plug

1 8914473   Spark plug wire kit, 90 degree boot for 1968-74, all 262 through 400 ci V-8 engines, except HEI distributor, special solid core high silicon cover

2.274 Pulley, fan; generator

1 3829387   Pulley, 302 through 350 ci W/S/H/P, 0.625 in. diameter, 0.672 in. shaft diameter, one groove, 0.50 in. wide

2.361 Distributor, ignition

1 1111263   Distributor assembly, transistorized with ball type shaft for gear drive cam V-8, use on chain drive cam by exchange of lower gear to #1958599, use with ignition kit #3997782

1 1111267   Distributor assembly, transistorized with bronze bushing type shaft for V-8, use with ignition kit #3997782

1 1110985   Distributor assembly, dual breaker point type, with tach drive for 302-400 V-8

1 1103302   Distributor assembly, cap and coil assembly (HEI type for 362-400 V-8)

1 14044871   Distributor assembly, all Chevy V-8 for heavy-duty off-highway usage, this is an electronic distributor and has a special Tufftrided shaft riding on two sintered bushings. A hardened and concentric ground advance cam with reinforced weight pins produces a smooth exact timing curve for proper engine operation. The distributor is a non-tach drive type. The distributor has a high-output magnetic pickup and uses standard Chevy cap and rotor. The distributor is supplied with the vacuum advance locked out. This unit can be used with tach #10038474, amplifier #10037378, rpm limiter #10037379, changeover switch #10037376, ignition coil #10037381 and wire cable assembly #10037377 or 10039932

1 10037376   Changeover switch. This switch provides the means for operating two ignition units and changing from one to the other with the simple flip of a switch from inside the car, this unit will require two amplifiers #10037378. Use with distributor #14044871

1 10037379   Rpm limiter. The Soft Touch rev limiter plugs directly into the ignition unit and provides rev limiting as set by a plug in module. Use with distributor #14044871

1 10039933   Rpm limit module kit 5000 series. Use with rev limiter #10037379. Incudes five modules, 5000 rpm, 5200 rpm, 5400 rpm, 5600 rpm and 5800 rpm

1 10039934   Rpm limit module kit 6000 series. Use with rev limiter #10037379. Includes five modules, 6000 rpm, 6200 rpm, 6400 rpm, 6600 rpm and 6800 rpm

1 10039935   Rpm limit module kit 7000 series. Use with rev limiter #10037379. Includes five modules, 7000 rpm, 7200 rpm, 7400 rpm, 7600 rpm and 7800 rpm

1 10039936   Rpm limit module kit 8000 series. Use with rev limiter #10037379. Includes five models, 8000 rpm, 8200 rpm, 8400 rpm, 8600 rpm and 8800 rpm

2.367 Cap, distributor

1 1941551   cap, distributor (for use with dual point distributor) screw type

1 1971244   cap, distributor use with distributor #14044871

2.372 Shaft-pole piece-pole piece with coil

1 1960779   pole piece "rotating" with pick-up coil, can be modified to repair distributor 1111263 or 1111267

1 1964272   pole piece "stationary" with weight base, can be modified to repair distributor 1111263 or 1111267 (see replacement chart)

1 3998289   shaft-oil pump to distributor shaft all 302 through 400 ci V-8

2.383 Amplifier harness unit, transistorized ignition

1 3997782   transistor ignition unit (included the following parts 3955511 amplifier, 1111507 coil, 6288704 connector, 6297793-8901973 wire, 6297688 harness) use with distributor 1111263 or 1111267

1 3955511   amplifier asm, pulse for transistor ignition part of unit 3997782

1 8901973   wire, for transistor ignition

1 6297688   harness, for transistor ignition pulse amplifier, part of unit 3997782

1 10037378   controller box (amplifier) for heavy-duty off-road electronic distributor system, V-8 engines, use with distributor 14044871 and coil 10037380

1 10037377   ignition cable asm, to wire amplifier to distributor or dash-mounted unit, use with distributor 14044871 and coil 1007378

1 10039932   ignition cable unit, to wire amplifier to distributor on engine-compartment-mounted unit, used with distributor 14044871 and amplifier 10037378

3.265 Manifold, guard; engine inlet

1 14044836   Intake manifold aluminum, 1968-69 302 ci, 1970 350 ci W/S/H/P Corvette, high-rise, dual plane, for mounting Holley carburetor

1 14007377   Intake manifold aluminum, 1978-79 350 ci W/S/H/P Corvette for Quadrajet 4bbl carburetor, low profile type

1 10051103   Intake manifold aluminum, bow-tie 4 bbl Holley high-rise single plane open plenum. Fits raised intake ports of bow-tie heads

1 10051102   Same intake manifold as 10051103 but fits stock-sized intake ports

1 14096011   Intake manifold cast iron, Quadrajet 4 bbl high-performance manifold

3.270 Gasket, manifold to cylinder head

1 14038088   Gasket kit, all 302 through 350 ci W/S/H/P

3.402 Air cleaner, carburetor

1 6423907   Air cleaner, open element type with chrome cover, 14 in. OD, includes base #6422188, cover #6421832 and element #6421746 or A212CW

3.410 Fuel filter

1 854619   Fuel filter, large capacity inline

3.601 Manifold, engine exhaust

1 3797901   Exhaust manifold, left hand, all 1962-65 327 ci W/S/H/P Corvette, 2½ in. exhaust flange

1 3814970   Exhaust manifold, right hand, all 1962-63 327 ci W/S/H/P Corvette, 2½ in. exhaust flange. Generator mount on side of manifold

1 3846563   Exhaust manifold, left hand, all 1964-65 327 ci W/S/H/P Corvette, 2½ in. exhaust flange. Generator mount on end of manifold

3.900 Pump, engine fuel

1 6415325   Fuel pump, all 262 through 400 ci V-8, high capacity pump

3.935 Rod, fuel pump

1 3704817   Fuel pump push rod, all V-8

Sources

Accel Performance Products
Box 142
Branford, CT 06405

AC Spark Plugs Division
1300 N. Dort Highway
Flint, MI 48556

Air Flow Research Head Porting
10490 Ilex Avenue
Pacoima, CA 91331

Air Research TurboChargers
3201 Lomita Boulevard
Torrance, CA 90505

Alliance Cams
3528 Sagunto Street
Santa Ynez, CA 93460

American Racing
17600 Santa Fe Avenue
Rancho Dominguez, CA 90221

Baker Racing Engines
14122 Ironwood Drive NW
Grand Rapids, MI 49504

B&M Automotive Products
9152 Independence Avenue
Chatsworth, CA 91311

Batten Heads
27554 Wick Road
Romulus, MI 48174

Blower Drive Service
12140 Washington Boulevard
Whittier, CA 90606

Brodix Incorporated
Third and Maple Streets
Mena, AR 71953

Cal Custom
Mr. Gasket Co. Inc.
19914 S. Via Baron Street
Compton, CA 90220

Cam Motion Incorporated
2092 Dallas Drive
Baton Rouge, LA 70806

Cam Techniques
105 Cascade Boulevard
Milford, CT 06460

Canton Custom Oil Pans
9 Tipping Drive
Branford, CT 06405

Carrillo Industries Incorporated
34431 Calle Perfecto
San Juan Capistrano, CA 92675

Cloyes Gear & Products
  Incorporated
Box 511
Willoughby, OH 44094

Competition Cams Incorporated
3402 Democrat Road
Memphis, TN 38118

Competition Engineering
80 Carter Drive
Guilford, CT 06437

Competition Fuel Systems
3820 E. 44th Street, #410
Tucson, AZ 85713

Compucar
Box 291857
Fort Lauderdale, FL 33329

Crane Cams Incorporated
530 Fentress Boulevard
Daytona Beach, FL 32014

Crower Cams
3333 Main Street
Chula Vista, CA 92011

Cyclone Headers
19007 S. Reyes Avenue
Compton, CA 90221

Diamond Racing Products
23003 Diamond Drive
Mount Clemens, MI 48043

Edelbrock Corporation
2700 California Street
Torrance, CA 90503

Engle Racing Cams
1621 12th Street
Santa Monica, CA 90404

Erson Cams
550 Mallory Way
Carson City, NV 89701

Fuelish Parts Limited
Box 152
Hollywood, FL 33020

Gaerte Engines
601-615 Monroe Street
Rochester, IN 46975

Gale Banks Engineering
546 Duggan Avenue
Azusa, CA 91702

General Kinetics Incorporated
5161 Trumbell Avenue
Detroit, MI 48208

General Motors Parts Division
6060 W. Bristol Road
Flint, MI 48554

Hamburger's Oil Pans
1501 Industrial Way N.
Toms River, NJ 08753

Hays Clutches
8700 Brook Park Road
Cleveland, OH 44129

Hedman Manufacturing
Box 2126
Culver City, CA 90230

Herbert Cams
1933 S. Manchester
Anaheim, CA 92802

Holley Replacement Parts
 Division
11955 E. 9-Mile Road
Warren, MI 48089

Hooker Industries
1009 W. Brooks
Ontario, CA 91762

Induction Engineering
80 Carter Drive
Guilford, CT 06437

Iskenderian Racing Cams
16020 S. Broadway
Gardena, CA 90247

Joe Hunt Magnetos
11336-A Sunco Drive
Rancho Cordova, CA 95670

Lunati Cams & Cranks
4770 Lamar Avenue
Memphis, TN 38181

Mallory Incorporated
550 Mallory Way
Carson City, NV 89701

Mickey Thompson
11955 E. 9-Mile Road
Warren, MI 48089

Milodon Engineering
 Incorporated
20716 Plummer Street
Chatsworth, CA 91311

Moroso Performance Products
80 Carter Drive
Guilford, CT 06437

Mr. Gasket Company
 Incorporated
8700 Brookpark Road
Cleveland, OH 44129

Mr. Gasket Company
 Incorporated
Exhaust Division
19007 S. Reyes Avenue
Compton, CA 90221

MSD Ignition
Autotronic Controls
 Corporation
1490 Henry Brennan
El Paso, TX 79936

NOS Nitrous Oxide Systems
5930 Lakeshore Drive
Cypress, CA 90630

Offenhauser Sales Corporation
Box 32218
Los Angeles, CA 90032

Paxton Products Incorporated
929 Olympic Boulevard
Santa Monica, CA 90404

Performance Chevrolet Products
2995 W. Whitton
Phoenix, AZ 85017

Pete Jackson
1207 S. Flower Street
Burbank, CA 91502

Predator Carburetors
1975 S. Blackstone
Tulare, CA 93274

Racing Head Service
3402 Democrat Road
Memphis, TN 38118

Rhoads Lifters Incorporated
602 S. Main Street
Taylor, AZ 85939

Ross Racing Pistons
11927 S. Prairie Avenue
Hawthorne, CA 90250

Sealed Power Master
 Distribution Center
La Grange, IN 46761

Speed-Pro
La Grange, IN 46761

Stahl Headers
1515 Mount Rose Avenue
York, PA 17403

Storm Crankshaft Service
511 Homestead Avenue
Mt. Vernon, NY 10550

TRW Replacement Parts Division
8001 E. Pleasant Valley
Cleveland, OH 44131

Valley Head Service
19340 Londelius Street
Northridge, CA 91324

Venolia Pistons
2160 Cherry Industrial Circle
Long Beach, CA 90805

Vertex Magnetos
Ranco, Box D
Blue Bell, PA 19422

Weber Performance Products
 Company
2985 E. Blue Star
Anaheim, CA 92806

Weiand Automotive Industries
2316 San Fernando Road
Los Angeles, CA 90065

Index